## WHAT PROFESSIONALS AND PARENTS ARE SAYING ABOUT THE TRIM KIDS PROGRAM

"Drs. Sothern and von Almen together with dietitian Schumacher have produced a sound and practical book. . . . It is the formula that they used so successfully in a clinical setting that they have now adapted for home use. . . . Parents with an obese child who would like to help him or her live a happier and healthier life would do well if they first consult *Trim Kids*. I recommend it highly to them."

    —Claude Bouchard, Ph.D., Executive Director, George A. Bray Chair in Nutrition, Pennington Biomedical Research Center, Louisiana State University

"*Trim Kids* is an authoritative approach to understanding and treating children who are overweight. . . . One particular strength of the book is its comprehensive focus on physical activity . . . showing how exercise can be fun. *Trim Kids* also addresses the emotionally-charged topic of body weight with sensitivity. For these reasons, I recommend *Trim Kids* with enthusiasm."

    —David S. Ludwig, M.D., Ph.D., Director, Obesity Program; Associate Director, General Clinical Research Center, Children's Hospital, Boston, MA

"The Trim Kids Program is a proven, practical guide for parents to take specific, sequential steps to encourage healthy habits in their children. The authors have drawn upon their years of experience helping families set and achieve fitness goals. This book is filled with delicious but low-calorie recipes, fun activities that will burn calories and improve strength while encouraging movement, as well as behavior techniques aimed to support the child's (and family's) resolve. I highly recommend this book!"

    —Dennis M. Styne, M.D., Professor of Pediatrics, University of California Davis

"The strategies in *Trim Kids* are practical, effective, and fun for kids. I strongly recommend this comprehensive guide to parents."

    —Nancy Butte, Ph.D., Children's Nutrition Research Center, Department of Pediatrics, Baylor College of Medicine

"*Trim Kids* is a much-needed and unique comprehensive program for achieving healthy weight in children. It is based on years of research and appropriate behavioral principles. It has been tried and tested—and it works."

> —Michael I. Goran, Ph.D., Associate Director, Institute for Prevention Research, Professor of Preventive Medicine and Physiology & Biophysics, University of Southern California

"This book does an excellent job emphasizing that kids are not just mini-adults. Their opinions are important, and family interactions (especially parental support) are crucial to childhood maturation. I was also happy to see the recommendation on post-activity stretching, as well as the inclusion of games such as laser-tag."

> —American Association for Active Lifestyles & Fitness (AAALF), David Chong, Reviewer, Physical Activity Coordinator, Department of Health, Hawaii

"This book is not only practical, but lifesaving—and life-changing for kids who are overweight and in danger of serious health problems. My son, at age 11, weighed 212 pounds. Today, so far, he weighs 160 pounds and has grown more than 3 inches in height. His symptoms of beginning health problems have corrected themselves as a result of the weight reduction. I have lost 45 pounds myself! This program is phenomenal! It is a must-have if you are concerned about the weight, eating habits, and nutrition of your children and the rest of your family. Thank you to the authors and anyone involved with this effective book and the program that it contains!"

> —Annette M. Holtz, Holland, MI

"I cannot express enough my sincere thanks to the authors of *Trim Kids* for the success my child has had on this program. The diet, the exercise, and the behavior modification truly work. At age 9, my daughter weighed 132 pounds, was wearing adult-size clothes, and was teased by other children. Thanks to the Trim Kids Program, she has lost 32 pounds and is maintaining her goal weight. The results of this program are absolutely remarkable and definitely long-term. I highly recommend it to both overweight children and their parents (I lost 8 pounds myself following the program with my daughter). My daughter's self esteem has sky-rocketed. Her face lights up every time someone comments on her weight loss and how nice she looks. When asked how she did it, she proudly replies, 'I joined Committed to Kids and followed the Trim Kids program.'"

> —Rhonda Miller, Harvey, LA

# TRIM KIDS™

## The Proven 12-Week Plan That Has Helped Thousands of Children Achieve a Healthier Weight

**Melinda S. Sothern, Ph.D., M.Ed., C.E.P.**
**T. Kristian von Almen, Ph.D.**
**Heidi Schumacher, R.D., L.D.N., C.D.E.**

HARPER

NEW YORK • LONDON • TORONTO • SYDNEY

HARPER

HarperCollins books may be purchased for educational, business, or sales promotional use. For information please e-mail the Special Markets Department at SPsales@harpercollins.com.

First HarperResource paperback edition published in 2003

*Designed by Jennifer Ann Daddio*
*Illustrations by Alexis Seabrook*

The Library of Congress has catalogued the hardcover edition as follows:

Sothern, Melinda.
Trim kids™ : the proven 12-week plan that has helped thousands of children achieve a healthier weight / Melinda Sothern, T. Kristian von Almen, Heidi Schumacher.
p.   cm.
1. Obesity in children.   2. Reducing diets—Health aspects.
3. Exercise in children—Patients—Family relationships.   I. von Almen, T. Kristian.   II. Schumacher, Heidi.   III. Title.
RJ506.E18 S68 2001
613.7'042—dc21
2001024461

ISBN 0-06-018815-4
ISBN 0-06-093417-4 (pbk.)

17 18 RRD 20 19 18 17

# Dedication

This book is dedicated to the children and families who have participated in our programs over the past fifteen years. They have demonstrated the courage and perseverance to break the vicious circle of childhood obesity in their own lives. It is their commitment to health that has made Trim Kids possible. They are the true heroes. Through their trials and triumphs we have learned so much, and we are grateful now for the opportunity to share our experiences in this book.

We would also like to dedicate this book to our respective spouses, especially David Hebert and Sonja von Almen; our children, Samantha, Allyson, Jordan, Julia, and Dane; and our parents, James and Jerry Sothern, Mitzie and William von Almen, Ph.D., and Barbara and Peter Schumacher. Without their faith, encouragement, and support in us, this project would not have been possible.

# CONTENTS

# Acknowledgments

The authors gratefully acknowledge the expert guidance and support of Dr. John Udall and Dr. Mark Loftin, who were not only mentors but inspirations and role models for all of us. We wish to especially thank Mrs. Leslie Capo, whose long hours of hard work as our media coordinator at LSU Health Sciences Center have provided us with a multitude of opportunities to highlight our academic and clinical successes for the public, and whose individual belief in our work made this book possible. Our literary agent, Jeff Kleinman at Graybill and English, deserves special mention, not only for his work as agent but also for his untiring efforts and assistance with promoting the project, assisting with writing and editing, mediating, encouraging, and advising. We especially thank our editor, Toni Sciarra, for her many hours of hard work and for believing in this project and providing us with a venue to reach so many children and parents in need of help. We are grateful for the help and encouragement of our publicist, Shelby Meizlik, Drs. Keely Carlisle, Saundra Hunter, Stewart Clark, Stewart Gordon, Alphonso Vargas, Ricardo Sorensen, Robert Suskind, Wilma Longstreet, and Frank Greenway. We must also acknowledge our numerous colleagues around the country, especially Dr. William Dietz, who promote quality and comprehensive care for overweight children and their families, for assisting us in refining our clinical approach and treatment. We also thank our colleagues in the pediatric obesity field, especially Drs. Claude Bouchard, Michael Goran, Leonard Epstein, Thomas Rowland, and Oded Bar Or, for their years of research, paving the way for us to design and implement our studies. We gratefully acknowledge the support of the Louisiana State University Health Sciences Center, the Pennington Biomedical Research Center, the University of New Orleans, and the West Jefferson Medical Center. We also wish to thank our research assistants, interns, students, and business associates—especially Chris Singley, Connie Van Vrancken, Dr. Thomas Ewing, and Carole Lachney.

# Foreword

As a pediatrician and a specialist in gastroenterology and nutrition, I have seen firsthand the devastating physical and emotional effects that weight problems can have on children. The division of Pediatric Gastroenterology and Nutrition at the Louisiana State University Health Sciences Center in New Orleans sees many overweight children each year. Some may have life-threatening conditions; others have related diseases such as diabetes, bone and joint problems, and asthma. Almost all experience severe emotional trauma due to their overweight condition. Fortunately, my colleagues and I have had the pleasure of working alongside Drs. Sothern and von Almen and Ms. Schumacher in the Committed to Kids Pediatric Weight-Management Programs at Louisiana State University Health Sciences Center. We have witnessed the incredible transformation of overweight kids into confident, healthy, and happy children. It is through these authors' dedication that major strides have been taken in the treatment of this most prevalent of all chronic nutritional diseases in children.

This book, *Trim Kids,* represents over fifteen years of clinical service with the children of New Orleans. This volume also represents many years of research efforts in which I have had the privilege to be involved as a mentor and coauthor. What the authors have developed to serve the needs of these children and what they have learned through interacting with more than 1,000 overweight children and their families is now at your fingertips. If your child is overweight or at risk for obesity, please let Drs. Sothern and von Almen and Ms. Schumacher be your support system. We are committed to having a lasting, positive impact on the physical and emotional health of children and to breaking this vicious circle of inadequate exercise and inappropriate dietary and behavioral practices that lead to the childhood weight problems that affect so many of America's young people.

We are sorry that we are unable to speak and consult with each one of you individually. However, through the stories, tips, and information contained in this book, you will discover healthy ways to help your chubby toddler, child, or adolescent become trimmer in twelve weeks. When used along with the supervision of your pediatrician or family physician, our program can help you and your children to achieve *health for a lifetime*.

John N. Udall, Jr., M.D., Ph.D.

## A NOTE FROM THE AUTHORS

Dr. Udall is the Medical Director for the Committed to Kids Pediatric Weight-Management Clinic at the Louisiana State University Health Sciences Center. He is Professor of Pediatrics and Division Chief for the Department of Gastrointestinal Nutrition, Department of Pediatrics, Louisiana State University Health Sciences Center, and the Children's Hospital of New Orleans. He holds an M.D. from Temple University in Philadelphia, PA, and a Ph.D. in Nutritional Biochemistry from the Massachusetts Institute of Technology (MIT) in Cambridge, MA. He has served or currently serves on the:

- Editorial Board, *Journal of Pediatric Gastroenterology and Nutrition*
- Nutrition Committee, North American Society for Pediatric Gastroenterology, Hepatology and Nutrition
- Committee on Nutrition, American Academy of Pediatrics, Chicago, IL
- Executive Committee, American Board of Nutrition, Bethesda, MD

Dr. Udall has been instrumental over the past decade as a mentor to our research projects in the prevention and treatment of childhood obesity. He was recently awarded the Richard E. L. Fowler Professorship at the Louisiana State University Health Sciences Center.

# Introduction

When most of today's parents were kids, there were no computers, no video games, no cable TV channels, and few fast food restaurants. Back then, most kids spent their days riding bikes, climbing trees, and playing tag. The family got together at dinnertime, sat at the kitchen table, and ate a home-cooked meal. Until recently, only 5 to 10 percent of America's children were overweight.

Today, more than twice as many kids are overweight. That adds up to about one in four—or 10 million—children who are heavier than their ideal weight. There isn't a racial, ethnic, or age group that escapes this mind-boggling fact, and boys and girls are both affected. Obesity is thus the most prevalent nutritional disease of children and adolescents in the United States. Eighty percent of overweight ten- to thirteen-year-olds will become overweight adults. The more overweight a child is, the higher his or her risk for adult obesity and type II diabetes.

It's time to make some changes.

You may have known for a while that your child is overweight—maybe even obese—but you probably weren't sure how to combat the condition. Maybe your pediatrician has said he'd grow out of it or has recommended a low-fat diet; your friends may have suggested exercise; your mother may have made you feel guilty and even hinted that maybe he needs therapy. Maybe you've tried one or all of these approaches, and they didn't work.

No wonder: the issues are not simple. Having an overweight child can be difficult, embarrassing, and complex. The media bombards us with images of beanpole-thin, blemish-free, muscular people. Oprah and Rosie are helping to counteract the message that everyone is tiny; but for every healthy, yet not petite, celebrity there are many superthin supermodels. The images saturate our daily lives, pressuring families of overweight kids from every direction.

Then there are your child's peers. Although more and more kids today are overweight, this doesn't mean that they are rallying together against schoolyard ridicule. It doesn't cushion the pain of being called names, or dry the tears when, once again, your child is the last one picked for the school baseball team.

And finally, there *you* are. A concerned parent grappling with feelings of guilt, helplessness, maybe some anger, and plenty of worry. You know there's a problem, but like the hundreds of parents we've worked with, you vacillate about what to do. The notion that your child isn't the only overweight kid on the block may seem like a legitimate reason to wait until he grows out of it, or go with the flow. In truth, however, permitting your child to remain overweight is a choice you make. And with that choice, your child—and the vast majority of the other chubby kids—will endure difficult mental and physical struggles, as well as lose hope for a bright future.

That's because the dramatic medical and emotional problems that develop when your child is overweight will follow her through her teenage years and into adulthood. If you choose *not* to make changes while your child is still young, chances are she may suffer from any of several deleterious conditions, including low self-esteem, depression, isolation, asthma, diabetes, high blood pressure, high cholesterol, abnormal bone development, and sleep apnea.

What's more, the damage resulting from an overweight childhood is usually damage *done;* that is, it's typically irreversible, creating a lifetime of emotional and physical obstacles for your child. And that lifetime, statistically speaking, will end sooner rather than later.

That's the bad news.

The good news is that we now have scientifically supported, clinically proven methods that can help your child lose weight and keep it off. The step-by-step proven techniques in the Trim Kids Program will see your child through a positive and lasting transition that promises a healthier, happier childhood and adulthood.

You've already taken the first step toward meaningful changes simply by picking up this book. We welcome you and applaud your courage and commitment to change—and especially your choice to accept this challenge for the sake of your child.

## WHO WE ARE

For the past fifteen years, the Committed to Kids Pediatric Weight-Management Program at the Louisiana State University Health Sciences Center in New Orleans has conducted studies on childhood obesity and learned how to break the vicious circle of overweight and related problems in children. Our hands-on clinical setting has provided the perfect laboratory to discover what's unique about overweight children and how their families can help them make healthy changes to ensure that they grow into healthy adults. This program, which we have translated for home use into the Trim Kids Program, is one of the only multidisciplinary team approaches in the world for preventing and treating childhood obesity. Our short-term success rate is 90 percent; our long-term success rate is 65 to 70 percent.

We are a team of medical experts and scientists—an exercise physiologist, a registered dietitian, and a research psychologist—who have pooled our knowledge, time, and passion for finding solutions to childhood weight problems. Since 1993, we have trained more than 100 medical and health professional groups throughout the United States, Europe, Central and South America, and Asia in how to use our techniques. In 1997, because of the high demand for our services, we began conducting professional training seminars twice annually. To date, we have trained ten affiliate programs located in Arizona, Louisiana, Missouri, Texas, Washington, Illinois, and Ohio. Our website, www.Trim-Kids.com, provides information on childhood weight problems for parents and professionals alike. We have consulted and lectured about weight management for major international corporations, hospitals, and scientific organizations and have appeared on radio and television and in print nationwide.

Melinda S. Sothern, Ph.D., M.Ed., C.E.P., is the director of the Louisiana State University (LSU) Prevention of Childhood Obesity Laboratory at the Pennington Biomedical Research Center in Baton Rouge and also serves as director of the Pediatric Obesity Clinical Research Section and an associate professor of research at the LSU Health Sciences Center (LSUHSC) in New Orleans.

During her early career, when she was teaching physical education and coaching swimming and cheerleading, she first observed how terribly excess weight could affect schoolchildren. She developed a unique approach that provided opportunities for all children to participate in physical education and athletics, regardless of size or initial ability. During this time, she also assisted European sports medicine experts with exercise testing of elite U.S., European, and Australian competitive swimmers and began developing her interest in exercise physiology research.

Dr. Sothern directs the research efforts and treatment program of the Pediatric

Obesity division at LSUHSC. A licensed clinical exercise physiologist, she revolutionized the pediatric exercise science field with her work in physiologic function and childhood obesity, and moderate-intensity, progressive exercise for children with chronic diseases. The results of her research have been widely published in scientific journals including *Clinical Pediatrics, European Journal of Pediatrics, Journal of the American Dietetic Association, Pediatric Exercise Science, Journal of Investigative Medicine, International Journal of Pediatrics, Acta Pediatrica, Southern Medical Journal, Obesity Research,* and others.

Dr. Sothern has led her field in establishing standardized guidelines for prescribing exercise for children with increasing levels of obesity. Her work in motivating overweight children to be active, based on social cognitive theory, has set the standard for health promotion in children nationwide. She is best known for her work in promoting active play as a means of preventing and treating childhood obesity. She has been a member of the American College of Sports Medicine and the North American Association for the Study of Obesity for more than ten years and currently serves as chairman of the Pediatric Obesity Interest Group. Dr. Sothern is a scientific reviewer for the *Journal of Pediatrics, International Journal of Obesity, American Journal of Clinical Research, Medicine and Science in Sports and Exercise, Journal of Sport and Exercise Therapy,* and *Obesity Research.* She is also a member of the United States Centers for Disease Control's expert panel on childhood obesity.

T. Kristian von Almen, Ph.D., is an adjunct assistant clinical professor in pediatrics at LSUHSC and a child development specialist with the Family Advocacy Care and Education Services (FACES) program of Children's Hospital in New Orleans. Dr. von Almen served as local coinvestigator and intervention director for the Dietary Intervention Study in Children, a clinical trial conducted from 1988 to 1998 in six major U.S. cities and funded by the National Institutes of Health. This program demonstrated the safety and efficacy of a low-saturated-fat diet for lowering LDL-cholesterol levels in preadolescent children while maintaining adequate growth and development through their teenage years.

Dr. von Almen's interest in childhood weight problems began in 1986 when, as a postdoctoral intern, he began illuminating the psychosocial and intervention needs of overweight children and their families. His innovative approach to treating childhood weight problems through the use of family-based multidisciplinary programs, coupled with his emphasis on the A-Factor (positive Attention, Accountability, and Attitude) and relapse prevention program, have proved so successful that they are now used as models for clinicians and scientists worldwide. He is a coauthor of articles published in popular and scientific journals including *Journal of the American Medical Association, Health Psychology, Pediatric and Adolescent Medicine, American Journal of Disease in Childhood,* and *Obesity Research.*

Heidi Schumacher, R.D., L.D.N., C.D.E., is the chief clinical dietitian at Children's Hospital in New Orleans, where she has practiced infant, pediatric, and adolescent nutrition since 1988. Her passion for developing and expanding the nutritional component of the Pediatric Weight Management Program and her years of experience as a pediatric dietitian and Certified Diabetes Educator in a regional pediatric medical center qualify her as an authority on meeting children's nutritional needs while they reach their weight management goals.

Ms. Schumacher has developed and conducts weekly hands-on outpatient educational sessions for overweight and obese children and their families to inspire new ways of understanding, cooking, and eating food. Her one-on-one interactions with these families have enabled her to establish healthy diets and kitchen habits that families can easily integrate with their lives. She also enjoys creating nutritious, kid-approved recipes that satisfy children's taste buds, meet their energy requirements, and encourage healthy, low-fat eating. Ms. Schumacher's objective is to keep the *fun* in food selection, preparation, and consumption. As a Certified Diabetes Educator, she established the nutritional prescriptions and conducts both diabetes and nutritional education for children and adolescents with diabetes mellitus. Her passion is to help children and families to develop manageable dietary habits for optimal health and well-being.

Our combined knowledge, clinical research results, and years of inpatient and outpatient experience have given us a deep understanding of the unique challenges facing overweight children and their parents. But without your own active involvement and commitment to your child's well-being, the Trim Kids Program—or any program—cannot reap long-lasting results. You are the key to your child's success at losing weight and maintaining a healthy lifestyle. You will not be doing this alone, however. Through this book, we will guide you every step of the way so that you and your child will come out winners.

★ ★ ★ ★ ★

# PART ONE

## Setting the
## Stage for Success

# IS MY CHILD OVERWEIGHT?

When Jeff was four years old, his weight was normal. At six, he was slightly over-weight. By eight, he was a little more than chubby. Schoolmates teased him and left him out when they picked team members for sports. It didn't help that Jeff's knees and ankles hurt when he tried to run. His breathing was heavy, his face turned red, and he'd sweat buckets after just five minutes of basketball.

Being physically active hurt (so did the teasing), so Jeff spent less time moving and more time in front of the television, eating high-calorie snacks. The food helped him forget how uncomfortable he felt. Eventually, he avoided sports alto-gether, believing he couldn't keep up with the other kids. It wasn't long before he discovered video games, which became his greatest escape. Soon, it was difficult for him to do an activity as simple as climbing stairs.

Jeff's parents thought he would "grow into" his weight. But he didn't. By the time he was ten years old and came to our clinic, he weighed almost twice what he should for his age. A trip to our clinical lab revealed that although his muscle weight was normal and his bone density was average for a boy his age, 55 percent of his total body weight consisted of fat (a healthy range for boys his age is 16 to 25 percent, and male athletes often have below 12 percent).

Jeff's aerobic fitness score was 60 percent lower than that of other ten-year-old boys. He had difficulty walking faster than three miles per hour (four miles per hour is considered brisk walking). He became completely exhausted and couldn't continue to walk at a moderate speed after only five minutes.

Jeff was severely overweight. He joined our program, began eating differently, and began participating in an exercise program designed for his condition and specific needs. We worked with his pediatrician to structure a safe diet plan.

One year after entering our program, Jeff has maintained his 54-pound weight loss. He participates in track and field. His baseball team—with Jeff playing first base—won the district championship. The football team that didn't let him play the year before because he was too heavy won regionals with Jeff as quarterback. Meanwhile, Jeff's dad now walks two miles every morning. He claims that his son changed his life. Jeff's mother also decided it was time to tackle her own weight problem, and she credits her son as her biggest fan.

### Is My Child Overweight?

Your pediatrician is the best source for determining if your child is overweight. See pages 19–23 for information on how special growth charts can determine this.

Success stories like this fuel our work. So do the phone calls we receive every day from frustrated or anxious parents, health-care providers, and overweight children themselves. Since childhood obesity is a relatively new phenomenon, most people—including doctors—feel defenseless in the battle against it. To complicate matters, the methods that help adults lose weight usually don't work for kids. Our research and experience have taught us that children require a different approach to weight loss—one that can stop a vicious circle unique to overweight children. Our program features a kit of practical tools that can put an end to that circle, resulting in active, healthy, happy children.

## THE VICIOUS CIRCLE OF OVERWEIGHT IN CHILDREN

It takes only a few extra pounds on a youngster to make his clothes feel uncomfortable, his movement restricted, and his enthusiasm for physical activity plummet. When he slows down, weight gain speeds up.

In some cases, children begin gaining unnecessary weight between the ages of three and seven years. By then, they are spending a good deal of time sitting behind a desk at school. After school, they might play video or computer games, or watch several hours of television. Meanwhile, they may be eating fast food three to six times per week (the national average). With those habits, children can easily become overweight or chubby by age seven. Even so, they may not experience any physical repercussions (especially if they're under twelve), except when they exert themselves during active play. Then, they are likely to become short of breath, overheated, and to sweat heavily. At this point, an overweight child may begin to feel inadequate at sports or other physical activities. He participates less, developing a more sedentary lifestyle that exacerbates weight gain. If this vicious circle is ignored, he could easily become chronically obese. Excess weight in children is thus considered a chronic disease that requires lifelong monitoring (similar to diabetes and heart disease) as well as being a vicious circle that must be stopped.

> ## The Power of Parental Expectations
>
> A recent study found that if parents simply set a goal to reduce their child's TV-watching and then reward steps taken toward that goal, the child will lose weight. Also, as children spend more time outdoors, their total physical activity increases.

Some serious long-term consequences of childhood weight problems are emotional in nature. Overweight children are targets of early and systematic discrimination not only by their peers but also by family members and society as a whole. To make matters worse, overweight girls tend to mature physically earlier than their normal-weight friends. Early physical maturation has been associated with low self-esteem and low self-efficacy (a feeling of being unable to succeed at anything one does).

The Trim Kids Program addresses the vicious circle at all points through nutritional changes, increased daily activity, behavior modification, and formal exercise. The families who commit to the program are claiming victory. You can, too!

# FAMILY TIES

To understand what perpetuates the vicious circle of overweight, it's helpful to look at family profiles. Research has revealed that *parental overweight is the single most important predictor of weight problems in children under the age of six*. Heredity certainly comes into play, but it is not the dominant source of the condition. Genetic makeup may *predispose* the condition, but the child's environment *causes* it. Environmental components include:

- What foods, how much, and how often the child eats
- The family's attitude toward food
- The family's eating habits
- The types of activities the family undertakes, such as sports, watching television, computer games, family outings, dancing, or playing cards
- The emotional climate in the household

The family household environment in general has an enormous influence on the child's health and well-being. And scientists have found that it's both the parents' genetic background and behavior characteristics that largely determine their child's body fat. For example, children with overweight mothers often eat a higher percentage of fat than children with normal-weight mothers, because overweight mothers may influence the amount of fat their four- to seven-year-old children consume—the ages when the vicious circle of excess weight may begin.

Research also indicates that 62 percent of mothers with preschool children use food as a reward, a pacifier, or a punishment. Ironically, providing rewards for eating nutritious foods initially enhances preferences for those healthy foods but has a negative effect later when the reward is removed. For example, when a mother makes her child finish his broccoli so he can have an after-dinner sweet, that ultimately tends to reduce the child's liking for broccoli (or whatever the mandated food may be).

---

### Family Circles

- If both parents are of normal weight, the child has only a 7 percent chance of developing severe weight problems.
- If one parent is overweight, the risk of developing weight problems increases to 40 percent.
- If both parents are overweight, the child's risk of becoming overweight doubles to 80 percent.

Just about everyone falls unwittingly into such traps, and since science has only recently discovered the dynamics behind childhood weight problems, there's no way parents could have known enough to respond differently before now. Fortunately, the data we now have can enlighten us about how the cycle begins and how to stop it. The Trim Kids Program will help you provide positive reinforcement through verbal praise and nonfood rewards.

## ENVIRONMENTS THAT PROMOTE OVERWEIGHT KIDS

Although the United States has the greatest percentage of overweight children, industrialization and the adoption of Western lifestyles in Asia, Africa, and the Middle East are predisposing children in those cultures to weight gain as well. In Europe and Russia, where Western lifestyle habits are already established, childhood weight problems are common and are rising rapidly.

There is also a striking relationship between weight and social class. In the United States, adult Caucasian (but not other races) women from lower socioeconomic levels are seven times likelier to be overweight than women from higher levels. There may be a similar relationship in men, but to a lesser degree. Even so, children from all socioeconomic levels who complete our weight-loss program have good success rates. This suggests that if they are in a healthy environment, children from all backgrounds can manage their weight.

The bottom line: genes surely contribute to weight problems, but the family environment has the greatest impact on children's weight gain. The flip side of this fact forms the backbone of our program: *the family environment also has the greatest impact on the child's ability to* lose *weight, keep it off, and build a lifetime of healthy habits.*

## THE FAMILY AS A WINNING WEIGHT-LOSS TEAM

Through the Trim Kids Program, we'll show you, the parent, how to become your child's greatest *advocate and example*—promoting eating, exercise, and lifestyle strategies that the entire family can embrace. Along the way, we promise some fun for your child as she learns more about her body, food, exercise, attitude, and the relationship between them and her family. Years of working with families just like yours have shown that your family will gain not only physical health benefits but emotional ones as well.

In fact, the Trim Kids Program is so successful because we *require participation* of everyone in the immediate family, giving the overweight child

### Nature Versus Nurture

Experts agree that excess pounds appear when susceptible individuals are placed in adverse environments. So, even if your child is genetically at risk for being overweight, his environment can be adjusted to combat the predisposition. He may become chubby even with adjustments, but he needn't be doomed to a life of significant obesity and chronic health problems. Weight management through smart dietary choices, an active lifestyle, and behavior modification is the key.

the best chance of reaching and maintaining his healthy goals. There's also a simpler logic: we can't expect Chubby Charlie to eat a low-fat chicken salad while his sister Lean Jean gobbles pepperoni pizza. We've often seen problems develop in the first few weeks of our program if there is a discrepancy between what the family eats and what the overweight child is asked to eat.

## THE TRIM KIDS' SUPPORT SYSTEM

The idea of making lifestyle changes and becoming your child's advocate may seem overwhelming. That's normal, and we encourage you to talk to friends, family, or professionals to help overcome doubts or fears so you can work comfortably with the program. Regardless of what you're feeling, it is wise to approach this knowing there may be some difficult times ahead.

Guilt is one of the most common obstacles. Typically, parents with overweight children feel guilty, thinking they have passed on bad genes, bad food, or bad habits to their child. Embarrassment that their child is fat feeds their guilt. Some grieve that their child is suffering and that they've not been able to successfully help. Others try to ignore the painful issue, saying that there isn't really a problem.

The greatest weapon against guilt is power. By gaining the power to reverse the cycle of overweight problems, parents can change years of emotional and physical pain into productive, active steps toward healthy living. To that end, the Trim Kids Program provides:

- Support to make lifestyle changes
- Knowledge about how to successfully make the changes
- Understanding of what contributes to and combats the problem
- Specific steps you can take to ensure long-lasting changes
- Pride that you are helping initiate healthy changes in your child and family

Most important, you can trust that you are a normal person who has done nothing *wrong* to have an overweight child, and an *exceptional* parent by choosing to do something about it.

## QUESTIONS AND ANSWERS

**Q: *I've tried to get my child to lose weight before and nothing has worked. How will this be any different?***

A: Our techniques are tried and true. Our expertise is successful weight management and healthy lifelong results. Most important, we show you how to focus on what works rather than on what doesn't. We even provide strategies for those times when our suggestions don't work! There's never a single solution for every child. But we've found there's not a single child for whom there are no solutions.

**Q: *How do I know the program is safe?***

A: We are not only doctors, dietitians, psychologists, and experienced exercise physiologists but also well-established scientists. We have published articles in leading scientific and health-related journals explaining how the program works and why it is safe and effective. We also consider your child's overall health and medical history, rather than simply focusing on weight-loss goals. And we promote the program *only* in conjunction with a doctor's supervision.

*Q: Will I draw too much attention to my child's overweight condition if I use this book?*

A: That depends. If your child is younger, probably not. Most young children aren't as aware of the changes you're implementing or the negative social consequences of their condition. Older children may be more resistant because of peer pressure. They want to eat what their friends eat and do what their friends do—which may not include what our program calls for. Even so, if an older child is noticeably overweight (or obese), she is already receiving negative attention and will probably welcome help. If in doubt, read the book on your own, first. Then approach your child with facts about the condition. Explain that you found a book that can help. If she's interested, go for it. If not, wait. You can still make lots of changes in the family's diet and physical activities without having to formally enlist her in the program.

---

**TRIM KIDS TESTIMONIAL**

## A Parent's Perspective

"Before we started the program, Toby suffered a lot. We had tried other things to help him lose weight, but they didn't work. He wasn't happy. I wasn't happy. He was only ten years old, and he just wanted to be accepted by other kids. He was so isolated, and I didn't realize, until his schoolteacher called me, that he was teased all the time and didn't ever stick up for himself.

"Once he started the program, he began to lose weight right away. He blossomed emotionally because people started telling him he looked good. He became a different child. He had more energy, and he started excelling in ways he never had. The day I saw him run for the first time—it hit me. My son was running and loving it, and I knew everything was going to be all right."

---

*Q: What if my doctor says my child will grow out of the condition?*

A: Most pediatricians today are aware of the growing epidemic of childhood weight problems. If your child's condition is mild, the pediatrician may suggest waiting it out. That's fine. But ask the doctor for a definite time frame in which you'd like to see the situation change. Younger children should grow out of it within six months. Older children take longer, up to two years. If during that time your child's weight increases dramatically rather than slowly or holds steady as she grows, then it's time to take action.

**Q: *How long will it take for the program to work?***

A: Overweight children will typically take about six to twelve months to achieve a healthy weight. More overweight children will usually take longer. How closely your child follows her nutrition and exericse plan will also help determine how long it will take.

# EMBRACING THE ELEMENTS

## HEALTHY NUTRITION, PHYSICAL ACTIVITY AND EXERCISE, BEHAVIOR MODIFICATION

The Trim Kids Program takes a three-pronged approach to weight management and lifestyle goals. Our fifteen years of clinical research experience show that if any one of these elements is omitted from the regimen, it simply will not work. The elements include healthy nutrition, a commitment to exercise and more daily physical activities, and behavior modification.

Your level of participation in the program will greatly determine the level of your child's success. No matter what you say to your child, your *actions* and *attitude* will guide him. The primary changes you will need to make include:

- Shopping for and cooking healthier foods, as well as educating your child about healthy food choices
- Creating an atmosphere conducive to ongoing physical activity and supervising your child's exercise program while participating with him as much as possible
- Recognizing your child for the positive changes he's making

- Establishing goals and enforcing household rules that support meeting those goals
- Monitoring and cheering his progress

## NUTRITIONAL KNOWLEDGE

We make changing your eating habits as simple as possible. Our dietary guidelines use lists of food groups so that just a few easy-to-remember facts let you compare calories and fats and control portions. You'll discover:

- Which foods to buy and how to read food labels
- How to prepare nutritious low-fat meals
- Ways to encourage family members to try new foods while maintaining fun at the dinner table
- What it means to eat for optimum health and weight-management success

Since the program is flexible, you can even occasionally indulge in your favorite dessert or in pizza with everything on it. Meanwhile, you may discover a whole new menu of tasty treats.

## PHYSICAL ACTIVITY AND STRUCTURED EXERCISE

Everyone likes to have fun, but kids are *motivated* by fun. They'll do just about anything if it's playful—including exercise. You, too, can have fun with the exercise component of the program. As your child's coach, advocate, and example, you encourage movement and exercise in your child while becoming more active yourself.

That means that when you visit the sporting goods store to buy your child a pair of in-line skates, get some for yourself, too. When you turn off the television to prevent your child from "vegging out," suggest playing a family game of basketball (we'll share more ideas in later chapters). Create a new lifestyle that includes weekend outings such as hiking, biking, swimming, and skiing—anything that's physically active. Invite friends and family who also enjoy being active. They can help fuel the fire and keep things moving.

The truth about exercise is that children do it differently from adults, and for different reasons. We'll explain this concept and help you home in on the activities your child likes to do, and we'll describe how you can facilitate them. We'll ask you to create places both inside and outside your home where kids can romp around, have fun, and burn calories. Of course there will still be moments when your child sits watching television. But even then you can initiate something fun and physical—like standing up during commercials, taking your kid's hand, and boogying until you're both about to drop. The key to promoting more physical activity in your child's life is to incorporate simple activities into each day, as well as through dedi-

**TRIM KIDS TESTIMONIAL**

## A Parent's Perspective

"At first, Tyler was reluctant to start the program. But his grandmother really pushed it, so he finally gave in. He's matured so much since he began losing weight. He has more self-confidence. His feet and knees don't hurt him anymore, and he has more energy to do things.

"The first four months were hard. The family complained a lot. But now we shop together and eat together, I'm back into cooking, and it made me take back time for my family. Now Tyler reads food labels and knows what's good for him. We go out to eat once a month, but he orders what's healthy for him to eat. It's been good for all of us, and I've lost 36 pounds!"

cated exercises as part of the child's weekly routine. *All* physical activity burns calories.

Every child needs an exercise program appropriate to his age, current weight, condition, health, and personal interests. Severely overweight children simply cannot perform the same activities as other children, and even mildly to moderately overweight kids have limitations during long periods of exercise or when they try to go too fast. We'll show you how to

## Fit and Smart

Children who are physically fit are absent from school less often and may perform better academically.

introduce exercises at a pace that will not hurt your child or make him feel defeated. We'll show you how to make sure he experiences initial success—the cornerstone of all successful learning and change. Your job, especially when he first starts his exercise routine, is to act as both coach and admiring cheerleader.

## BEHAVIOR MODIFICATION

Before you expect your child to change his habits, take a moment to evaluate your own. Start with the words you use when speaking to yourself, to your child, or to others.

You may believe there are *bad* foods, habits, and emotions. We believe there are only *healthy* and *unhealthy* foods, habits, and emotions. As you gear up to become your child's greatest advocate, lose the value judgments—of yourself, your child, and others—and reword your perspective in terms of what's *healthy* and *unhealthy*.

The next time your child is sulking and reaches for food to console himself, refrain from thinking or saying, "Don't eat that! You'll just put on more weight!" Rather, try to redirect her—for example, try saying, "Hey, how about we go for a walk and talk about school?"

And finally, when you hear unkind remarks about your child—from people you know or people you don't—respond to them as though they have made an unhealthy comment. To the remark, "Gee, that kid is chubby," you could reply, "That's very insensitive. He's working hard on being healthy and happy. Please keep your comments to yourself."

It's also necessary to change some of your own behaviors, habits, and routines. If you've been passive so far, you no longer can be. You will need

---

### TRIM KIDS TESTIMONIAL

## A Child's Perspective

"People were mean to me. They told me I was the fattest dude in the world, and they always picked on me. I felt pretty bad. I wanted to go into the program, but I was very nervous. I was afraid I wouldn't lose weight and afraid I might gain some. But my sister told me I have more willpower than anyone else in the family. So I told myself I wouldn't sneak food. I do standing push-ups against the wall and stomach crunches [pages 183, 332], and I ride my bike at least twenty or thirty minutes twice a week. I've lost 25 pounds, and I feel different. I used to be shy because I was afraid people would call me names, but I'm not nervous anymore. So I have more friends. I didn't know I had strength until I did the program."

—Benjamin, age ten

to commit to this program as the team leader, viewing your overweight child as the star player and the rest of your family as members of the support team. If you approach family-oriented physical activities, new ways of cooking and eating, and problem solving as a labor of love rather than as a burdensome obligation, you will have more energy to start and maximize the benefits of the program.

You'll have plenty of support along the way. We support you by:

- Helping you shift from a negative to a positive focus regarding weight, food, and activity. Your entire family will gain skills for maintaining a sense of control, achieving mastery, and feeling comfortable about the program
- Teaching practical steps for eating and exercise that will make your family feel better physically and mentally

- Recognizing the need to honor family traditions while also supporting the goals of the overweight child
- Helping you and all family members shed years of unhealthy habits so that you can become a happier, healthier family

That sums up the basics that keep our program focused on success: an improved nutritional and eating regimen, increased daily physical activity and structured exercise, and other behavioral changes. Put those under the umbrella of your commitment and encouragement, and your child *will* beat the odds of growing up unhealthy and overweight. Along the way, lots of things can improve, including:

---

**TRIM KIDS TESTIMONIAL**

## A Parent's Perspective

"My eldest son has a weight problem, but his brother, Chad, is a beanpole. Chad's only seven years old, so it was hard for him to understand why we began eating more healthfully. One night he said, 'What happened to our three-thing dinner? We're only having a two-thing dinner.' I didn't realize what he meant until someone pointed out that before we started the program, we'd have three things on the plate: a meat, a vegetable, and a high-calorie starch. I no longer serve high-calorie starches all the time, and Chad didn't understand that. From then on, I always prepared two vegetables so he could have his three-thing dinner. And now Chad reads food labels and understands fat and sugar grams. Still, we take him out to have a hamburger once a week so he doesn't feel deprived."

- Your child's health
- Your child's self-esteem
- Your relationship with your child
- Your family's overall dynamics
- Your understanding and knowledge of what drives the vicious circle of weight problems, and your ability to find and follow through with solutions
- Your own peace of mind as you help save your child from discrimination and a bleak future
- Your feeling of being in control: your family will no longer be driven by the issues of your child's health and weight problems

We'll help dispel myths about childhood weight problems—myths that too many families and children believe. In the end, your child will be equipped to handle the disease for the rest of his life. But this can happen only if everyone is ready for a change. If you suspect that your child may not be ready, or if you think you may not be ready, take a moment to check your commitment. Turn to page 91 in "Week 1" and check your commitment rating. If now is not the time, come back to the program later when you and your family are truly committed.

## QUESTIONS AND ANSWERS

*Q: Won't this program be expensive since it involves buying healthier products and exercise equipment?*

A:   Initially you may see an increase in your grocery bill, because some products that are low in fat or sugar can be pricier than bargain brands. Keep in mind, however, that by avoiding fast foods and restaurants, you will be saving much more than the little extra you're spending on a few select products. And buying exercise equipment of any kind is optional. As you move into the program, you'll see how to avoid those costs and still help your child stay active.

*Q: I'm afraid that committing to the program will make my life harder. It sounds as though implementing these changes will be a hassle.*

A:   The program is designed ultimately to make your life easier. True, you'll need to spend more time communicating with your child and more time preparing food. But you'll find the time you spend with your child very rewarding, and we'll show you "quick and dirty" recipes so your life won't be terribly disrupted. You'll also learn how to set limits and redirect your child away from unhealthy choices. That will eventually free you from some of the hassles you're dealing with now.

**Q: *I'm afraid that I will damage my daughter emotionally by paying so much attention to weight.***

A: You will cause much more harm, physically and psychologically, by not taking action than by taking constructive action. Our experience reveals that children and families feel much better about themselves and each other after they participate in the program—not worse. The good feelings are both psychological and physical. The new family household rules will also eliminate some of the weight issues.

**Q: *I'm a single working mother, and I hardly have enough time to make my bed, much less spend so much time, energy, and effort on something like this. How can I manage it all?***

A: Any change appears more difficult at the outset than after it has been established. We're not asking for hours per day from you—but hours per week. If you look closely at your schedule, you'll probably discover that you are making choices about how you spend your time that you weren't even aware of. For example, if you usually watch television to unwind, you could now unwind with your child on a casual walk. These are choices you already make, and making different choices won't require much more of your time. Your fears and uncertainty are normal. The rewards, however, far outweigh the sacrifices. Also, in no time you'll find you're a pro at this, and ultimately you will feel a greater sense of control and effectiveness as a parent.

# 3

# GEARING UP AND
# GETTING STARTED

## WORKING WITH A DOCTOR

Weight problems are medical conditions. As such, they require the help of a physician. Indeed, the primary relationship you must maintain throughout the program is with your child's doctor. Some studies indicate that when children are put on a diet, their growth may be temporarily delayed. Close monitoring of the child's height and growth during weight reduction programs is critical for the health and safety of every participant.

In week 1 of the Trim Kids Program, you will have the doctor plot your child's height and weight on a growth chart and assist you in figuring out just how much weight is reasonable for your child to lose. You'll tell the doctor that you are interested in starting this program and would like to enlist the doctor's help in doing so. He or she may wish to run additional tests to ensure that this program will be safe for your child to follow. You'll also

### The Power of Medicine

A recent study showed that preschool children who were taken for frequent visits to their pediatrician or family physician were less likely to be overweight than those with less frequent visits. Your pediatrician is your most valuable asset in preventing weight problems in your child.

make a follow-up appointment three months from the date you start the program, or as your doctor suggests, so that the doctor can assess your child's progress.

## FIND OUT IF YOUR CHILD IS OVERWEIGHT

With your child's pediatrician or family physician, you'll need to ascertain how overweight your child is, and her risk of becoming an overweight adult. Plotting your child's weight and height on the U.S. Centers for Disease Control (USCDC) body mass index (BMI) growth charts helps the doctor determine what percentile best describes your child in relation to other children in the same age group.

Healthy body weight corresponds closely to height percentile. For example, if your child is at the 90th percentile on the USCDC BMI growth charts, she is considered at risk for overweight because her score is above the 85th percentile. Children whose BMI scores are above the 95th percentile on the charts are considered overweight.

Reviewing these percentiles with your child's doctor can also verify that your child is slowly developing a weight problem. By observing his weight over a one- to three-year period, you can see how his condition is progressing. A greater increase in weight percentile relative to height percentile over time suggests a potential problem. But you also need to keep in mind that for every inch your child grows, it is normal to gain an average of 3 to 5 pounds. This fact becomes very important after weight loss. Working with and communicating regularly with your child's doctor ensures that your calculations are accurate and will give you necessary assurance that your approach to weight loss is appropriate for your child's medical history and optimum health.

In addition to the height-weight percentile charts, there are several other ways to assess how much of your child's weight consists of fat, lean muscle, or bone. They are:

- *Body mass index (BMI):* This is a simple number that corresponds well with body fat, derived from an equation based on your child's height and weight. As you will soon learn (pages 23–24), the four "levels" of the Trim Kids Program—Red, Yellow, Green, and Blue—are derived from the BMI. You can figure your child's BMI using the following formula:

Your child's weight in pounds: _____ ÷ 2.2 = _____ kilograms

Your child's height in inches: _____ × 2.54 ÷ 100 = _____ meters

Weight in kilograms = _____ ÷ (height in meters _____ $^2$) = _____ BMI score

*Example: Paul is twelve years old, weighs 120 pounds, and is 48 inches tall.*

*Step 1: Divide his weight by 2.2 (120 ÷ 2.2 = 54.5 kilograms).*
*Step 2: Multiply his height by 2.54 and divide by 100 (48 × 2.54) ÷ 100 = 1.22 meters.*
*Step 3: Now divide his weight in kilograms by his height squared (height × height).*
*Weight in kilograms = 54.5 ÷ (height in meters squared [1.22 × 1.22])* = 54.5 ÷ 1.49 = <u>36.6</u> BMI score. If you compare this score with the table below for twelve-year-old boys, you'll find that Paul would be at Level I, Red, because his score (36.6) is more than the score (26) listed in the column "Level I—Red."

Now compare your child's BMI score with the numbers in the chart on pages 21–23. (Please note: there are separate charts for boys and girls.)

If you're having trouble using this formula, see your pediatrician—or go to the U.S. Centers for Disease Control's website at www.cdc.gov, where there are plenty of tables to help you.

- *DEXA or underwater weighing:* These are the most accurate ways to measure how much of a person's weight is fat, muscle, and bone. They tend to be costly, but they can generate valuable information. DEXA measures bone density and weight and estimates muscle and fat weight. Underwater weighing uses Archimedes' principle of water displacement to determine the percentage of body fat. Both have only a 1 to 2 percent error rate.
- *Skinfold analysis:* Although this technique must be performed by a trained health-care professional, it's still the least expensive method for determin-

ing fat, muscle, and bone weight. A special tool is used to measure the thickness of the area between skin and muscle to estimate how much of the weight is fat. You should know, however, that this method is not 100 percent accurate; it has a 3 to 5 percent error rate.

- *Bioelectrical impedance analysis (BIA) test:* This process yields the same information as the skinfold test and has the same error rate, but it usually costs more. It uses a very low electric current to determine body fat.

Sometimes excess weight may not be fat but heavy bones or strong muscles. These tests will help you differentiate among fat, lean muscle, and bone weight so you can more accurately determine how much weight loss is appropriate (since fat weight is the primary reason to engage in a weight loss program). It's especially important to have these tests performed if your child is very active in sports, seems muscular, or has large bones.

## BODY MASS INDEX CHARTS*

*Boys 5–17 years of age*

| Age | Level I—Red | Level II—Yellow | Level III—Green | Level IV—Blue |
|---|---|---|---|---|
| | Severe Overweight more than 97th % BMI | Overweight more than 95th % BMI | At Risk for Overweight more than 85th % BMI | Healthy Weight 50th to 85th % BMI |
| <5 years | See your pediatrician | See your pediatrician | See your pediatrician | See your pediatrician |
| 5 years | more than 18 | more than 18 | more than 17 | 15–17 |
| 6 years | more than 19 | more than 18 | more than 17 | 15–17 |
| 7 years | more than 20 | more than 19 | more than 17 | 16–17 |
| 8 years | more than 21 | more than 20 | more than 18 | 16–18 |

| Age | Level I—Red | Level II—Yellow | Level III—Green | Level IV—Blue |
|---|---|---|---|---|
| | Severe Overweight more than 97th % BMI | Overweight more than 95th % BMI | At Risk for Overweight more than 85th % BMI | Healthy Weight 50th to 85th % BMI |
| 9 years | more than 23 | more than 21 | more than 19 | 16–19 |
| 10 years | more than 24 | more than 22 | more than 19 | 17–19 |
| 11 years | more than 25 | more than 23 | more than 20 | 17–20 |
| 12 years | more than 26 | more than 24 | more than 21 | 18–21 |
| 13 years | more than 27 | more than 25 | more than 22 | 19–22 |
| 14 years | more than 28 | more than 26 | more than 23 | 19–23 |
| 15 years | more than 29 | more than 27 | more than 24 | 20–24 |
| 16 years | more than 29 | more than 28 | more than 24 | 21–24 |
| 17 years | more than 30 | more than 28 | more than 25 | 21–25 |

*BMI scores are rounded to the nearest 1.0.

## Girls 5–17 years of age

| Age | Level I—Red | Level II—Yellow | Level III—Green | Level IV—Blue |
|---|---|---|---|---|
| | Severe Overweight more than 97th % BMI | Overweight more than 95th % BMI | At Risk for Overweight more than 85th % BMI | Healthy Weight 50th to 85th % BMI |
| <5 years | See your pediatrician | See your pediatrician | See your pediatrician | See your pediatrician |
| 5 years | more than 19 | more than 18 | more than 17 | 15–17 |

| Age | Level I—Red | Level II—Yellow | Level III—Green | Level IV—Blue |
| :---: | :---: | :---: | :---: | :---: |
| | Severe Overweight more than 97th % BMI | Overweight more than 95th % BMI | At Risk for Overweight more than 85th % BMI | Healthy Weight 50th to 85th % BMI |
| 6 years | more than 20 | more than 19 | more than 17 | 15–17 |
| 7 years | more than 21 | more than 20 | more than 18 | 16–18 |
| 8 years | more than 22 | more than 21 | more than 18 | 16–18 |
| 9 years | more than 23 | more than 22 | more than 19 | 16–19 |
| 10 years | more than 25 | more than 23 | more than 20 | 17–20 |
| 11 years | more than 26 | more than 24 | more than 21 | 18–21 |
| 12 years | more than 27 | more than 25 | more than 22 | 18–22 |
| 13 years | more than 28 | more than 26 | more than 23 | 19–23 |
| 14 years | more than 29 | more than 27 | more than 23 | 19–23 |
| 15 years | more than 30 | more than 28 | more than 24 | 20–24 |
| 16 years | more than 31 | more than 29 | more than 25 | 21–25 |
| 17 years | more than 32 | more than 30 | more than 25 | 21–25 |

*BMI scores are rounded to the nearest 1.0.

# THE MEANING OF THE TRIM KIDS COLOR CODES

The needs of overweight children vary, so we have created four distinct levels that correspond to the severity of a child's condition and the specific considerations for a child in that weight range. So, for example, children who fall into Level I (Red,

Severe) will do different physical exercises in the Trim Kids Program from those in Level III (Green, At Risk for Overweight). As your child loses weight, he will graduate to a new level (or color) of the program. One reason we use the colors is to accentuate positive accomplishments. That means when a severely overweight child in the Red level loses enough weight to graduate to the Yellow level, he is reminded that his initial short-term goals have been met.

The color-coded levels are broken down as follows.

- **Level I, Red**: This level includes children with severe overweight conditions or those with medical problems due to their weight. Their BMI is higher than that of 97 percent of other children in this country.
- **Level II, Yellow**: This is for children with overweight conditions who have special needs related to diet, behavior, or fitness.
- **Level III, Green**: Many children at risk for overweight will be at this level when they start the program. It is also designed to help stop the onset of overweight conditions.
- **Level IV, Blue**: This regimen keeps your child healthy for life and is the goal of the overall program.

If your child's weight problem is severe (the Red level), your pediatrician may request additional medical tests and assessments. These tests typically screen for problems with endocrinology, genetics, cardiology, cholesterol, insulin, thyroid or other hormones, blood pressure, the respiratory system, muscles, or bones that can accompany severe weight problems. If your child is already seeing a specialist and is under treatment for a medical condition, you can discuss with your pediatrician the relationships between existing treatments and medications and your child's weight-loss goals.

Your doctor may also have resources for enlisting the help of an exercise physiologist, physical therapist, registered dietitian, and psychologist if you feel the need.

## CHILDREN AT RISK

As children grow and enter school, weight becomes a strong predictor of whether or not they will become overweight adults—in fact, 80 percent of overweight twelve-year-olds will become overweight adults. That's why it's so important to establish healthy habits early, and to begin monitoring a weight gain as soon as you notice it.

Even if your child isn't currently overweight, it's easy for her to gain unhealthy weight without anyone's being aware of it. One way to assess whether she may develop a problem is to observe her behavior:

1. Is she always hungry?
2. Does she never seem to be satiated?
3. Does she choose to watch television rather than play outdoors?
4. Does she seem awkward or resistant when trying new sports, dances, or other physical activities?
5. Is she shy or withdrawn around other kids, or even isolated?

If you answered "yes" to most of these questions, your child could be on the way to troublesome weight gain. Keep an eye on her and make mental notes about how she develops. It's not always easy to notice weight gain when you are around someone every day. Ask a friend or family member who sees your child intermittently to help decide if a problem is developing. Or, if she wears baggy clothing, encourage a trip to the pool and take a good look while she's in her swimsuit. You may feel awkward at first, but the sooner you catch the problem, the easier it is to remedy.

It's easier to follow a weight-management program when the child is young, so start as soon as you can. Older kids already have some independence: they know what they want to eat at the movie theater; they have figured out ways to avoid exercise. You have more influence over younger kids, and you can teach them early to be health-conscious.

## PHYSICAL ACTIVITY AND DIETARY RISK QUESTIONNAIRE

We've created a simple questionnaire that will help you understand your child's activity and eating habits. It will also reveal how much activity may be lacking, and guide you in what needs to be introduced.

# Physical Activity Questionnaire

*First, let's rate your child's physical activity. Circle the number that best describes your child (circle only one number):*

0. Sits most of the time. Occasionally he walks around slowly.
1. Likes to bowl, play billiards, go fishing, do puzzles, color, and play board games or marbles. But he likes television and video and computer games more.
2. Sometimes rides a bike or plays in the swimming pool. Or he'll dance or do some other indoor physical activity or sports about once or twice a week.
3. Plays on a sports team or goes to a dance or other indoor physical activity two or three times per week. Sometimes plays outside but doesn't run very much.
4. Plays on a sports team, dances, or does another indoor physical activity two or three times a week. Plays outside one to three times a week. Likes to run. Spends at least two to three hours on weekend days practicing or playing outside at a park, at a swimming pool, or in a gym.
5. Plays chase, tag, basketball, soccer, or some other indoor or outdoor game three to four times a week. Or he is on a sports team or involved with dance, gymnastics, or a martial arts team that practices three to five times per week. Really likes to run. Practices or plays at least five to six hours on weekend days.
6. Plays chase, tag, basketball, soccer, or some other indoor or outdoor game five to six times per week. Or he is on a sports team or is involved with dance, gymnastics, or a martial arts team that practices four to six times per week. Would rather run than walk anytime. Practices or plays almost all day on weekends.
7. Plays chase, tag, basketball, soccer, or some other indoor or outdoor game every day, or is on two or more sports teams or is involved with dance, gymnastics, or a martial arts team that practices every day. Would rather run than walk anytime. Practices or plays all day on Saturday or Sunday.

List the numeral you circled above:_____

# Dietary Risk Questionnaire

*Now rate your child's eating habits. After each statement, circle the number that describes your child. (Circle only one number.)*

| Eating Habits | Unhealthy | Less Healthy | Healthy | Your Child's Score: |
| --- | --- | --- | --- | --- |
| My child eats fast food (hamburgers, fried chicken or nuggets, french fries, bacon, sausage, biscuits) . . . | 0<br>More than three times per week | 1<br>More than once per week | 2<br>Less than once per week | |
| My child drinks sodas and fruit drinks . . . | 0<br>More than three times per week | 1<br>More than once per week | 2<br>Less than once per week | |
| My child eats chips or nachos . . . | 0<br>More than three times per week | 1<br>More than once per week | 2<br>Less than once per week | |
| When it comes to vegetable intake, my child . . . | 0<br>Dislikes most vegetables—eats them less than once per week | 1<br>Likes a few—does not eat vegetables more than three to five times per week | 2<br>Likes a variety—eats vegetables more than five times per week | |
| When it comes to breakfast, my child . . . | 0<br>Skips breakfast most of the time | 1<br>Skips breakfast some of the time | 2<br>Never skips breakfast | |

| Eating Habits | Unhealthy | Less Healthy | Healthy | Your Child's Score: |
|---|---|---|---|---|
| The snacks in the pantry currently include . . . | 0<br>Chips, nachos<br>Hot dogs, salami,<br>Vienna sausage<br>Frosted cookies,<br>Brownies<br>Sweet rolls,<br>Frosted snack cakes<br>Soda, fruit drinks<br>Ice cream bars | 2<br>Fruit<br>Crackers—graham, wheat<br>Popcorn, pretzels,<br>Unfrosted cereals, oatmeal<br>Granola bars, trail mix<br>Nuts, peanut butter<br>Cheese (part-skim), skim or low-fat milk<br>100 percent fruit juice | | |

*Total what you circled on the Dietary Risk Questionnaire:*_____

Add your totals from the Physical Activity Questionnaire and the Dietary Risk Questionnaire:_____

- If the score is *greater* than 7, your child is less likely to be at risk, but it's still a good idea to periodically monitor your child's eating and activity level.
- If the score is *less* than 7, your child may be at risk of becoming overweight.

Follow the guidelines in this book to help halt the development of weight problems. Work with your child's pediatrician to develop an individual plan if your child is already overweight.

# 4

# FROM FATTENING
# TO FULFILLING
# FOODS

Sharon is a single working mom with three kids. Her two eldest are both physically fit, active girls. One is on a soccer team; the other is heavily into gymnastics. Her youngest, Blake, is more of a bookworm. The girls find rides to their after-school activities, while Blake spends his time at the school library doing homework or playing on a computer until Sharon can pick him up. He usually munches on a candy bar or gulps down some soda while he works.

After picking up Blake and before fetching the girls, Sharon regularly stops at one of several fast-food places for a take-out dinner. Blake likes to eat his on their way to gather the girls. Then, when they get home, Sharon eats while answering phone calls, and the girls eat in front of the television. Blake sees their french fries and burgers and craves something more, so he goes to the refrigerator and pulls out his dessert. He drinks some juice and eats some chips before bed as a kind of ritual.

After a few years of this, Blake's sisters are still active and fairly healthy. But Blake weighs 200 pounds at age ten and couldn't make it up the stairs at Disney World when the family vacationed there. His blood pressure is elevated, and he's headed for a life of misery.

## FOOD FACTS: FINDING YOUR WAY OUT OF THE FAST-FOOD JUNGLE TO A FRESH-FOOD GARDEN

The idea of coming home and preparing a big meal isn't at the top of most parents' list. Busy parents have come to rely heavily on fast food or packaged prepared foods that are typically high in fat and calories.

The Trim Kids Program has a different agenda. We suggest that you shop for and cook nutritious foods, and eat as a family whenever possible. We urge you to read food labels, exercise portion control when necessary, and learn a basic system to keep track of how much and what kind of food is enough for your child's particular condition and weight goals. We'll provide dozens of easy-to-prepare recipes, lots of cooking tips that speed up the process, and innovative ways to weave these new cooking and eating habits into your life week by week. We will also include healthier choices of restaurant and convenience foods to help accommodate parents' busy schedules.

### The Basic Rules of Healthy Eating

Feeding your child foods that are lower in fat and sugar and higher in fiber will help her feel full faster, automatically reducing the number of calories she consumes. This basic step will help curb her craving for high-fat or high-sugar foods. From now on, hand her high-fiber foods including whole grains, fruits, and vegetables. Consume *less* of these foods:

- High-calorie snack food such as chips, frosted snack cakes, pizza snacks, breakfast pastries, and nachos
- Fast food
- Processed (white) bread and bread products
- Regular mayonnaise, butter, or margarine
- High-calorie meat such as fried chicken, sausages, and ribs
- Sodas, fruit drinks, sport drinks
- Candy, ice cream, cookies, and cakes

### FAST FOOD

Given the leading role that fast foods play in today's world, it is wise to take a close look at what those juicy burgers, greasy fries, and sweet sodas contain—and how they are contributing to your child's condition. That way, it becomes easier and easier to eat less of them.

## SOME FAST-FOOD FAT FACTS

| | Amount | Average Fat Grams | Average Calories | Percent of Fat Calories |
|---|---|---|---|---|
| Croissant sandwich | 1 | 46 | 600 | 69% |
| Cheeseburger | 1 | 40 | 700 | 51% |
| Chicken tenders | 6 pieces | 18 | 375 | 43% |
| French fries | Large | 25 | 550 | 41% |
| Chocolate shake | Medium | 7 | 320 | 19% |
| Pizza | 1 slice | 20 | 350 | 51% |
| Fried chicken breast | 1 | 28 | 470 | 54% |
| Fried chicken sandwich | 1 | 35 | 600 | 52% |

When you consider that a healthy caloric intake for an average, normal-weight ten-year-old child is 1,600 to 2,200 calories per day, with no more than 30 percent (about 60 to 70 grams) of fat calories, an average meal at one of these places could easily rack up enough calories (up to 2,000) to fill an entire day—and then there's the fat content! In addition, these foods tend to replace more nutritious foods (whole grains, fruits, and vegetables), which are lower in fat and may even have a protective cholesterol-lowering effect. No wonder children who commonly eat fast foods have a higher risk of developing clogged arteries similar to the arteries of adults five times their age. It doesn't take long to do serious damage when you rely on junk food as a staple.

In addition, like so many other things we eat, these foods also consist of refined flour, preservatives, and inordinate amounts of sugar or sodium. Such foods:

- Have been stripped of their true nutritional value
- Have been pumped up with artificial ingredients to make them juicier (or higher in fat)
- Often contain additional preservatives
- May be prepared with unhealthy fats and excessive amounts of sodium, which can contribute to the development of heart disease

## OVEREATING AND PORTION CONTROL

Part of your child's problem may be a need to consume more food to feel full. Unlike thinner kids, many of the overweight kids we see apparently don't have the same mechanism to self-limit how much they eat. That results in a higher overall caloric intake, especially when they eat fast food and other junk foods.

We don't know why they can't stop. Children from the same family can have different degrees of control over how much they consume. One sibling may feel full and stop after eating a reasonable portion, while another doesn't feel satisfied and continues to eat.

We do know that diets high in fat and sugar can trigger the release of certain chemicals in the brain that actually increase craving and appetite. Changing your child's diet so that it includes less fat and less sugar can help alleviate this cycle over time. Reteaching the body portion control, especially when weight loss is indicated, also helps to prevent excessive caloric intake. Over time, limiting portions (if indicated) and decreasing fat and simple sugar intake retrains the body to decrease secretion of the chemicals that trigger these cravings.

### Thin Isn't Always Healthy

Some children are frustrated because they know other kids who can eat as much as they want but never get fat. Our reply to this common cry is, "Just because they're skinny doesn't mean they are healthy!" Good nutrition is a cornerstone to good health, and losing weight is often a result of eating well. No matter how old or young, fat or thin a person is, healthy eating habits reduce the risk of heart disease and certain cancers. The Trim Kids Program is ultimately about maintaining life-long health, not only about weight loss.

## SUGAR IS SWEET, BUT . . .

What most people either don't know or don't want to know about sugar is that although sugar is fat-free, it is not free of calories. So when your child bypasses high-fat cookies for fat-free cookies, be mindful that he'll probably still eat too many, perceiving anything "fat-free" as "safe." When we consume more calories than we need, even in the form of sugar, it is stored as fat in the body. This mechanism perpetuates a craving for sugar or carbohydrates in general by causing the brain to secrete chemicals that insist on *more!*

Reducing the amount of simple sugar in your child's diet is an important component to achieving weight-loss goals. It may surprise you to learn that soft drinks, artificially flavored fruit drinks, and sports drinks can skyrocket your child's sugar intake to hundreds of grams per day. It is fairly common for kids we work with to have been drinking more than *1,000 calories per day* in sugar-laden beverages! That's because a 16-ounce fruit drink can contain more than 70 grams of sugar, or more than 15 spoonfuls. That's the same amount of sugar as in three pieces of cake!

Although natural fruit juice is nutritious, it can be a source of too much fruit sugar and plenty of calories. A 12-ounce glass of grape juice contains 60 grams of fructose (fruit sugar) and more than 200 calories. Until now, you may have thought your child's food intake was the main reason for his weight gain, when in fact it could be the amount of sugar-containing beverages he is drinking. One of the participants in our program lost 2 pounds during her first week in the program simply by replacing soft drinks with water.

On the Trim Kids Program, your child will automatically consume less sugar. This doesn't mean she'll never get to eat another piece of cake or

### Types of Sugar

Food labels list ingredients in order of quantity. The first ingredient, therefore, is what the product mostly contains, the second is the next greatest ingredient, and so on. Beware of these types of sugars if they are listed within the first three ingredients of a food or beverage.

- White sugar
- Sucrose
- High-fructose corn syrup
- Dextrose

never drink her favorite beverage again. She just won't be able to have it as often and will learn to consume a safe, reasonable portion.

## THE LOWDOWN ON FAT

Fat, especially in infants, is an important nutrient for development. But fat contains more than double the calories of other nutrients and can easily result in an excess of calories when too much is consumed. This is especially true for children over two years of age. The American Academy of Pediatrics and the American Heart Association make this recommendation: dietary fats generally should not be restricted in the diets of children under two years of age because they are important to the development of the brain.

To be heart-healthy, fat also has to be the right kind—such as a monounsaturated fat. All fats are high in calories and can add extra pounds, but unhealthy fats, such as saturated and hydrogenated fats and trans fatty acids, can also increase the risk of high blood cholesterol levels and heart disease. Unhealthy fats are found in "junk" food and fast food, primarily because of the types of oils used in preparing these foods. Other sources of unhealthy fats include fatty animal products, whole milk and dairy products, butter, and margarines containing hydrogenated or partially hydrogenated vegetable oils. Reading food labels will help you and your child to differentiate between healthy and unhealthy fats.

Also keep in mind that as you reduce the amount of fat your child eats to a healthier range, his craving for fatty foods will decrease, making it easier to adhere to the dietary recommendations.

As we've noted, not all fats are unhealthy. Read through the following definitions, then follow the suggestions for cooking with the fats that will nourish your child's body rather than increase his girth.

## Less Healthy Fat Choices

*Saturated fat:* Saturated fat is the culprit in raising blood cholesterol and increasing the risk of heart disease. Whenever possible, avoid excessive amounts of foods containing saturated fats. It's easy to remember which foods contain saturated fat, because these fats are usually harder at room temperature. Foods containing saturated fats include:

- Meat fat
- Poultry skin
- Whole-milk dairy products
- Cream
- Lard
- Coconut oil, palm oil, cocoa butter
- Butter and margarines containing hydrogenated vegetable oils

*Hydrogenated fats:* Unsaturated (healthier) fats can be turned into saturated fats through a process called hydrogenation. This process also creates by-products called trans fatty acids that can raise the level of LDL ("bad") cholesterol. Liquid vegetable oils that are made harder (hydrogenated or partially hydrogenated) will contain a greater amount of saturated fat and trans fatty acids. Shop for oils that list the first ingredient as liquid vegetable oil rather than partially hydrogenated vegetable oil. Foods that typically contain hydrogenated fats include:

- Margarine
- Packaged products (check the list of ingredients for the words *hydrogenated* or *partially hydrogenated vegetable oils*).

### Culprits: Saturated Fat

| | Total Fat | Saturated Fat |
|---|---|---|
| Sausage biscuit | 29 grams | 10 grams |
| Pizza (2 slices) | 25 grams | 11 grams |
| French fries (medium portion) | 20 grams | 10 grams |
| Bacon (3 slices) | 12 grams | 8 grams |
| Sausage, ribs, greasy beef (3 ounces) | 20 grams | 7 grams |
| Chicken breast with skin, fried | 19 grams | 6 grams |
| Margarine or butter (1 tablespoon) | 14 grams | 4 to 8 grams |
| Cheese (1 ounce) | 9 grams | 5 grams |
| Whole milk (1 cup) | 8 grams | 5 grams |

## Healthier Fat Choices

*Monounsaturated fats:* These fats may actually protect against heart disease, but they are still high in calories—so use them in moderation for weight control while knowing they are the better types of fat for your child. You'll find monounsaturated fats in:

- Olive, peanut, and canola oils
- Avocados
- Most nuts
- Peanut butter (choose one that does not contain hydrogenated vegetable oil)

*Polyunsaturated fats:* These fats are preferable to saturated fats and can be eaten in moderation, although monounsaturated fats are preferable. Many vegetable oils are polyunsaturated, such as soybean, sesame, sunflower, and cottonseed oils.

## FILLING UP WITH FIBER

It's important to introduce more fiber into your child's diet. Fiber is found in whole-grain bread and grain products, beans, fruits, and vegetables. By definition, "fiber" is the part of these foods that we cannot digest or absorb. There are a host of benefits to eating it, including:

- Stabilizing blood sugar fluctuations. The carbohydrates in many high-fiber and whole-grain foods are metabolized more slowly than those in other foods. This slow metabolizing can also decrease postmeal cravings.
- Relief of constipation. Fiber draws water into the digestive tract, resulting in softer stools that are easier to pass. Be sure to drink 6 to 8 glasses of water per day.
- Lowering the level of LDL cholesterol level in the blood. Consuming foods containing soluble fiber can literally help to "move" cholesterol out of the body.
- Promoting a feeling of fullness. Fiber is bulky, making you feel fuller. This can help reduce overeating.

### How Much Fat Is OK?

A question frequently asked is, "How much fat should I eat in a day?" In general, average total fat intake should not exceed about 60 grams per day. A typical fast-food meal can contain more than 40 to 50 grams of fat; a stick of butter contains about 100 grams.

To determine how much fiber your child should eat, add five to the age of your child. So a child who is eight years old should be consuming 13 grams of fiber. Most adults should consume at least 20 to 30 grams of total fiber per day. If you have not been doing this, you should work up to it gradually, as the body must become accustomed to digesting larger amounts of fiber.

Good sources of soluble ("cholesterol-lowering") fiber include oatmeal, oat bran, barley, avocado, broccoli, brussels sprouts, carrots, collard greens, sweet potato, beans (any kind), split peas, lentils, apricots, figs, prunes, flax seeds, and sunflower seeds.

## HIGH-FIBER FOOD CHOICES

| Type of Food | Average* Fiber Grams |
| --- | --- |
| Beans | 6 to 8 grams |
| Bran, oat cereals | 3 to 11 grams |
| Brown rice, pasta | 4 grams |
| Whole-grain bread products | 2 to 6 grams |
| Oatmeal | 4 grams |
| Fruits and vegetables | 2 to 3 grams |

*Average serving size: 1 cup where applicable.

## THE ADVENTURE OF SHOPPING FOR GROCERIES AND READING LABELS

As your family grows into the Trim Kids routine, you'll find that planning meals, shopping for groceries, and learning to read labels together will make each task more enjoyable. You are helping your child understand nutrition, portions, and how food relates to how she feels—both physically and emotionally.

Sit down with your family, or at least with your overweight child, and ask her which healthy foods sound most appealing. Make a comprehensive grocery list of

TRIM KIDS TESTIMONIAL

## A Parent's Perspective

"I was glad to start the program with my child because it took the pressure off of me to be the bad guy for trying to change my daughter's habits. I knew I would do the program with her so I could support her, but I didn't think I would stay with it very strictly. Well, I've gotten into a pretty good exercise program, but more than that, I'm excited to know about nutrition. I'm much more of a health advocate now. It's not as though I didn't know about this stuff before, but now I've *experienced* it. I feel much, much better, and that makes me want to do it even more. I feel better about myself, both because of what it's done for me and because of what it's done for my daughter."

what you know you must get, and which foods she wants to try. When you're at a store, avoid the candy aisle, and lead her instead to the fruits and vegetables section. We encourage the child to be involved in the food selection process, within reasonable limits and guided by the parent. For example, instead of telling your child to "pick out a snack" you may want to say, "Pick out the fruits that you would like to have." The more she's involved in planning and choosing her menu, the more responsibility she'll take for the program, and the more gratifying it will be.

While shopping, make it a habit to read food labels. Teach your child what each category represents, and which ones most apply to her. Pay special attention to the serving size, as it may surprise you how small a product's serving size is in relation to its nutritional values. Bear in mind that the percent values on the nutrition label are based on an average 2,000-calorie-per-day intake and may need to be adjusted for your child. Notice the amounts of total fat and saturated fat per serving. Remember to avoid products high in fat.

### Fat: A Rule to Memorize

15 grams sugar–5 grams total fat. In general, if a product contains more than 15 grams of "sugar" or 5 grams of "total fat" per serving, or both, it may be too high in sugar, fat, or both.

Don't be swayed by the promotional claims splashed across the front of packages. Manufacturers tempt you to buy a product by describing it as low-fat, nonfat, reduced-calorie, and so on. Reading the nutritional label on the side or back of the product is all you need to focus on. You'll learn how to do this in "Week 6" (page 240) of the Trim Kids Program.

# REARRANGING THE KITCHEN FOR A SAFE FOOD ENVIRONMENT

By making healthy food choices at the grocery store, you'll make your home food environment less conducive to overeating. Here's why: you can't eat something that's not there. Foods that are high in fat and sugar can be *temptation foods* for your child. We all have our individual "temptation foods"—calorie-packed foods that we crave and cannot resist. Having many of these foods readily available in the home can set up the child for failure. The very best way to support your child's new eating habits, therefore, is to limit the availability of these products in the home.

This process is called *cue elimination*. Such foods actually cue your child to want them. If he doesn't see the foods, he will be less inclined to ask for and crave them. Removing unhealthy foods also prevents conflict because you do not have to say "no" when he reaches for a temptation food. Instead, when your child asks for temptation foods, you can end the

> ### FDA-Approved Food Claims
>
> The Food and Drug Administration (FDA) permits several specific food claims on products. Beware of products bearing other claims and always check with your dietitian or physician if you have specific questions.
>
> - Foods low in total fat and saturated fat may reduce the risk of heart disease and cancer.
> - Oatmeal, oat bran, and whole oat products make the FDA-approved claim of lowering cholesterol.
> - Milk and other foods containing calcium, such as fortified juices, reduce the risk of osteoporosis.

conversation quickly by saying, "We don't have that in the house right now. So would you like an apple, or some rice cakes?" Offering alternative choices of healthy foods gives your child a sense of control and reminds him that even if he can't have ice cream, he can still have a choice. Keeping these foods away from the house also sends a message to the whole family that everyone is going to be healthier, not just the overweight child.

Be aware, however, that severe restrictions may actually promote a greater desire for the prohibited foods, especially in younger children. Let the child have an occasional temptation food away from home, but be careful about portions. Keeping his favorite high-fat foods out of the house enables you to allow them

### A Parent's Perspective

"Think of this program as a new way of life that will benefit and extend your child's life, as well as your own. Don't think of it as a diet program so much as the right way your body works. You'll live a better life, improve the quality of your life, and have more energy, and you won't feel deprived. It's energizing. You're happier with more positive goals."

occasionally as part of a fun family outing.

Temptation foods that are occasionally kept in the home should be purchased in smaller amounts, such as individual portions, when possible. For example, instead of keeping a big bag of chips in the pantry, keep a box of individually wrapped packages. Then, when you allow your child the treat, it will come in a downsized, more reasonable portion. Many foods are available in small or single-serving packages, including chips, ice cream bars, cookies, and desserts. Also, experiment with lower-fat versions of these products. To save money, you can buy the cheaper super-size packages but divide the contents into half-cup portions in zipper bags.

Always make sure that favorite low-fat or "free" foods are well within reach and available to him when he's hungry.

## SURVIVAL AT RESTAURANTS

With today's busy schedules, dining out is part of most people's lives, and it still can be as long as you and your child plan ahead and make appropriate choices. Wait until you are familiar and comfortable with the types of foods and portions your child can eat in the Trim Kids Program before venturing out to a restaurant. Stay clear of places that dole out huge portions of primarily high-fat foods. Agree with your child on what he wants to eat before you go out—preferably when he's not feeling hungry—or you may run into an unexpected high-calorie binge. Refer to the plans in "Week 10" for more on healthy eating outside of the home.

# PUTTING ON THE FOOD BRAKES: WHERE TO BEGIN?

The dietary changes your child will need to make depend on how overweight he is. You can start implementing healthier food choices for any child, including:

- Choosing better fast foods and snacks
- Keeping healthier food products at home
- Reducing fat intake (high-fat snacks; fast food; regular mayonnaise, butter, and margarine; high-fat meats)
- Drinking less sugar—in the form of soft drinks, fruit drinks, and excessive consumption (more than 12 ounces per day) of fruit juice
- Increasing fiber intake (whole grains, beans, fruits and vegetables)

More seriously overweight children and adolescents may also require a calorie restriction. These would include children at the Yellow or Red level (refer to pages 23–24 for a discussion of the Trim Kids color codes). Some children at the Green level may also require calorie restriction initially, depending on the family history and on the child's growth, puberty status, and her weight trend over a period of time. Be sure to coordinate this process with supervision by your child's physician, especially at the outset of the program.

Calories are restricted by limiting the amount of food (portions) that your child eats. Excessive fat and sugar intake easily results in a greater calorie intake, but large portions of high-carbohydrate foods such as bread, rice, pasta, and potatoes can also heap on more calories than the body needs. Portion control also helps to teach the body to normalize food intake over a period of time.

You will learn about weight-loss calories and meal plans in week 2 of the Trim Kids Nutrition Plan and Portion Control Plan.

# 5

# ENCOURAGING PHYSICAL ACTIVITY: LET THE CHILDREN PLAY!

"Now I'm an exercise machine! I can do anything!" Michael says proudly, tossing a basketball toward a hoop and scoring another two points.

Four years before making that basket, Michael came to us as one of our youngest patients. He was only 5½ years old and already his weight condition was severe.

Although our program was designed for seven- to seventeen-year-olds, we agreed to treat him because his condition was so severe. In fact, his sleep apnea was so bad that it was considered life-threatening. Excess fat prevented normal breathing and sleep at night. Because of this, he would often fall asleep during the day.

After a thorough medical exam, we determined that at 140 pounds and only 46 inches (just less than four feet) tall, Michael was more than twice his ideal body weight. He began the Level I program (Red), which included following a structured exercise plan designed

### Genetics That Operate When You Don't Move

Scientists have discovered something called a "thrifty gene." People who have this genetic profile are more likely to develop obesity—and, even worse, type II diabetes—if they live in an environment that promotes a sedentary lifestyle combined with an overabundance of food. Sounds like America!

especially for him, along with a special medical nutrition plan. We also worked with his family to find new habits that would increase the time he spent moving around, burning calories.

Because Michael's condition was extreme, it took him a full year to meet his goals. But four years later, he has maintained a 70 percent weight loss. Not only is he much healthier, but the grin on his face as he shoots another basket reveals that he's a much happier person, too.

## THE EVOLUTION OF EXERCISE

For centuries, we used our muscles and relied on our physical prowess every day. Indeed, our bodies were designed for bending, reaching, running, squatting, throwing, jumping, swinging, walking, pushing, climbing, swimming, and much more. Our survival depended on having lithe, active, strong, and flexible bodies. Up until about one hundred years ago, we spent most of our lives moving.

The industrial revolution changed that. It enabled us to stay home, open a package or can of food, and sit by the fire for a cozy dinner. It wasn't long before we gathered before the television rather than the fire or the kitchen table. With the advent of the information age, we're moving less than ever. By sitting before a computer, television, or desk, for the first time in human evolution, we are behaving in a physiologically abnormal way.

> **Move It or Lose It!**
>
> Studies of the effects of prolonged bed rest or weightlessness (in astronauts) have taught us that by not carrying our weight around, we lose muscle tissue. Just as a leg gets thinner when it's put in a cast, so our muscles get smaller if we aren't active.

Amazing what can happen in a single century.

What's even scarier is what's currently happening in a matter of five to twenty years to the kids who are living a sedentary life. When your child spends the majority of his time in front of the tube, at the computer, or even reading a book while sprawled on the couch, his muscles may begin to atrophy—muscles become less dense and less able to sustain muscular contractions, and may actually get smaller. This leads to *sarcopenia,* the precursor to irregular bone development, diabetes, high cholesterol, and other physiological, metabolic, structural, hormonal, and neurological health disasters. Some researchers believe that fat may be a natural by-product of sarcopenia.

Research shows that children's muscles develop in many different ways and perform specific roles or movements. We like to refer to this as *muscle intelligence*. A sedentary child only uses the muscles required for walking, lying down, and sitting. By not activating the other muscles in his body, he will eventually *lose the ability to awaken the intelligence in the neglected muscles*. Consequently, by the time he's an adult, he will be uncoordinated and may become physically *unable* to perform certain physical functions.

> ## Windows of Opportunity
>
> Infants learn language in eighteen months to two years. When adults attempt to learn a new language, it can take far longer. The same is true with learning a musical instrument or learning how to swim. Show four-year-olds the move, and they'll get it sooner than an adult will. That's because the window of opportunity to learn and integrate new skills is much greater in the brains of children than in adults. Muscles depend on the brain, too. Waiting until adulthood to use muscles poses a far greater challenge than putting them to work during childhood.

This points to why it is so important for children to be active, firing up every muscle group in their growing bodies. It's as though exercising the muscle implants a computer chip in the brain that says, "OK, all the muscles that are necessary to do this movement have just been activated. We know which ones, when, and how fast to contract them, and this is what they do." Once the message is received and practiced (this is somewhat like learning the alphabet), the memory lasts a lifetime. In the end, physically active children will grow into adults with astute muscle intelligence, or strong physical prowess. Those children who never tapped in to their different muscles become physically disadvantaged adults.

Working all the major muscle groups also helps develop a healthy heart, lungs, cells, and immune system, thanks to the vast network of interchangeable systems that make up the body. No one part of the body is isolated from the next; each has an impact on the other.

Because developing as many muscles as possible has so many health benefits, it's better for children to cross-train—that is, do a variety of activities—rather than do a single type of exercise all the time. In fact, exercise physiologists and experienced coaches do not start intense training in any one sport until a child is at least twelve years old. If the child has awakened all her muscles by then, she will enter a specific sport with more agility and skill than if she had been concentrating solely on a single sport during her early childhood. This approach also prevents overuse injuries and sports "burnout."

Waking up unused muscles in your child's body is simple. Adopting physical activity as a way of life will enable your child to jump hurdles she didn't even know existed.

## THE JOYS AND BENEFITS OF PLAYFUL EXERCISE

The Trim Kids Program asks that your child practice both a formal exercise plan and daily activities that promote aerobic movement. Motivating your child to do this can be easy once you understand kids' relationship with movement.

First, think about why adults exercise. Typically, we do it to improve our health and appearance, to relieve stress, to escape from the world, for solitude, or to spend time with a friend. Consider, too, that adults tend to exercise over long, continuous periods. We go for an hour's run or walk. We play three hard sets of tennis over two hours. We swim steadily for a mile. Once we've "felt the burn" and put in our time, we're finished. We go back to the office, the kitchen, or the car and resume our relatively sedentary day.

When it comes to exercise, kids are wired very differently from adults—both physically and emotionally. They have an immature metabolic system that is well suited for short periods of vigorous movement. That's one of the reasons the game of tag is so popular. It answers their specific physiological need to run very fast for very short periods, then stop and rest—burning about 350 to 400 calories per hour. This stop-and-go approach, as every parent knows, can last throughout an entire day.

### Young Hormonal Systems

Before children reach puberty, they don't have the circulating maturation hormones that will enable them to exercise very vigorously for long periods of time. Children twelve years and under should not be forced to participate in adult exercise classes or activities.

Tag also answers kids' emotional needs—their primary objective in all forms of movement: to have *fun!* To heck with cellulite or solitude—they want to play! That can happen by themselves with the appropriate toys or equipment, or with others. If you're worried that being playful won't burn enough calories, here's news for you: playing burns more calories than structured exercise. So as you consider how to get your kid up and around, think fun, and think short, intense spurts. And think about this: since obesity is primarily an environmental disease, you'll need to change the environment that surrounds your child to prompt more fun activities. This starts, as they say, in your own backyard.

## CREATING OUTDOOR FUN

Take an inventory of your yard. Is there a swing set? A sandbox? A wading pool? A sprinkler with an attachment for playing with water? If not, get busy! Your child can engage in the great outdoors in many ways. Her age will determine her interests. Older children love to climb rope swings or ladders leading to a tree fort in which they can play endlessly. They also enjoy competition, sporting games (basketball, baseball, badminton, croquet, miniature golf), and tag, tag, and more tag! Younger kids enjoy playing knights in shining armor with an open field for battle. They like balls of all sizes. Building makeshift houses out of cardboard boxes provides endless adventure. Or they'll pull a wagon full of their favorite things.

Enter into this knowing that it may be a process of trial and error. Maybe for your child's first six to eight years, watching television was her idea of fun. She may have to explore different corners of a new world of activity before she finds the right fit. Bear with her. Your patience will pay off enormously.

If you don't have a yard, find the nearest park. Even older kids enjoy monkey bars, swings, teeter-totters, tunnels, flying kites, and the wonderful playground equipment so many parks offer. Take her to a grassy area and throw a Frisbee, pitch some baseballs, or ride bikes around the periphery of the park. The only hard and fast rule is *find activities your child likes and do them!*

## CREATING INDOOR PLAY AREAS

Once you create an activity area outside, your child will probably spend most of his time there. But winter always comes, and in most places that means he's coming back inside. No problem. A little rearranging will do wonders. Transform his bedroom or a room you don't use much into an "imagination station" (see page 179 for further details). Enlist your child's help to create a fun atmosphere. Pull a few old mattresses into the room so he can jump from one to the next. Bring in a boom box and clear a space for dancing. Or, if he's younger, designate an area for soft balls, Hula Hoops, and jump ropes. No child we know can resist a small indoor trampoline surrounded by fluffy pillows. Hopscotch is always in vogue. Believe it or not, kids still love the game of Twister™. You can play, too! Or try a piece of technology that actually gets kids out from behind the computer: a Power Pad. It's connected to both the child's body and the computer, so it records his actions and shows them on the screen, in the form of abstract images. This can make hours of interesting physical twists and turns, and it ends up as techno-art!

Get your child's opinions and help and spend as much time as necessary putting the room together so your child *wants* to be there. Of course, you are invited to do some playing, too, which will inspire your child to play even more.

Here's an idea to act on sooner rather than later: younger children actually enjoy doing household chores. Ask your youngster to help you make the beds in the house, help you transfer clothes from the washer to the dryer, put the dishes in the dishwasher, or water the plants. Even sweeping and vacuuming have a nearly mystical appeal to young children.

The goal is to provide as much opportunity as possible for your child to play, move, and burn calories. Always be certain to select activities that are safe for your child's age and level of fitness.

## WHAT EXERCISE EQUIPMENT SHOULD I BUY?

You don't have to buy anything to create effective play areas. Sometimes just rearranging the furniture and cleaning out the toy box will give you great ideas. Work within your budget, and if you're not comfortable purchasing anything, don't. If you're excited about getting some sports items for your child, wait until he demonstrates a commitment to the Trim Kids Program and then get a new scooter, in-line skates, a baseball bat, or a skateboard as a reward. Whenever possible, give your child things that will increase physical activity.

By all means *don't* purchase expensive equipment that adults rely on for exercise such as treadmills, stationary bikes, or cross-country ski machines. You'll fare much better if you wait to see what your child really enjoys, and invest in that. Consider purchasing an automatic pace counter (DIGIWALKER™). This is a small device like a pager, worn on the hip, that measures how many steps you take in one day. You can help your child set daily and weekly goals and increase gradually over time. Refer to the exercise activity ideas list in "Week 3" (page 160) for other inexpensive ideas for equipment that promotes increases in physical activity.

## MAKING ACTIVE CHOICES: MINUTE BY MINUTE, DAY BY DAY

Making some simple changes in your house and yard is just one way to encourage burning fat. Making new choices each day also greatly contributes to your child's level of activity and how many calories your child burns. Here are some choices you can make on a daily basis:

- Whenever you go shopping with your child, park at the far end of the lot and walk to the store. If you're shopping for groceries, ask your child to push the shopping cart; then both of you can return it to the store when you're finished.
- Allow your child to watch a favorite television show *on one condition*: she has to stand up and dance or move around for the duration of every commercial. Otherwise, turn off the TV. If she's watching a video, tell her you'll pause it every 30 minutes so she can walk around the block or do her abdominal crunches (page 332). If there's an argument, no more video.
- If your teenager is a telephone talker, say, "You can *talk as long as you walk.*" This may require a cordless phone, but it's a worthwhile investment. The moment she sits down, the conversation is over. Although you can't necessarily monitor her conversations, you can make surprise visits to make sure she's moving. Or direct her to walk the length of the house so she'll keep popping up at your end of the house. Remember, if she sits down, it's over!

• Have a garden? Ask your child to help plant, water, and weed it. If it's a vegetable garden, choose the juiciest tomato or reddest raspberry and present it to your child as a thank-you. A pretty flower expresses appreciation, too.

> ### The Thirty-Minute Rule
>
> Research indicates that concentration and work performance begin to decline after thirty minutes of intense mental activity (like studying). Take a break for just five to ten minutes every thirty minutes and watch your performance improve!
>
> And don't forget—these small movement periods burn an extra 2,000 to 3,000 calories a week!

These may seem like insignificant choices, but they are not. *All activity burns calories.* Sitting burns only about 30 to 50 calories per hour, but standing burns twice that much: 60 to 110 calories per hour. Just walking slowly burns 120 to 200 calories per hour. Even shaking a salad dressing or beating eggs will use more energy than being a couch potato.

Companies that make video and computer games spend millions on advertising. Their goal is to see your child sit (motionless) before their merchandise all day long. We've had clients who could do amazing things on the computer but who had never learned to ride a bike or swing a bat! Remember, you don't have to wait for holidays to purchase toys, games, and equipment that encourage movement. Start rewarding your child with fun new things as soon as he begins meeting his goals.

## CALORIES BURNED PER HOUR BY VARIOUS ACTIVITIES (Approximate Values Based on a 120- to 150-pound Individual)

| | | | |
|---|---|---|---|
| Badminton (singles recreational) | 310 | Calisthenics | |
| | | Low | 245 |
| | | Medium | 395 |
| | | High | 585 |
| Baking (using mixer) | 100 | Card playing | 80 |
| Basketball (half-court) | 495 | Carpentry work (light) | 205 |
| Bicycling (15 mph) | 370 | Checkout-counter work | 120 |

| | | | |
|---|---|---|---|
| Dancing | 385 | Raking leaves | 200 |
| Dinner preparation | 120 | Resting (seated) | 50–65 |
| Domestic work (cleaning windows, scrubbing floors, no pause) | 225 | Running in place<br>50 to 60 steps per minute<br>90 to 100 steps per minute | <br>455<br>585 |
| Driving car (automatic, light traffic) | 85 | Shopping | 150 |
| Eating | 80 | Skiing cross-country (5 mph) | 625 |
| Golf (foursome, 9 holes, 2 hours) | 225 | Skiing downhill (continuous) | 530 |
| Handball (2 people) | 695 | Skipping rope (50 to 60 skips per minute) | 455 |
| Hunting (not sitting) | 400 | Standing—light activity (dishwashing, etc.) | 120 |
| Jogging (5.5 mph) | 585 | Standing—no movement | 90 |
| Lawn mowing (power) | 225 | Swimming<br>30 yards per minute<br>45 yards per minute | <br>375<br>615 |
| Making beds | 185 | Table tennis (recreational) | 270 |
| Office work | 130 | Telephone talking (sitting) | 80 |
| Painting house | 185 | Tennis (singles) | 380 |
| Personal toilet (washing, shaving, dressing, combing, etc.) | 180 | Walking<br>2 mph<br>3½ mph | <br>165<br>280 |
| Playing pool | 140 | Washing cars | 205 |

| Washing clothes (washing machine) | 145 | Weeding | 270 |
|---|---|---|---|
| Washing dishes (dishwasher) | 100 | Window cleaning | 205 |
| Watching TV | 30–50 | Writing | 80 |

# DESIGNING A FORMAL EXERCISE ROUTINE

We have discovered that just *telling* families to be more physically active is not enough. Most overweight kids need weekly structured exercise goals. As with casual fun and play, allow your child to choose the exercise activities she most enjoys to make up a formal exercise routine. Otherwise, she probably won't stick with it. We've found there is an enjoyable exercise for *every* child—even bookworms and computer addicts. It may take time to discover, but the greater variety of activities she is exposed to, the more likely she is to find one she likes.

Every child who participates in the Trim Kids Program will engage in a tailor-made exercise program. And each child will succeed in reaching his goals. How do we know? Because the program is designed that way. In the beginning, we make absolutely sure that the goals each child establishes are *easy* to accomplish. Some parents are concerned that the workout is too easy. But ten years of laboratory research have shown that every child is metabolically unique, and that children will continue the program only if they:

- Have fun
- Start off slowly and easily
- Feel safe
- Experience initial success

It's that initial success that motivates the child to keep going. And each child has his own level of ability, which parents and children must respect. Refer to the exercise safety rules in "Week 1" on page 97 before you begin.

Severely overweight children will have a more difficult time exercising than

## As Weight Goes Up, Fitness Goes Down

Research in our own laboratory showed us clearly that children with different weight levels have different capacities for exercise—especially when carrying their weight (when they walk, for example). Normal-weight children could walk at 3.5 miles per hour for long periods of time without becoming too tired. Chubby kids were able to do this for about half the time. Kids who needed to lose more than half their body weight could not walk at 3.5 miles per hour for five minutes!

moderately or mildly overweight kids. Consequently, they should start out doing less, at a slower pace, and fewer times per week. It's perfectly all right to begin with one or two days a week of approximately twenty minutes of exercise and increase the amount of activity weekly as the child sheds pounds. The Trim Kids Program will automatically do this for you—you'll learn how in "Week 1" (pages 96-99). And your child doesn't have to do all twenty minutes in one go. Ten minutes in the morning and ten in the afternoon or evening will still burn the same number of calories.

It's best for severely overweight children to start out doing exercises that support their extra body weight, such as swimming or riding a bike. The water supports the child's body weight while he moves his arms and legs to burn calories and strengthen muscles; a bike supports his upper body while his leg muscles rotate the pedals to burn calories. After he's lost some weight and improved his fitness, he can gradually move to weight-bearing activities like walking, dancing, and field sports.

## Play Now! Homework Later!

When children get home after a day at school, their brains are tired, but not their bodies. They've already been confined during the long, often tedious day in a relatively sedentary environment. They need a break to enjoy physical activities and let off steam.

From now on, hand your child a big glass of ice water, then tell him to go outside and walk, ride a bike, skate, play ball, jump rope, or play tag. If the weather's bad, tell him to do some dancing, go to his imagination station, or play a round of indoor basketball. Make sure he does between thirty and sixty minutes of moving around before starting to do his homework.

Moderately overweight children should begin with non-weight-bearing exercise, and gradually alternate with weight-bearing activities. They can participate in walking or playing tag, for example, or basketball, as long as they take frequent rests when necessary. Again, they can *gradually* work up to longer walks and fewer rest stops.

Mildly overweight kids or those at risk for becoming overweight can safely participate in most activities, but even that little bit of extra weight may slow them down somewhat, so pacing is important. If an activity seems too challenging, encourage your child to slow down but not to stop moving. Gradually work up to higher speeds, harder movements, and longer durations.

Consider enrolling your child for one or two afternoons a week in an activity such as structured dance, martial arts (for example, karate), or gymnastics (only for chubby or mildly overweight children). This will help foster friendships with other children who are active, and it will give you a break from having to supervise an entire exercise program. Make sure you speak to the coach or teacher beforehand to discuss your child's special needs.

Remember, even if your child is just slightly overweight she may be at risk of becoming an overweight adult. If you introduce more activity in her life now, she'll have a better chance of staying trim when she's older. Activity she learns as a child will follow her well into later years. Seek every opportunity to provide her with active playtime. Refer to "Week 1" for specific exercises geared especially to your child's needs and level of fitness.

## THE BODY'S METABOLIC ENGINE

We've mentioned that young children are perfectly suited for short bursts of high-energy movement. Any mother of a preschool child knows this firsthand. Outdoor tag is a good example (burning about 350 to 400 calories per hour!). Unfortunately, the spontaneous activity of young children decreases as they get older. We don't know if this is a natural occurrence or if it's a result of their changing environment. For overweight and even slightly chubby kids, activity may be less frequent because they can't keep up with the demands of certain sports, dances, or group games. In addition, their metabolic system—the engine of the body—is different. Using a car as a metaphor, we can say that chubby and overweight children run out of gas sooner because the excess weight makes the engine run harder to move the car forward. A small car can go farther than a large truck on the same amount of gas.

Regardless of weight, your body has three types of engines (or metabolisms), much as a car has three gears: one for fast takeoffs, one for start-and-stop driving, and one for highway driving.

- Medium-slow: This engine enables movement for long stretches of time. This is the engine that's fired up for aerobic exercises. It uses a combination of oxygen, fat stored in the body, and sugar (or carbohydrates) for fuel. After about twenty minutes of activity at the same speed, your body begins to use more of the stored fat for fuel. If you haven't eaten for several hours, it will gobble up even more of that stored fat. The longer you maintain the medium-slow speed, the more calories and fat you will burn.

  Since overweight children have more stored fat than others, they can exercise in the medium-slow engine for hours without running out of gas as long as their pace stays low and consistent. But they must keep it slow and steady for a long period of time. It's all right to use the fast engine for a moment as long as it's brief and they return to the easier pace.

- Fast: This engine taps into the body's anaerobic capabilities. "Anaerobic" means "without air"—this engine depends not on oxygen but primarily on sugar stored in the muscles (glycogen) for its fuel source. You kick-start this engine whenever the speed of your activity increases to a higher level.

  Your chubby child can use the fast engine until the workload becomes too difficult. At this point a substance called lactic acid will build in his muscles, making his muscles burn and feel tired. His breathing rate will also increase because he is trying to take in more oxygen in order to shift gears and begin using the medium-slow engine again. Unfortunately, because the fast engine is anaerobic, trying to take in more oxygen by breathing faster will not help. Your child's body will not allow him a shift to the medium-slow aerobic engine unless he slows down.

  The fast engine has a very small fuel tank. It takes only between three and five minutes for your child to run out of gas. Unless activity is reduced to a speed or level to allow a shift to the medium-slow engine again, your child will be physically unable to continue.

The fast engine is great for short periods of exercise that promote strength and power. Sprinting is one example. So are stomach crunches (page 332).

- Superfast: Skilled and powerful athletes such as Olympic weight lifters, jumpers, and sprinters use the superfast engine. It relies on chemicals made from fuel stored directly in muscle fibers and immediately ready for use. The tank of the superfast engine is even smaller than that of the fast engine. When kids turn on that engine, they will run out of gas in only ten seconds!

Your child can increase the size of the tank in each of these engines by engaging in regular exercise training, increasing how often ("frequency") and how long ("duration") he spends being physically active during any given week. Doing this will allow him to exercise for longer periods in all of the metabolic engines.

Don't rush the process! The heavier your child, the longer it will take for him to comfortably use and improve his engines. Chubby children take at least three months to experience a noticeable change, and at least six months to reach their full potential for improvement. Heavier kids will take longer. Be patient, and always refer to the color-coded guidelines in the Trim Kids twelve-week plan as you gradually add more exercise. To pace the effort better, help you child practice taking his heart rate. We show you how on page 152.

Finally, listen to your child. When she's exercising and says she's tired, that means *she's tired!* If she says she's hurting, that means *she's hurting!* Allow her to slow down or stop to catch her breath, then gently prod her back into moving at a pace that is more comfortable. You may think she's faking discomfort, but she's probably not. If you get irritated with her

> ### Exercise Keeps Dieting Children Healthy
>
> If you're having a hard time getting your kid off the couch, don't sit back with satisfaction that he has at least restricted his caloric intake. Individuals who diet but don't exercise may lose not only fat but also lean muscle—which is crucial for their health, growth, and development. If you continue to restrict your child's diet without requiring him to move around, you'll end up with physical disorders, an unhappy child, and medical complications.

limitations, remember: excess weight is *physically* disabling. Children need encouragement, not criticism.

## STRENGTH AND FLEXIBILITY

Aerobic exercise is great for a healthy heart and lungs. But if your child engages only in aerobic exercise, she'll be missing two critical components: strength and flexibility. What good is a car with a great engine but no tires, hood, top, or doors? Muscles provide the framework for your child's engine and must be strong to prevent injury. A bone is only as strong as the muscle attached to it.

Muscles must be exercised with some kind of weight at least once or twice a week to keep them tight or toned. This happens through the force of resistance, or strength training. Children can strengthen their muscles through lifting weights (cans of soup will do), or by simply lifting a limb or another part of their body (as in modified push-ups). Strength training will become a regular part of their routine in the Trim Kids Program.

Strengthening exercises result in toned muscles. Toned muscles are metabolically active tissues: they burn more calories than fat *even when the child is not moving.* In fact, a toned muscle may burn 20–30 calories per hour to maintain itself, whereas fat tissue may burn only 2 to 10 calories. Strong muscles are a lot like a furnace. The stronger the muscle, the more intensely the furnace burns. This furnace is called the metabolic rate.

Ask your pediatrician or family physician about which kinds of strengthening activities are safe for your overweight child. His growing bones and developing joints may be at risk of injury if he asks too much of his body by strenuous lifting, pushing, jarring, or pulling. Even jumping could cause harm. Severely obese children should participate only in strength exercises that offer good support for their joints. The exercises in the Trim Kids Program were designed especially for overweight children.

If your child is not overweight, get your pediatrician's or family physician's approval, make sure the equipment is in good repair, and encourage your child to strengthen her muscles by:

• Climbing trees
• Swinging on monkey bars

- Jumping on a trampoline
- Swinging on a swing set
- Skipping rope
- Playing hopscotch
- Climbing into and out of a swimming pool
- Participating in gymnastics
- Dancing
- Learning a martial art

Strength training has many other health benefits: it may prevent bone fractures, arthritis, and diseases like osteoporosis, diabetes, and heart disease. It will make your child look better: strong muscles under her skin will make her look toned and fit.

A car runs more efficiently when it is in alignment. The same holds true for the human body. The function of flexibility is to maintain balance. When your child was born, she was in perfect proportion. She was symmetrical—the left side was identical to the right, the front of the body was in balance with the rear. After years of using one part of the body more than another, imbalances occur. This can result in poor posture, unfit appearance, or injury and pain in a bone or joint. In week 7 of the Trim Kids Program, you'll find a flex test to check your child's posture.

Flexibility training, or stretching, is just as important as aerobics and strength training. Inflexible joints and muscles inhibit your child from participating in activities to her fullest potential. Inflexibility can also lead to chronic muscle and joint disorders. If you participate in stretching exercises with your child, you will also be helping yourself offset chronic pain and disease.

Stretching can be done often and almost anywhere. We encourage it during television time. Make sure you arrange the room in which your child watches TV so that she can sprawl on the floor and perform her stretches. In the Trim Kids Program, we show you safe stretching exercises that she can do anywhere.

Be sure your child always stretches after aerobic or strengthening exercises.

---

## Strength Training: Great for Mom and Dad, Too!

*Blood pressure responses:* Sensible strength training does not produce adverse blood pressure responses. Arm exercise increases systolic blood pressure by approximately 50 percent. Anyone with high blood pressure should begin at 40 to 50 percent of maximum strength.

*Heart rate response:* Heart rate may double during a set of strength exercises. Heart rate returns to normal shortly after resting.

*Body Composition Response:* Body composition improves as a result of strength training. Research indicates that untrained men and women typically add 3 pounds of muscle after two months of strength exercise. At the same time they may lose from 1 to 2 pounds of fat, depending on their diet.

### Parents Say the Darndest Things!

One day during weight-management class, Dr. Melinda was talking with parents about how important it is to have their child follow the Trim Kids exercise video at home.

Mr. Harris, one of the parents, raised his hand. "What should I do? I'm trying to get David to do the video, but he won't stop playing basketball outside to come in!"

"Basketball burns more calories than aerobic dancing," Dr. Melinda said, "and it works just as many muscle groups. Let David play!"

This will prevent soreness and possibly even injury. Stretching is also a great way to unwind at the end of the day.

## MOTIVATING YOUR CHILD TO BECOME MORE ACTIVE

When kids know they're going to have fun—and succeed—with their exercise program, they cheerfully accept it as a new way of life. Likewise, when they experience variety and flexibility within the program, they feel more able to comply with it. So, keep in mind that if your son is supposed to walk for a total of twenty minutes per day, he can do ten minutes in the morning and ten in the afternoon if that's easier. If walking isn't his game, but he enjoys riding his bike, he can do that instead. Adaptability and creativity are especially helpful in the beginning of the program. You may ask for more structure later on, but at the beginning, you can offer plenty of leeway.

On the days when your child seems to drag, don't wait for him to initiate or choose an activity. If you leave it up to him, he'll probably revert to the couch or a computer game. As his coach, you can either tell him what to do or—better yet—give him several choices. For instance: "Go do your abdominal

### TRIM KIDS TESTIMONIAL

## A Child's Perspective

"Before we got into the program, my dad took me jogging with him, but I couldn't keep up and he'd get mad. I wasn't losing any weight so I didn't want to do it. Then, Dr. Melinda showed us the best kind of exercise for me. I was glad to hear that swimming was a good choice—and not laps, but just playing in the pool—because it burned lots of calories. I even like the stationary bike, now. So now I exercise a lot because I know it makes me lose weight."

crunches." Or: "You can choose to rake the leaves or shoot some baskets." Pitting chores against more fun activities yields great results!

As we've suggested before, it's a good idea to enroll your child in group activities outside the house. These will help him feel like he's part of a peer group and will give you a break. Just be sure it's an activity your child really likes, and speak to the teacher or coach first. Make sure he'll support your efforts and is sensitive to your child's physical restrictions.

> ## Activity Relieves Stress
>
> When children and adults are stressed, their brains release different types of chemicals. Exercise manages these stress-inducing chemicals in the same way as mood-altering drugs. Exercise also releases dopamine, endogenous opiates, and serotonin—the chemicals that give us the sensation of well-being. Next time your child is feeling blue, go outside and throw a Frisbee or ride bikes together and see how her mood improves.

Allowing your child to choose her favorite sport or activity—even if it changes four times a year—will give her the confidence to work as a team member. As your child loses weight, she may be motivated to show everyone what she is truly capable of doing.

Mary is a good example of this. Although her father was an avid bicyclist, Mary and her mother preferred to stay home. As time went by, both of them became overweight.

Upon joining our program, Mary discovered that she loved to swim. She tried out for the swim team, but the 52 seconds it took her to complete the 50-meter freestyle put her in last place. The 30 extra pounds she carried were too much to pull, and she simply couldn't qualify.

Mary was persistent, however, and worked diligently on developing new eating habits and exercising regularly. She even started biking with her dad. After reaching her goal weight a year later, Mary completed the 50-meter freestyle in an amazing 32 seconds, which qualified her for state competitions. What's more, she and her father went together on a 75-mile bike ride to raise money for charity.

## MONKEY SEE, MONKEY DO

The more you participate in the exercise component of the program, the better your child's chances for success. In fact, we've found that if parents *don't* join along with their children in activities, the child will eventually quit doing them.

If you walk with her, she'll walk more. If you clap each time she jumps rope, she'll jump more. If you get in the pool with her, she'll stay in longer. Your participation and your praise count, big-time.

Being an example can also mean creating your own unique exercise program. Is there a dance class you've always wanted to take? How about karate lessons? Have you tried tennis? By committing to your own exercise routine, you'll demonstrate that fitness is now a way of life for you, too.

Follow the same rules you ask of your child, and you'll be amazed at the progress you make. Start out slow and easy. Choose activities you enjoy. Reward yourself with a new pair of shoes, that fancy swimming suit you eyed, or a new pair of skis.

Plan weekends around family fun and fitness. Spend at least one weekend day doing something active—a trip to a water park or a venture to mountains where you can fish, row a boat, rent a horse, or bicycle. City life offers plenty of choices, too. Spend the day at the zoo. Visit a children's interactive museum or a laser tag center. When planning next year's family vacation, consider a beach with kid-friendly pools, swimming with dolphins, cross-country skiing, or a hiking trip. Be creative and don't give in to the old desire to go somewhere and "veg out."

Even a televised sports event can spark family-oriented physical activity. On the day that a football game is going to air, for example, take the family outside and spend the first quarter tossing a football among yourselves. Then, go inside and watch the second quarter. During halftime and the third quarter, resume the family game outside. Go back in to watch the fourth quarter so you know who wins.

In the end, your family will be the real winners. That's because *participating* in sports is far healthier than *watching* them. Studies show that if parents engage in physical activities, their children will grow up to be active, too. Likewise, if parents spend their leisure time being observers—watching sports on television—chances are their kids will grow up to be observers, too.

Furthermore, exercise is preventive medicine: it prevents a long list of diseases and contributes to a vital, longer life. It's inexpensive, it's fun, and it has few, if any, side effects. Creating an atmosphere of ongoing physical activity is the best gift you can give to yourself and your kids. After all, who can argue with being happy and healthy?

To recap, here are our favorite tips to keep your child physically active:

- Ask your child to walk *briskly* whenever and wherever he walks.
- Create an environment for active play both inside and outside the home.
- Participate in activities the entire family can enjoy together.
- Expose your child to as many different kinds of activity as possible in a nurturing, nonintimidating environment.
- Provide opportunities for normal-weight children to safely climb, run, and jump to help develop muscle strength and bone density. Consult a physician about which activities are safe for your overweight child.
- Don't impose adult exercise goals on young children, who have an immature metabolic system.
- Reserve at least one day each weekend dedicated to fun family fitness activities.
- Don't draw attention to sedentary activities. Rather, spend your energy praising your child when he chooses to be active and play.
- Require that when he watches television, he has to do some kind of exercise or movement during commercials. If he's watching a movie or video, turn it off every thirty minutes and ask him to dance, jump rope, or do crunches (page 332) for five or ten minutes.
- Offer choices: vacuum your room or walk the dog; shovel snow or dance in your room; rake the leaves or go for a bike ride.

Parents must be very cognizant of their children's behavior in order to prevent excess fat from creeping into their lives. In the 1960s and 1970s, when today's parents grew up, playing tag outside, climbing trees, riding bikes, and playing sports (300 to 400 calories per hour) were considered normal. Parents today view normal childhood activity as watching TV, playing video games, or surfing the net (30 to 50 calories per hour).

Sitting for hours on end is not normal. Our bodies will not permit this sedentary lifestyle. We were perfectly designed to walk, run, jump, and climb. Early humans did just that: climbing to get food, walking to find water, and running away from wild animals. Industrialization and the resulting technological advances have, over time, created an environment that is physically unnatural for the human body.

If you don't move, you may not become overweight, but you will become sick. The health benefits of regular exercise or physical activity read like an encyclopedia of disease prevention. Almost every chronic disease (such as heart disease, diabetes, or asthma) has been related to inactivity. Even if you're not interested in preventing your children from becoming overweight, you surely must be concerned with their health.

Remember: anything is better than sitting! Let your children play!

## QUESTIONS AND ANSWERS

*Q: What's the best kind of exercise for my child?*
A: It's the kind your child wants to do and enjoys—with some limitations.

*Q: What kind of exercise equipment should I buy my child?*
A: None. You should buy games, sports equipment, and things that promote play.

*Q: Are there activities that may harm my child or cause injury?*
A: Yes. Children have an immature metabolic system and immature bones and joints. High-intensity exercise for long periods of time is not recommended for children under twelve. Heavy weight lifting and aggressive contact sports are not safe for young children. Your overweight child is even more at risk because of the excess weight he or she must carry.

*Q: My child is really overweight but wants to do gymnastics, soccer, basketball, or another challenging sport. Should I let him? If he fails, won't that make things worse?*
A: Yes, if your child fails or gets hurt, it will make things worse. Start by participating in these activities with your child at home and at a pace that is safe and appropriate. Then explore options and talk to coaches about providing the nurturing environment your child needs. If the coach is not willing to accommodate your child's needs, go someplace else.

**Q:** *If my child is active outside for long periods of time, should I give him sports drinks?*

A:   No. Sports drinks contain sugar and far too many calories. Water is better. Give him about eight ounces of water for every half-hour of exercise. He can drink more if it is hot or if the activity is very challenging.

## 6

# MAKING BEHAVIORAL AND LIFESTYLE CHANGES

By this time next year, you and your child will have made some significant and positive changes. Most people feel that change is more manageable and comfortable if they undertake it incrementally. The Trim Kids Program allows you to make changes one at a time.

Before actually introducing change, it's important to understand what's going on *inside* your child. Get a sense of her concerns and fears. Recognize that your child is the center of this change, and as such, may feel responsible for everyone else's experience of it, as well as feeling anxious about having to conform to it. Understanding her point of view will help you inspire her to change.

## EASING YOUR CHILD'S FEAR AND DISCOMFORT

Typically, children who participate in our program have similar fears. They usually sound something like this:

- I'll *never* get to eat my favorite foods again!
- I'll *never* get to watch my favorite television shows again!

- I'll have to do *really hard, boring* exercises and they'll hurt *really bad!*
- This won't work! I'll *always* be fat!

If your child expresses any of these concerns, be reassuring—yes, things will be *different*, but the changes she makes will be manageable and fairly flexible.

Let her know, for example, that she won't have to forever pass up those sinfully delicious ooey-gooey cookies that you both love. True, she can't have cookies every time you visit the mall, but there will be times when you can share one or even get a whole one apiece. The important difference between how things used to be and how things are now is that you can no longer buy and eat three cookies each, then take two dozen home. It just doesn't work that way.

What does work is being *flexible* about letting her have her favorite things, while also being *firm* about limitations. That means limiting how often you allow treats, and how much of the treat you allow (i.e., portion control). We're thrilled to report that allowing your child some treats *actually makes the program work more effectively*. When kids go into it knowing that they won't be denied their favorite things *forever and ever*, they are more inclined to stick with the rules and reach their goals.

Even though most kids know they can, on occasion and in moderation, delight in their favorite foods and watch their favorite shows, this assurance doesn't obviate the deeper issues some overweight children face, including feeling ashamed, scared, embarrassed, alone, different, and out of control. Many parents don't perceive the depth of these feelings, since their overweight kids have developed good comic comebacks to taunting and teasing. The truth is that a weight problem is neither a pretty nor a popular condition. Studies show that chil-

---

**TRIM KIDS TESTIMONIAL**

## A Child's Perspective

"I was nervous at first. I didn't know what I would have to do. But I started losing weight in the first week—3 pounds. That's what made it easy for me. Losing weight made me want to stay on the program. The hardest part was eating new foods. I'd bring stuff to school—tuna fish and salads and stuff like that—and my friends kept asking me what I was eating. Pretty soon I discovered the new foods weren't so bad. And since I stopped eating school lunches and started playing more outside, I've lost 39 pounds. So the program is a lot easier for me. I really feel so much better about myself. It's not as hard as you think it's going to be. I have a lot of fun with it."

—Graham, age eleven

dren as young as kindergarten regard excess weight as something *ugly, stupid,* or *dirty*. So even if your child feels no *physical* ill effects from his weight, you can bet that he feels emotional despair—even if he doesn't express it. Not only is he excluded from sports he'd like to try but probably also from social gatherings he longs to join. That's tough for any kid, and chances are your child absorbs more social rejection and judgment than most.

If, during the program, you feel that your child's self-esteem is not improving as he loses weight, consider seeking professional help. You might start with a visit to a counselor yourself first, then decide whether or not your child could benefit.

## PROBLEM SOLVING

When you talk to your children about hurt feelings, remember that your objective is to find solutions, help figure out how to implement them, and remind your child that you are there—that you will do whatever's necessary, within reason, to get through these difficult times.

When your child is able to be specific about his feelings, do as much problem solving as you can. If he's being harassed by a schoolyard bully, ask what steps your child has taken so far to deal with it, and the kind of results he's gotten. If he's tried to ignore the teasing and walk away, and that hasn't worked, suggest the support of his teacher or principal. Sadly, too often adults allow hurtful playground comments because they are simply unaware of the severity of the problem. If your child has tried on her own to get help from adults at school and if she hasn't been success-ful, you need to intervene. Bullies, we have come to learn, are often emotionally unstable. It shouldn't be your child's responsibility to handle the situation alone.

There may be times when steering your child away from unhealthy food and

> ### TRIM KIDS TESTIMONIAL
>
> ····················································
>
> ### A Parent's Perspective
>
> "My twelve-year-old daughter started talking about how inadequate and unattractive she felt. She didn't think she was as good as other children. We started the Trim Kids Program and she began los-ing weight. The other day she told me, 'It's making me a better person.' She's more open. She started attending a new school and no one called her fat. She can shop at stores with regular sizes where she likes the clothes. It's made a huge difference in our lives."

encouraging physical activity will elicit a grunt of resentment and stubborn reluctance. When that's the case, remind him that his current condition did not develop overnight. Getting into better shape also won't happen overnight. Emphasize that the teasing and unkind remarks from other children are a result of his previous eating habits and inactivity, and that if the jeering is to stop, he'll have to adhere to the plan. Reiterate the health issues, too. But remember that young children are motivated by things that will make them grow taller, be smarter—like their superheroes. Older kids are more motivated by things that will improve appearance or sports performance.

The first two or three weeks of the program are usually the most challenging. Your child is accustomed to the *old you,* who allowed her to eat half a gallon of ice cream. Now you're telling her she can't have any until next week. New program, new limits. Let us warn you: she's going to test those limits. She'll pull out every conceivable trick from her *I Can't Live Without Ice Cream* book, and you're going to have to stand firm, enforcing the rules you established. She may cry, bribe, manipulate, threaten, and verbally abuse you. Objections may fly like missiles. Acknowledge them, and overrule them—not to fulfill the role of household dictator but to support the actions necessary to attain the goals that will ultimately save your child from a future of physical and emotional ailments.

> ### TRIM KIDS TESTIMONIAL
>
> ## A Parent's Perspective
>
> "My husband and I thought my teenage daughter would grow into her weight, but she didn't. So I was excited about starting the program. The problem was that she didn't think she was overweight, since she was only about 20 pounds too heavy. I had to convince her that she needed help. The dynamics at our house became difficult. Finally, she said, 'You think I'm fat!' I had to say, 'Yes, you are.' It was the hardest thing I've ever had to say. But that was in the beginning. Once she started the program, it began to work. Now she's met her goal weight, and she's walking around her school lunchroom advising her friends about what they should and shouldn't eat. She's a lot happier, and we're closer for it."

When you stick to your "no," she begins to realize that you mean it. Then, the next time you say "no," her protests won't be as adamant or as loud. The time after that, she may just shoot you a murderous look. After that, she'll say, "Then what *can* I have?"

Standing firm isn't optional. It's essential. And it will make your job much eas-

| | |
|---|---|
| **TRIM KIDS TESTIMONIAL** | |

## A Parent's Perspective

"I didn't cook much before starting the program. I worked late most of the time, and I wasn't sure how I was going to be there for my daughter. But, step-by-step, I began making changes. I told my boss I was going to leave the office by five o'clock each day. I started taking the kids grocery shopping with me. And now we eat together every night.

"We also spend more time together on weekends. Mostly we swim, play baseball, and ride bikes. I don't yell at them anymore when they're running around the house having fun. All these changes were worth it because my daughter's health and future were at stake. I've also changed as a parent—I'm now a better one."

ier in the long run if you start the program meaning what you say, and saying what you mean.

## PARENTAL CONCERNS: CAN I CARRY THIS OFF?

We encourage you to approach the program with the same tenacity as when you learned to ride a bike. You'll feel off balance sometimes, take a few spills, and endure some scrapes, bruises, and bumps. But what motivates you to get back in the saddle is that the benefits of learning to ride are worth the painful falls. The same holds true with the Trim Kids Program. After a slipup in diet or activity (some call it cheating; we prefer to call it a treat), you have to decide if the changes you're going for are worth getting back on track. Once you see the delight in your child's face when she's lost her first few pounds, we trust you'll agree that it is, absolutely, worth it.

## THE A-FACTOR

To help you stay focused on your role as advocate and example, we've come up with the A-Factor. If you get confused about what to do next, or are worried that you don't have what it takes, consider these four words:

Attention
Attitude
Accountability
Availability

### Attention

In the Trim Kids Program, we reward *positive behavior* with *positive attention*. But Americans are trained to respond to negative behavior with negative attention. See if this sounds familiar: Your three-year-old throws a tantrum, and you put down whatever you're doing to see what's up. Whether you comfort her, yell, act irritated, or put her in time out, what matters is that she got your attention by acting in a negative way.

Now let's say your child is playing quietly, making up a song, or impulsively cleaning her room. Do you put down everything you're doing to praise her behavior? Most people don't. Some parents may not even notice the positive behavior. Or, if they do, they smile quietly, say nothing to the child, and go about their business.

And we wonder why our kids have tantrums!

In the Trim Kids Program, we've found that giving children positive attention for behavior that supports their weight-loss goals can reap incredible results. Likewise, scorning their unhealthy behavior can be detrimental. Up until now, you may have admonished your son for eating that entire bag of cookies or refusing to go outside and play or watching too much TV. From now on, however, you need to train yourself *not* to lecture him when he slips. Instead, give him attention when he does something right. Each time he makes a choice that supports his new lifestyle, pat him on the back, both literally and figuratively. In Part Two, we'll give you tips on how to stay constructive while responding to inevitable slips.

Your primary charge is to be positive, upbeat, encouraging, and empathetic, and help build your child's belief in himself. Hold back the criticism when he loses ground, help him identify healthier options (we'll show you how), and acknowledge him when he's successful.

### Attitude

Perhaps the most substantial change we ask of parents is to change their attitude. Take an honest look at what you think about the health food movement, those exercise buffs you see running down the parkway, and the little hearts next to certain food items on menus at restaurants.

Whether your past responses have been positive, negative, or neutral, now is the time to reframe your attitude so that *you are the health food movement! You are an exercise trainer! You are always a positive force!* Start living by the principle that you are committed to health, a cutting-edge parent leading your family into the fabulous world of fitness. You are, in fact, a trendsetter! Boo television commercials that promote unhealthy foods. Cheer your child on for eating a new high-fiber, low-sugar cereal or completing his first twenty-minute walk. Remind your family that healthy choices are the key to vitality and quality of life. Listen to your child when the going gets rough, and help shore up his confidence so he stays with it. Root for him all the way, both in actions and in words.

### Accountability

If the only professional help you enlist is from a pediatrician, then it will be up to you to:

- Regularly weigh your child
- Fill out the forms in each week of Part Two
- Set weekly goals
- Evaluate past goals
- Continually assess how your child is progressing

Keeping close track of your child's physical changes and emotional commitment, and whether or not your child is meeting her goals, will reveal how well she's doing. If she hasn't lost any weight in four months but she's grown a half-inch, then you can assume things are advancing. If, on the other hand, she's gained 5 pounds without growing, you must be accountable to the program and figure out what to do next. Other family members also need to adhere to new house rules. If they don't, it's up to you to rally the troops and talk about solutions. The operative concept here is to find solutions *as a family* so that you can continue to support the efforts of your overweight child. We'll provide techniques for handling both weight gain and reluctant family members. Please understand that if you don't give importance to record keeping or self-monitoring, neither will your child. Research shows that just writing down what you eat makes you eat less.

### Availability

In this age of working parents and endless distractions, it can seem impossible to carve out quality time for children. It's not impossible, though, and for the sake of your child's healthy future, you're going to have to make it a priority. In between cheering him on or noticing how his face looks thinner, you'll need to be available for conscientious food shopping and cooking, and to launch more physical activity around the house. It won't take long, though, before you are comfort-

able with your new lifestyle and begin
enjoying the benefits that unfold from
within your child, your family, and
yourself.

One of the greatest gifts you'll get
from the time you spend with your
child is a new understanding of how
to solve problems together. When
you meet with your child to assess
progress, you will both determine
what needs to be tweaked and how
to go about it. You'll be amazed at the

> **TRIM KIDS TESTIMONIAL**
>
> ......................................................
>
> ## A Parent's Perspective
>
> "The program has brought us closer together, even
> after tough times. My daughter has actually said,
> 'Thanks, Mom. You've really been there for me.' It
> gets easier when your child sees results in herself,
> and you see changes in the dynamics of the family."

answers he comes up with when you ask the right questions. Being available to
help nurture his own inner resourcefulness will serve him throughout life. You'll
probably find that these problem-solving skills will have a positive impact on other
areas and challenges of your family's life, as well.

## MAKING CONVENIENT AND HEALTHY CHOICES

With all that parents must accomplish these days, the need for convenience has
increased exponentially. Although certain lifestyle habits will change, you can
still maintain a good deal of convenience while following the Trim Kids Program.

We're parents, and we know how tempting it is to pull into a Burger King
when you're on a road trip. It's quick, it's easy, and the kids like it. But most grocery stores now offer fruit or salad bars and deli sections replete with low-fat,
healthy foods. Getting out of the car allows you to stretch, and when your hungry
child is presented with some of his favorite healthy foods, he'll forget about the
fried foods he used to eat.

We're also aware of how convenient it is to have your child in front of the television when you want to get something done that requires your full attention.
Consider this: your child could be equally diverted by jumping on a trampoline,
roller skating, jumping rope, riding his bike, dancing, or shooting baskets in the
driveway. You still get a moment to yourself, and instead of sitting and watching

television and burning about 30 to 50 calories per hour, your child can be active and burning about 300 to 400 calories per hour.

### What We Do for the Family

It may be comforting to know that it is easier to mobilize change in your child than it is in your own life. That's because we tend to care more about our children's future than our own. We can oversee the child, offer support, and envision a happier, healthier life for our child more effectively than we can for ourselves. This can be a positive factor that motivates you to keep your child on track.

When it comes to introducing new foods, have a little *fun!* Your child is always up for fun, so bring a new brand of it to the kitchen table. Write food reviews. Give grades to the new foods, and promise your child that those that receive A's will become regulars on the menu. A month later, bring out the report cards from the beginning of the program. Notice if any of the grades have changed. At the same time, if she gives brussels sprouts an F, don't force them on her. Your child won't like everything, but if you approach new foods and eating habits with an open mind, she will eventually follow suit.

## ESTABLISHING ATTAINABLE GOALS

Setting goals for your child is an integral part of the program, and a tried and true technique for implementing new routines and habits. The best way for your child to be successful and for you to be comfortable policing the situation (without feeling like a bad cop) is to start with easily attainable goals, simple steps that your child can handle. Here are some suggestions:

- Make sure the goals you and your child set are specific, easy to measure, and easy to accomplish. ("I'll ride my bike for ten minutes two days this week.")
- Avoid setting vague or unrealistic goals. ("I am going to stay on my diet this week" or "I'll stay on it until I lose 30 pounds.")
- Focus on what you *can* have rather than what you *can't*. (Instead of saying, "I won't have ice cream for dessert this week," say, "I'll eat fruit this week for dessert.")

- State what you *will* do versus what you *won't* do. (Instead of saying, "I won't be a couch potato," say, "I will walk half a mile on Saturday.")
- Most important, reward your child frequently with positive comments and mutually agreed–upon material items as she reaches her goals.

With each day that your child meets her goals, pour on the praise and support her into the next step. It's a process that will need to be reviewed and updated each week. In the weeks that she doesn't reach her goal, praise her for the changes she did incorporate. Talk about why the goals she had set were difficult to meet. Together, figure out if new goals need to be established, or if you simply need a new approach or strategy to achieve a difficult goal. But it's always better and easier to set reachable goals initially. Remember, if you give them less to do, they'll do more.

# HOUSEHOLD RULES: FLEXIBLE AND FIRM

Although you and your child work together to create goals, you alone enforce the household rules essential for attaining those goals. The best way to get your child to cooperate with the rules is through rewards and consequences.

Take an honest look at which rules you feel strongly about (firm rules), and which ones you may be willing to bend (flexible rules). This fits with our idea of being flexible about *how often* you serve up goodies, but being firm about *how much* your child gets.

Here are some examples of typical *firm* rules:

- No television until you've completed your exercise program or played for thirty minutes.
- No homework until you've played outside for thirty minutes. (Not all rules will be hard to maintain!)
- Take only one serving. Seconds should be vegetables only.
- Eat breakfast every morning before leaving the house.
- Try at least three bites of each type of food on the plate.

Some ideas for more *flexible* rules could include:

- Eat with your nondominant hand. (If your child is right-handed, ask her to eat with her left hand, and vice versa.) This will automatically slow your child down.
- Chew each bite fifteen to thirty times.
- Put your fork down after each bite.

The difference between firm rules and flexible ones is their degree of importance. The need for reward and consequence is also based on importance. If, for example, your daughter sticks to her exercise program without a hitch, then it is appropriate to reward her so she feels recognized. Maybe a trip to the water slide? New clothes? Fancy athletic shoes? And always a sincere pat on the back, recognizing her hard work.

If, however, she neglects her exercise program and puts up a fight about doing it, you will need to impose a consequence. Remind her that the reward you've agreed upon will have to wait until she fulfills her end of the bargain. If she continues not to adhere, you may have to deny phone privileges or insist that she abide by her regular bedtime rather than an extended bedtime on the weekend.

Flexible rules, in general, don't prompt either a reward or a consequence. So, if she chews her food thirty times, there's no need for a material reward. Make sure, however, that you acknowledge her effort by making a positive comment. Similarly, if she chews her food only five times, there's no need to impose a consequence.

Following through with consequences isn't always fun, but as we've pointed out, the most dramatic reactions will occur within the first few weeks

---

**TRIM KIDS TESTIMONIAL**

## A Parent's Perspective

"There may be family members or grandparents who refuse to do the program. One of my relatives told me she thought I was getting carried away. But I told her I didn't agree and asked her to please not minimize our effort. It doesn't matter what other people think, really. And I wouldn't allow them to fool with me or with the health of my child. In the end, my child is thinner, healthier, and happier. Now she's patting *me* on the back."

when you enforce the rules. After that, it will get easier and easier if you stay consistent.

## FAMILY AS TEAMMATES OR SABOTEURS

When you first introduce the program to your family, your overweight child may not be the only nervous participant. Even if she is scared, on some level she knows that she needs to make changes to be happier and healthier.

Her siblings, however, may not share the same emotional or physical issues and may resent being asked to join in the effort. Your partner may also be uncomfortable initially.

The best way to respond is to educate them about what's at stake. Appeal to their love and concern for the overweight child. Point to the disturbing statistics of what happens to children who grow into overweight adults. Explain to the thinner children that junk foods with empty calories don't build muscles or make them grow taller—that the new healthier foods are for everyone, though for different reasons.

Reassure them that life as they know it will not come to an abrupt halt. There will even be something in it for siblings. Using the same strategies of reward and consequence that you apply to your overweight child, remind siblings that being more active will lead to a healthier, more fit family. Or maybe a new bike. Or more trips to the amusement park. Or later bedtime hours. You'll get their attention and support if they know there's also a payoff for them.

Let them know, too, that you promise to take them out occasionally to their favorite fast-food restaurant as long as they join their heavier sibling in his healthy choices of salad or grilled chicken.

Typically, we've found, more fathers than mothers feel resistant to change. Once again, home in on the issues. Remind the reluctant partner of how painful it is to see your overweight child come home from school in tears, and how much pain she lives with each school day while the adults are insulated in the world of work.

You can still make lots of changes that don't require his help. Some things he won't even notice. Serve lean ground beef. Use fat-free sour cream in a recipe instead of regular sour cream. You can even change from whole to a lower-fat milk without his knowing it. To do the "milk switch" simply keep the whole milk container in the fridge, use half of it, then refill the carton with 2 percent milk. After a couple of weeks, start buying only 2 percent milk. Later, mix the 2 percent milk with 1 percent, and 1 percent with skim. Within weeks, you'll all be drinking skim milk, and no one will even know it—until you break it to the family, at which time you can start using the right container!

Change may come more slowly to some family members than others, but the once-reluctant member very often comes on board without even realizing it. When you reveal the new low-fat ingredients in the meals he's been enjoying, and share how much fun you had exercising with your child that day, he'll probably lighten up and participate.

## BACKSLIDING

Nobody's perfect, and everyone needs a break now and then. At some point, your child may stop losing weight and, in fact, start gaining. This is fairly typical, especially in growing children. First, check with your child's pediatrician to see if the extra pounds may be due to normal growth. Remember that for every inch your child grows, he will gain 3 to 5 pounds. Research shows that the key to getting back on track is how you deal with the setback. Typically, those who beat themselves up over the setback have the hardest time maintaining lasting change. Instead, help your child talk about—or "externalize"—these setbacks, which will make him feel some sense of control over the situation. One way to externalize a situation is to verbally express what happened. "What could I do? I didn't plan to go to the movies today *and* I didn't plan ahead. How could I know that they would be out of dill pickles and diet soda? I had to get a regular soda and I wanted something to eat, so I chose nachos and cheese."

**TRIM KIDS TESTIMONIAL**

### A Child's Perspective

"Doing this made me realize I could do more than ever before. My grades went up. Guys are talking to me. I have more friends. I got more confidence when my dress size dropped. It felt so good."

—Nancy, age fourteen

If the backslide persists, consider giving your child a vacation from his new lifestyle. That may be the best thing to do if, after gaining a couple of pounds, you hear him say, "I knew I couldn't do it. I'm a failure and I'm tired of this. I'll never be able to stay on the diet." If you feel the same way, you definitely need a break.

Remind your child that vacations are valuable and necessary, and that he can take a week off. Discuss the idea of a vacation with your entire family. Then, set a specific date when you will resume the program.

★　★　★　★　★

# PART TWO

# The Trim Kids
# Twelve-Week Program

Part Two is divided into twelve weeks that include worksheets,
weekly forms to fill out with your child, appropriate exercises
for the color-coded levels of our program, weekly menus, and
more. The appendix contains forms you'll copy for weekly use.
As you familiarize yourself with the program, be sure to
look through "Forms You'll Need" so you're working
with all the necessary tools. Time to get busy!

# Week 1

# READY, SET, GO!

## TRIM KIDS ROAD MAP FOR WEEK 1

*This week we'll help you get started. Each week is divided into four sections: "Time to Stop and Think," providing essential background on what we'll be covering that week and behavior modification tips; "Time to Get Active," dealing specifically with the exercise and activity part of our program; "Time to Eat," containing key nutritional information, menu plans, shopping lists, and recipes; and "Time to Sum Up," in which you and your child evaluate the week's progress and problems.*

*You'll begin this week by determining your child's weight level with your pediatrician or family physician. You'll then figure out your child's level (Red, Yellow, Green, or Blue) for the Trim Kids Program. You'll also learn how to monitor progress using the Trim Kids Record Forms:*

1. TRIM KIDS WEEKLY REPORT AND GOAL SHEET
2. TRIM KIDS AEROBIC ACTIVITY AND FOOD CHECKLIST
3. TRIM KIDS STRENGTH AND FLEXIBILITY WORKOUT CHART

*We'll provide tips on motivating your child and family to meet the challenge of the Trim Kids Program, and determine whether you're committed to going through with it. You'll write out an eating schedule, and we'll walk you through the goal-setting process.*

*This week you'll learn how to make exercise and activity a way of life. We'll show you safe exercise techniques for warming up and cooling down, and what types of activities are best for your child. Each week, you'll learn a new aerobic activity, a new strength activity, and a new flexibility exercise.*

## SECTION 1: TIME TO STOP AND THINK

## INITIATING PARENTS

To officially kick off your role as coach, here's a quick preview of how to be your child's sounding board, exercise coach, and dietitian. You may want to post a copy of these pointers somewhere easy to see, so you'll have a daily reminder of your new role.

## Commandments for a Committed Coach

1. I will guide my child to success by acting as her greatest example, an advocate, a mentor, and a cheerleader.
2. I will listen to my child without interrupting. I will let him know I am listening, and I will help him solve problems when they occur.
3. If I feel judgmental toward my child, I will say nothing negative. Instead, I will keep the thoughts to myself and do my best to be supportive.
4. I will consider and respect my child's individuality. I will adjust the program to meet her physical and emotional needs.
5. If my child becomes defiant or depressed during this process, I will contact a professional.
6. I will ensure my child's success by following the appropriate color-coded suggestions, and by making sure she can follow them with ease.
7. I will focus on what my child does right and give positive responses whenever he demonstrates his commitment to the program.
8. I will help my child select activities he enjoys so that he has fun and wants to keep active.

9. I will participate with my child in the program as much as possible because I know that my involvement will greatly determine her success.

10. Every day, I will help my child pick the best times to exercise so there is flexibility as well as a structured routine.

11. Every day, I will create opportunities for my child to be more active. I will provide a variety of choices such as riding her bike, raking leaves, cleaning her room, dancing, or vacuuming. Being more physically active will become a family priority.

12. I will make sure my child warms up and cools down each time she exercises.

13. I will review my shopping list before I go to the store so that I can buy the healthiest foods for my family.

14. I will rearrange the kitchen so my child has easy access to healthy foods and cannot reach or see the few high-calorie foods that remain in the house.

15. I will cook healthy, low-fat, low-calorie foods for my family. We will eat together whenever possible, introduce new rules for eating, and keep mealtime fun and adventurous.

16. I will keep track of my child's progress with a weekly weigh-in and by monitoring his eating and activity records. I will praise him for making healthy food and activity choices; otherwise I will encourage him to keep on trying when he hasn't.

## WHAT TO EXPECT FROM THE PEDIATRICIAN

The time has come for your first visit to the pediatrician as part of the program. He or she will record your child's height, weight, and circumference measurements. Both boys and girls will need to have their waist and hips measured. The pediatrician will then determine your child's body mass index (BMI) and optimal weight range (see pages 20-23). This will determine which level of the program to follow (Red-Severe, Yellow-Moderate, Green-Mild, or Blue-Maintenance; see page 24 for guidelines). The doctor may also ascertain your child's blood pressure, cholesterol, and triglyceride levels and undertake any other necessary laboratory tests.

Record these values on the *Trim Kids Initial Measurements* form provided below.

## Trim Kids Initial Measurements

Name _____ Age _____ Today's date _____

Initial height _____ Initial weight _____

Healthy body weight _____ Goal weight _____

Body mass index (BMI) _____ (refer to chart on pages 20-23)

Level of overweight _____ RED _____ YELLOW_____ GREEN _____ BLUE _____

Waist circumference _____ Hip circumference _____ Blood pressure _____ % Fat _____

Laboratory values:

Triglycerides _____

Total cholesterol _____ HDL _____ LDL _____

Ask the doctor any questions you have, and clearly agree on your intentions and strategies for attaining the weight-loss goals. This is also the time to discuss medical conditions your child may have that need to be monitored. If you feel you need extra support, ask the doctor to recommend a registered dietitian, exercise physiologist, psychologist, or social worker. Most important, make sure that the doctor will be available to answer questions if you become concerned about your child's health as you follow the program. Before leaving, make an appointment for three months in the future to assess progress—or sooner, as your physician requires.

If you decide to work with an exercise physiologist, request an exercise fitness evaluation to assess your child's muscular strength and endurance, flexibility, cardiorespiratory endurance, and physical activity levels. Be sure the exercise physiol-

## Cholesterol and Children

A high level of total blood cholesterol, especially LDL or "bad" cholesterol, can increase the risk of coronary artery disease or heart disease. New studies show that fatty deposits in the blood vessels can begin developing in childhood. Dietary intervention needs to begin when your child is quite young, at about three years of age.

Here's what you should know about cholesterol so you can discuss it with your physician:

- Total cholesterol: This total is made up of several fractions including LDL and HDL cholesterol and a very small fraction called VLDL cholesterol. The total cholesterol level should be less than 170 in children.
- LDL cholesterol: This is the *bad* cholesterol, which increases the risk of forming fatty deposits in blood vessels. LDL should be less than 110 in children.
- HDL cholesterol: We call this *good* cholesterol; it reduces the risk of fatty deposits in blood vessels. HDL cholesterol should be greater than 35 in children.

ogist is aware of your child's color-coded level and performs the exercises that are suited to his condition.

# RECORD KEEPING: MEASURING SUCCESS

Keeping close tabs on your child's eating habits, activities, and weight enables you to measure progress and determine if he will attain his goals. If your child is able to write, don't do the record keeping for him, but keep an eye on what he's recording since those records are your measuring sticks to monitor his success. *It is absolutely essential that your child get used to filling out these records. Our research has shown us that children who do this—and their families—are far more likely to work through our program successfully.* Once she gets used to the process, it will become second nature to complete the records.

For each week, there are short forms and charts pertinent to the focus of that week. In addition, you'll complete three major forms which are the backbone of our program. You should photocopy them—one for each week—and have them readily available.

1. TRIM KIDS WEEKLY REPORT AND GOAL SHEET (page 384): At the beginning of every week, your child needs to be weighed, and the weight recorded. Always weigh her in the same clothes, on the same day of the week, and at approximately the same time of day. You'll also record

weight she's lost, the problems she's encountered during the week, and goals she sets for the coming week. Give positive reinforcement *only* for weight lost or maintained, but try to focus more attention on healthy behavior, such as trying new vegetables or a new physical activity, rather than on the child's weight. If your child gains weight, encourage her to try again the next week. Nonfood rewards are helpful. *Never* ridicule or criticize your child for gaining weight or stepping outside the program. Instead, discuss the result and make adjustments where necessary. If something occurs that you feel ill-equipped to handle, consult a professional for advice. Follow this same process for the next eleven weeks. If your child has medical concerns, or if you're working with a registered dietitian or other health professional, you may want to visit the pediatrician more frequently. This will simply assure you—and the doctor—that things are progressing in a healthy manner.

2. TRIM KIDS AEROBIC ACTIVITY AND FOOD CHECKLIST (page 386): Every week, your child will keep tabs on his aerobic activities (we'll give suggestions and guidelines for him to follow), and the "food unit portions" he can, and does, eat. It's important that your child understand the Trim Kids system of portion control, and you'll soon learn all about it.

3. TRIM KIDS STRENGTH AND FLEXIBILITY WORKOUT CHART (page 388): Every week your child will learn a new strength exercise and a new flexibility exercise. These exercises are cumulative—meaning that your child will learn a new exercise each week and will practice that exercise as well as the exercises she's learned in previous weeks. She'll track her progress on this chart.

# INITIATING CHILDREN: ACCEPTING THE CHALLENGE

Take however much time your child needs to understand your explanations of each component of the program. Age will determine how easy it may be for her to absorb this, but research shows that children eight years and older should be able to grasp these concepts without much difficulty. Ask your child to fill in the blanks below, to help her become aware of exactly what is motivating her to lose weight.

*List three reasons why you want to lose weight:*

1. _____
   _____

2. _____
   _____

3. _____
   _____

## CHANGING BEHAVIOR THROUGH SELF-MONITORING

Our clinical experience over the past fifteen years tells us that the majority of children in the program lose weight the first week by simply monitoring their eating and activity—even before they are given recommendations for diet or exercise! This is due to something called the Hawthorne effect: by observing any behavior, we change what we do.

In this program, we explain to your child that learning to monitor her own behavior will help her become aware of what she's doing to help or hinder her weight loss. Explain this to your child. Touch on these points:

1. The Trim Kids Program is about change—specifically, about learning to change unhealthy eating and exercise habits into healthier ones.
2. In the nutrition portion of the program, you will learn about food selection, cooking, and eating habits so that the amount and kinds of calories you eat will keep you healthy but enable you to lose weight.
3. The exercise component of the program will help you change your physical habits so it's easier for you to move around and play.
4. You'll learn about behavior modification that will help you make all these changes. You'll be able to see what you do that's unhealthy, understand why you do these things, and learn how to do other, healthier things instead.

5. When you try something new—like in-line skating, ice skating, or a new food—it takes practice. This will, too!

6. The first behavior modification exercise you'll learn is how to become a *self-monitor*. That means you are going to notice or observe how much you eat and how much you exercise. When you become a good self-monitor, you can identify:
   - What and how much you eat
   - How much you exercise
   - Situations that cause you to overeat
   - Situations that cause you to be underactive

7. Overeating and being physically inactive are the behaviors that keep you from losing weight. When you recognize them, you can replace them with other, healthier behavior.

8. Beginning today, you'll be filling out the following forms each day (see "Record Keeping," page 84, if you have more questions):
   - TRIM KIDS WEEKLY REPORT AND GOAL SHEET (page 384), which will record your weight, your accomplishments, your goals for the next week, and your problems in the previous week.
   - TRIM KIDS AEROBIC ACTIVITY AND FOOD CHECKLIST (page 386), which will record how often, how long, and how hard you exercise aerobically each week. Beginning in week 2 you will also record what you're eating, how much your eating, and how many times you eat.
   - TRIM KIDS STRENGTH AND FLEXIBILITY WORKOUT CHART (page 388), which will record how you're progressing on our specially tailored exercises.

Explain to your child that when he learns to monitor his eating habits, he may discover that he eats for lots of different reasons. Your child's reasons may include these.

**EXTERNAL URGES**
- Being somewhere that makes him want to eat—at a party, a movie theater, or a special event like going to the circus or to a restaurant
- The sight or smell of food
- Being around people who are eating

• Sometimes activities he's engaged in can make him want to eat—for example, watching television, studying, or reading.

**INTERNAL URGES**
• Hunger
• Craving a food
• Moods and feelings that lead him to the refrigerator, such as boredom, sadness, or burnout

**AS HE BECOMES AWARE OF HIS EATING HABITS, HE NEEDS TO RECOGNIZE:**
• Where he eats
• What he eats
• How much he eats
• How fast he eats
• How often he eats

---

### Rules for Eating

1. Chew more—fifteen to thirty times per bite.
2. Eat slowly. Taste your food and enjoy each bite.
3. Take smaller bites.
4. Do not take seconds—except for vegetables.
5. Leave some of every type of food on your plate. (This really is OK.)
6. Take smaller portions.
7. Leave the serving bowls of food in the kitchen.
8. Use a smaller plate.
9. Try to put your fork down after every bite.
10. Eat at least three bites of every food.
11. Drink a large glass of water fifteen minutes before each meal.

---

Explain to him that he'll begin this week to follow the Trim Kids rules for eating.

Sit down with your child and fill out the form below to begin replacing unhealthy eating habits with other activities.

# Four Golden Rules for Altering Eating Behaviors

*Follow these four golden rules for healthy eating habits:*

1. **Eat on a schedule.** Don't eat at any other time. Plan your schedule, write it down, and stick with it!
   - Breakfast            time _____
   - Morning snack       time _____
   - Lunch                time _____
   - Afternoon snack     time _____
   - Dinner               time _____

2. **Eat in one place.** When you're at home, always eat at the same place, usually the kitchen or dining room table. Do this for all meals, drinks, and snacks. It's only OK to drink water anywhere, anytime.

3. **Don't do anything else while eating.** From now on, you may not watch television, study, read, or play while eating.

4. **Create your list of alternative activities.** Make a list of practical and enjoyable activities that you can do instead of eating.

   **Alternative activities (What I can do instead of eating!)**

   _____  _____
   _____  _____
   _____  _____
   _____  _____

   Include activities you can do both inside and outside. Examples include taking a walk or bike ride, listening to music, reading, or drinking a large glass of ice water or another sugar-free beverage. Keep this list handy so you can refer to it when you feel tempted to eat between your scheduled meals.

# GOALS, SUCCESS, AND COMMITMENT

The Trim Kids Program sets both long-term and short-term goals to help kids achieve success. Start by establishing what your child's *long-term goals* may be. Typically, they include:

- Losing a specified amount of weight (such as 20 pounds)
- Fitting into smaller-size clothing (dropping two to three dress sizes)
- Filling out the daily food and activity records
- Graduating to the next color level of the program
- Walking one mile nonstop
- Including one fruit and one vegetable at every meal
- Running without getting tired
- Playing a quarter of a game of basketball nonstop

## Defining Your Short- and Long-Term Goals

*Trim Kids Long-Term (1-Year) Goals:*

My long-term goals are:

_____

_____

*Examples:*

- My long-term goal is to reach my healthy body weight by the beginning of the next school year.
- My long-term goal is to reduce my waistline by 5 inches by the summer.
- My long-term goal is to finish a 10K race.

*Trim Kids Short-Term (12-Week) Goals:*

My short-term goals are:

_____

_____

Examples:
- My short-term goal is to lose 10 pounds.
- My short-term goal is to drop one dress size.
- My short-term goal is to walk ½ mile without resting.
- My short-term goal is to try three new vegetables.

Setting goals improves your child's chances of success only if the goals are practical and attainable. As you track his progress, you'll be able to tell if he's on course. Establishing new goals or reassessing old ones is also a good time for him to voice hopes and fears about how he's doing, what he thinks about the program, and how he feels about the changes. If he encounters rough times, encourage him to focus on accomplishments he has enjoyed, and express your belief and pride in him.

As you begin the program, ask yourself who in your family makes household rules. If the children in your house—rather than the adults—seem to set the rules, then your child will probably have more problems initially adhering to the Trim Kids Program. It's essential that you establish only rules you know you can enforce. Your child's success depends on this.

We find it helpful for parents and children to rate their level of commitment on a scale from 1 to 100, at the beginning of the program and at twelve-week intervals. A rating of 1 means you're not interested in changing; a rating of 50 means you're moderately interested; 100 means you're very interested. If the whole family can't honestly rate their motivation at 50 or higher, then the time to begin the program is later—not now. Resistant children or parents often sabotage weight-loss efforts for the whole family. So take a moment to answer the following questions and decide for yourself if you, your child, and your family are truly ready.

## Commitment Rating

*Child—Rate yourself on a scale from 1 to 100 (circle one) as you answer each question:*

*How much do you want to lose weight right now?*

| 0 | 25 | 50 | 75 | 100 |
|---|---|---|---|---|
| Not at all | A little | Somewhat | A lot | Very much |

*Parents—How much do you want your child to lose weight right now?*

| 0 | 25 | 50 | 75 | 100 |
|---|---|---|---|---|
| Not at all | A little | Somewhat | A lot | Very much |

*Parents—How much do you want your family to lead a healthier lifestyle?*

| 0 | 25 | 50 | 75 | 100 |
|---|---|---|---|---|
| Not at all | A little | Somewhat | A lot | Very much |

## BENEFITS AND SACRIFICES

Although undertaking a lifestyle change as comprehensive as this one requires sacrifices, you will receive many benefits. Now, ask yourself, "Is it worth my time and effort?"

### Sacrifices and Benefits

*Make a list of the sacrifices you think you'll make and the benefits you think you'll enjoy on the Trim Kids Program.*

**Sacrifices:**                                    **Benefits:**

_____          _____

_____          _____

_____          _____

_____          _____

_____          _____

_____          _____

Don't forget that the sacrifices are mostly food-related, while the rewards range from better health (no more sore knees or getting out of breath from climbing the stairs) to social acceptance (no more teasing or being picked last for the team).

*Is the time right for you?*

If the benefits seem to be *more important* to you than the sacrifices, and if you feel like making the commitment to begin the Trim Kids Program, then *now is the time for you!* Decide whether you will begin the Trim Kids Program now: _____.

# BEHAVIOR SUBSTITUTION

Establishing short-term goals is a proven way to help people accomplish what they're after. Short-term goals need to be reasonable and attainable but challenging enough so that your child is making positive, significant strides. Remember, too, that you must reward your child when he takes the steps necessary to reach the goal, providing a positive incentive and recognition for a job well done. Likewise, if he strays from the program, you need to impose appropriate consequences.

## A Parent's Perspective

"My thirteen-year-old daughter walked into my bedroom one day and asked, "Mom, do you think I'm fat?" I was caught completely off guard, but I managed to answer, "Honey, you're probably somewhat overweight but you're certainly not fat." That was the first time I had to actually face the problem head-on. But I didn't really know what to do. I tried bringing her to an adult weight-loss program, but she was bored and felt out of place. When she came home crying from school one day, I thought, That's enough! I'm taking her to the pediatrician!

"That's where I should have started. Dr. Graham evaluated her and told us exactly how overweight she was—which wasn't very much, when we considered her height. He then discussed the many options that were available to us. He assured us her problem wasn't a medical one at this point, but if we didn't address it now, it would inevitably become one. We scheduled a follow-up appointment before leaving his office and got started looking into appropriate plans the very next day."

Tell him that the doctor helped figure out his goal weight, which you used to set a twelve-week goal weight (a 10 to 15 percent loss, for example). Then say something like this: "Now we will take small steps every week toward meeting that goal through weekly exercise, nutrition, and behavior modification goals."

Make a list of specific unhealthy behaviors such as eating high-calorie snacks after school or watching cartoons all day Saturday. Our mission is to try to change these unhealthy behaviors one at a time. Read over the list of substitute activities below that you can do instead of engaging in the unhealthy behaviors. Add items that you particularly enjoy. Once you've changed a behavior, stick with the new behavior and we'll work on changing another behavior.

For each behavior that you change or each goal that you reach, we'll do something special like go to the zoo or the pool. Or maybe we'll get you a new pair of in-line skates, a jump rope, a compact disc you can dance to, or karate lessons!

## Substitute Activities

Exercise!  
Walk  
Jump rope  
Dance  
Do aerobics  
Bicycle  
Run  
Talk on the phone while walking around  
Write  

Sing  
Play outside  
Shop  
Play a game  
Read  
Clean your room  
Visit a friend  
Run errands  
Drink a large glass of water  

## Your Own Behavior Substitutions

*Make a list below of the "low-calorie behaviors" you tried this week:*

_____

_____

_____

_____

*Make a list below of the "high-calorie behavior" that you used to do:*

_____

_____

_____

_____

## Rewards for Accomplishing Goals

| Instead of . . . | Try . . . |
|---|---|
| Video game | In-line skating |
| Box of candy | Jumping rope or lifting hand weights★ |
| Television | Bicycle |
| Board game | Hopscotch★ |
| Radio or tape player | Mini-trampoline★ |
| Magazine | Frisbee |
| Handheld sports game | Volleyball |
| Sports video | Football |
| Fast-food gift certificate | Skating event gift certificate |
| Movie video | Exercise video |

★Not appropriate for Red level.

## Write Five of Your Own Rewards

| Instead of . . . | Try . . . |
|---|---|
| _____ | _____ |
| _____ | _____ |
| _____ | _____ |

_____     _____

_____     _____

····················································
## SECTION 2: TIME TO GET ACTIVE
····················································

## MOVING RIGHT ALONG: MAKING EXERCISE AND ACTIVITY A WAY OF LIFE

Remember that having fun motivates your child. Explain that the changes in and around your house will invite more fun into his life, and that you want to provide him with as much fun and activity as possible. Reassure your child that the structured part of the exercise program was designed with his needs in mind, that it will be somewhat challenging, but that he will succeed at it.

Describe the four color-coded levels to your child (page 24), identify which one he's in, and explain that there is a different exercise and eating program for each color. Let him know that when he reaches his first weight-loss goal he will graduate to the next color code, and that the objective is to attain his long-term goal weight and be a lifelong member of the Blue level.

As you will see, our exercise plans are laid out according to your child's level. Certain issues, though, are common to all the levels. They are:

- Warming up
- Cooling down
- Safety tips

### TECHNIQUES FOR WARMING UP

Before you do any type of exercise, you'll need to warm up for at least five minutes at the beginning of each session. Warming up is simple: move each part of your body in a slow, controlled manner. When you slowly move an arm, a leg, or a shoulder, your heart sends blood to that body part, delivering fuel to the muscles and tissues that are in motion. Moving your arms and legs helps the heart pump blood throughout your entire body, preparing your body for more movement. Try the suggestions below, or make up your own!

### Some Warm-Up Suggestions
- March in place for three to five minutes
- Do arm circles forward, then back, twenty times
- Do ten modified jumping jacks or "side jacks": instead of jumping, alternate placing each heel out to the side on the floor while the arms go above the head
- Tap each foot twenty times; then rise on your toes ten times

### TECHNIQUES FOR COOLING DOWN

Five to ten minutes before you complete your exercise—whether it's riding your bike, jogging, swimming, walking, or dancing—you need to start cooling down. Do this gradually until you are maintaining a slow, easy pace. Continue at this pace for the last ten minutes or so of your workout.

Cooling down is important because your body needs time to return to its normal heart rate and breathing pattern. Otherwise, the blood traveling to your exercising muscles will *pool*, or remain in the muscles. This can make you feel dizzy or nauseated, and you may experience painful muscle cramps.

Cooling down is just like warming up. You simply move your arms and legs slowly after exercising, and your blood leaves the muscles and returns to the heart and lungs. Your legs even have a built-in pump to help with that process, but you have to keep them moving for the pump to work.

Slowing down before stopping your exercise also helps bring your temperature back to its normal range. That's why it's called cooling down!

No matter what exercise you're doing, always slow the pace for the last five to ten minutes.

### SAFETY TIPS

Be sure to emphasize these, no matter what your child's level is!

- Stop exercising if you feel any discomfort in a muscle or joint. It's normal to feel a gentle burning sensation, but if the pain is worse than that, stop

immediately! You'll need to report it to your teacher, coach, exercise physiologist, or doctor the next time you see him or her.
- Do the exercise exactly as instructed. The exercises in this book have been
designed especially for you, and you shouldn't change them.
- Be sure to record your daily activity on the forms in the appendix.

## WEEKLY EXERCISE ACTIVITIES

Each week, you will find two types of activities:

1. Weekly aerobic activity
2. Weekly strength and flex exercises

Each activity includes recommendations as to how often, and for how long, your
child should perform it. These are meant to be *realistic goals*—they're also the minimal
goals. If your child wants to do more—great! Usually if you give children less, they'll
do more. Then you can really praise them for going over and above, and this really
helps them achieve "mastery"—a feeling of having accomplished something special.

Let your child choose activities she wants to do from the list below. We'll give
you additional ideas every week.

## Trim Kids Aerobic Activities

### *Red-Level Activities*

*Do* only *activities that support your excess weight, such as:*

| | | |
|---|---|---|
| Swimming | Arm crank★ | Recline bike |
| Cycling | Seated (chair) aerobics | Snorkeling |
| Stationary bike | Seated or lying circuit training★ | Water jogging or aerobics |

★If you're not sure what these are, talk to your pediatrician about the proper technique and equipment you will need.

### Yellow-Level Activities

*Alternate the Red-level activities with these:*

Interval walking★    Swimming             Cycling
Strength-aerobic     Arm-specific aerobics  Water jogiing or aerobics
  circuit training   Interval indoor-
Recline bike         outdoor games★

★Walking or playing with frequent rests. Keep your arms moving as you rest legs and ankles. Gradually work up to longer periods of activity and fewer rest periods.

### Green-Level Activities

*Do activities that will burn the most calories, such as:*

Outdoor-indoor games  In-line skating or   Tennis or racquetball
Field sports            ice skating        Martial arts
Brisk walking         Jumping rope         Skiing
                      Hiking

### Blue-Level Activities

*Choose from any of the activities listed above. Kids in the Blue level can perform most physical activities safely and with ease. We'll give you more ideas in the next eleven weeks.*

WEEK 1 AEROBIC ACTIVITY: RECOMMENDED GOALS
- **Red Level:** The exercise goal this week is two days per week for twenty minutes each day.
- **Yellow Level:** The exercise goal this week is two days per week for twenty to twenty-five minutes each day.
- **Green Level:** The exercise goal this week is three days per week for twenty to thirty-five minutes each day.
- **Blue Level:** The exercise goal this week is three days per week for thirty to sixty minutes each day.

Write your goal in the TRIM KIDS AEROBIC ACTIVITY AND FOOD CHECKLIST (page 386). This is the minimum amount of aerobic exercise that you should perform this week. In the spaces indicated, have your child list the activities she accomplished this week and how long she did them. If you know her heart rate, write it in the space provided.

Now it's time to get moving! Choose an activity from the list on pages 98 and 99. Be sure it is suitable for your child's level of fitness. For example, if she is in the Red level advise her to choose swimming and cycling—the activities that are the easiest and healthiest for her condition.

Check to make sure your child is performing the activities for the length of time and the number of days per week suggested above. She should do them at a moderate or medium pace and be able to talk without strain while exercising. If her breathing becomes rapid or labored, instruct her to slow down. Check her heart rate to determine if she's attained 55 to 65 percent of the maximum age-predicted heart rate (see page 152).

Remember: The Trim Kids Program establishes the *minimum* goals for each week to ensure that your child achieves initial success—which is crucial to her confidence and ongoing participation in the program. This week, make sure she can complete the activity without difficulty and that she is *having fun*!

Encourage your child to do as much playing as possible. Let her know that playing burns even more calories than structured exercise. Weave her favorite playful activities into daily life. Work with her to create appealing indoor and outdoor play areas. Be imaginative! Resist the urge to push, thinking more will be better. If she can do it, great. But if you assign less, she may do more.

### WEEK 1 AEROBIC ACTIVITY: AEROBIC VOLLEYBALL

Gather the family or a group of overweight neighborhood kids and set up a volleyball game. You'll need some music to make it complete—along with these few additional guidelines:

• When the opposing team scores a point, the receiving team has to do ten aerobic moves to the music such as aerobic dance moves (like side jacks—page 97)—the twist, the grapevine, and the cha-cha) while the ball is retrieved.

- When the serving players get a "side out" (they lose the point and the serve to the opposing team) they have to do ten dance movements to the music.
- It's also fun to have all players walk, jog, or dance around the court at the end of each game.

See the MPEP Step (page 358) for ideas on other moves.

### WEEK 1 STRENGTH AND FLEX EXERCISES

Each week, your child will learn a new strength exercise and a new flex exercise. In week 6, we'll start the process of exercising with weights.

Children under fourteen should begin at the lowest intensity. No matter what the child's age, you should focus on the child's technique.

Read the directions below aloud to your child as she does each exercise. Eventually, she will know them by heart and do them without your instruction.

## Strength Exercise 1: Leg Extension, Sitting

Sit in a chair with your arms at your sides. Bend your knees at a ninety-degree angle with your feet flat on the floor. Gently flatten your lower back.

Slowly extend both your legs from the knee while keeping your upper legs stationary for two to four seconds. Do not lift your hips. Extend your legs fully until your upper front thigh muscle is completely contracted, but *do not lock your knees.* Keep your ankles and feet relaxed. Great! Now take about four seconds to return to the starting position. Do eight to twelve repetitions. This exercise strengthens your front thigh muscles (quadriceps).

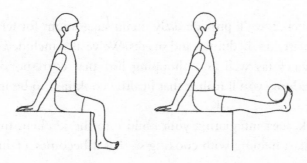

### Flex Exercise 1: Shoulder Stretch

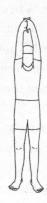

Stand with your feet about eighteen inches apart. Now bend your knees slightly. Push your hips forward just a bit. Keep your stomach muscles tight. Inhale as you raise both arms above your head with your upper arms just ahead of your ears. Interlock your fingers and turn your hands inside out. Stretch upward at a slight angle forward. Hold this position for fifteen to thirty seconds. Lower arms and relax. Repeat this process one more time, holding this position again for fifteen to thirty seconds.

Perform these new strength and flex exercises at least once, but preferably twice this week. Record your progress on the TRIM KIDS STRENGTH AND FLEXIBILITY WORKOUT CHART in the Appendix ("Forms You'll Need"), on page 388. Every week, you will add another exercise to your program.

Don't forget to fill out your TRIM KIDS AEROBIC ACTIVITY AND FOOD CHECKLIST on page 386, and try the aerobic activity of the week with the entire family.

·············· **SECTION 3: TIME TO DINE** ··············

# NUTRITION NUTSHELL: COOKING AND DINING; RESURRECTING FAMILY TRADITIONS

Starting in week 2, we'll provide daily menu suggestions for feeding your family a healthy breakfast, lunch, dinner, and snacks. We've also included a selection of easy-to-follow recipes (as well as a shopping list) that correspond with that week's menu. Before long, you'll realize that healthy cooking can be integrated into your life with ease.

This week, start integrating your child into the kitchen. Invite your child (or children) to start helping with cooking so that it becomes a family affair. Cooking together also keeps your child active. Show him the difference between slicing and dicing. Remind him why you're cooking the nutrient-rich foods you chose, rather than pizza or a frozen dinner. If your child shows absolutely no interest in culinary activities, suggest that he go outside and play. Then, try using the time you spend cooking to unwind from your own day.

If your child claims he's "starving" just before dinner is ready and wants a snack, ask him to drink a big glass of water instead of eating something solid. This is a great way to tease the body into thinking it has eaten something. Be firm, though. Snacking just before dinner isn't wise. Water, or a low-calorie food such as vegetables, will have to do.

When dinner is ready, call the entire family to the table. Your family will be prepared to come, since you will have already established some new rules about how the family eats. No more eating on the run. No more meals in front of the television. No more chowing down while standing up. That's because *how* we eat is nearly as significant as *what* we eat.

Indeed, *everything* your child eats should be at the kitchen or dining room table. Studies show she'll eat less if she can't do it while running around or while zoning out in front of the tube. Even if she just wants a glass of milk and an apple, tell her she must sit down—without a book or toy—and drink or eat it at the table. The only exception is if she wants water while riding her stationary bike or doing some other form of exercise.

We encourage the entire family to follow these practices whenever possible because they build family dynamics. Remember, this is a family program. You can't eat in front of the nightly news while your child eats alone at the table!

Also, when you're at the table together, you can monitor your child's eating habits more closely. How can you know how *fast*, how *much*, or precisely *what* he's eating if you're not sitting there with him?

If you have conflicting schedules, making it impossible for everyone to sit together for family meals, be sure at least one parent or sibling can eat with your overweight child. And don't rush him or make him feel it's a chore to be there. Sit down, relax, enjoy each other's company, and help him learn and integrate his new mealtime habits.

If you want to take your family out to dinner—go ahead! But be sure to look at our recommendations in "Week 10" (page 336), where we discuss dining out in detail.

# ENLISTING SUPPORT

Spread the news to friends, relatives, teachers, and others that your family has begun the Trim Kids Program. Accept their praise and support. Most likely, everyone will want to see you succeed. Ask other overweight children if they would be interested in playing team sports once a week or joining in other fun activities. Go for it! The more the merrier!

Also, it's helpful for anyone who supervises your child to know that he is following the program. Make a copy of the letter on page 392 in the appendix ("Forms You'll Need"), ask your pediatrician or exercise professional to sign it, and send it to your child's physical education teacher, coaches, or other appropriate people.

## Trim Kids Weekly Checklist

| *Did you remember to:* | *Yes* | *No* | *Will do it by* |
|---|---|---|---|

Visit your child's physician, determine child's overweight level and appropriate color code, and record measurements and weight on the TRIM KIDS INITIAL MEASUREMENTS form?

Fill out TRIM KIDS AEROBIC ACTIVITY AND FOOD CHECKLIST?

Fill out TRIM KIDS STRENGTH AND FLEXIBILITY WORKOUT CHART?

Have your child list three reasons for wanting to lose weight, and fill out the Alternative Activities form?

Establish long-term goals?

—— —— ————

Fill out Commitment Rating form and the Benefits and Sacrifices chart?

—— —— ————

Review warm-up and cool-down procedures?

—— —— ————

Complete all appropriate exercises?

—— —— ————

Perform the aerobic activity of the week?

—— —— ————

Perform the strength and flex exercises of the week?

—— —— ————

Parents: after you weigh your child and fill out the weekly forms, be sure to set eating and activity goals for week 2.

Now that you know the basics of the Trim Kids Program, it's time to learn about the specifics of our nutritional component.

# EATING MEALS AND SNACKS THE TRIM KIDS WAY

## TRIM KIDS ROAD MAP FOR WEEK 2

*You'll start the week by filling out the Trim Kids forms, as you learned to do last week. (Remember to weigh your child!) Review last week's goals and have your child write her accomplishments. Reward your child for meeting her goals. Discuss any problems or questions with her. This week you'll begin the Trim Kids Nutrition Plan. You'll determine your child's individual plan, and we'll describe what kind of food, and how much food, your child should eat each day. You'll learn to keep track of what she eats, using the* TRIM KIDS AEROBIC ACTIVITY AND FOOD CHECKLIST. *A weekly menu plan, detailed recipes, and a weekly shopping list are provided.*

## SECTION 1: TIME TO STOP AND THINK

Earlier, we offered broad initial steps for introducing healthier eating habits to your child. Now, we're going to home in on specific eating guidelines that you will need to enforce every day. Whenever your child sits down to eat this week—be it a meal or a snack—ask her to:

*Slow down. Taste your food and enjoy each bite!*

- Take smaller bites.
- Try to put your fork down between bites.
- Try to chew more, swallow, and then pick up your fork or spoon for another bite.
- Pause during the meal. Start with a brief pause (thirty seconds) and gradually increase the time to one, then two, and finally three minutes. Use this time to discuss how your day went, learn about how the day went for other family members, and so on.
- Try to eat with your non-dominant hand. If you usually hold your fork with your right hand, try eating with your left. This will slow your eating automatically!

*Be open to the adventure of new tastes! Introducing The Three-Bite Rule*

- Let your child know that you'll be trying several new foods. Remind him that this can be fun.
- Implement the three-bite rule: everyone has to take at least three bites of every food on the plate.

## TRIM KIDS TESTIMONIAL

Every year we invite our program graduates to attend our holiday party. This year we were thrilled to see Jack—one of our very first patients—now twenty-two, a ten-year veteran. He was healthy, trim, and very handsome to boot! He brought his girlfriend and was excited to introduce us to her. We, of course, took the opportunity to let Jack act as a role model for our current patients. What he said, though, surprised *us* most of all:

"Ten years ago I was 65 pounds overweight. My mom brought me to this program and I lost all the weight before the year was up. I started playing football and then I hurt my knee. I couldn't exercise, so I gained 40 pounds back, but after my knee healed I still kept playing sports. I knew I could look better but I just didn't want to commit to losing the weight again. Then I started college and I wanted to be as fit as all the other guys. I pulled out my old books and started eating right again. I joined the gym and started working out. Every day I could hear Ms. Heidi saying, 'If it's under 5 grams of fat or 15 grams of sugar, go for it,' and Dr. Melinda saying, 'Don't forget to warm up, and don't go too fast. Increase a little each week.' Or Dr. Kris saying, 'Stay positive and focus on your accomplishments.' And you see it worked!"

The beauty of teaching children healthy nutrition and fitness habits now is that even if they get that "glazed" look as if they're not listening, don't worry. They are, and they're soaking it all up. They'll remember later when they're ready.

- After trying all the foods, give each food a grade. A means it's great, B means it's pretty good, C means it's just OK, D means it's not very good, and F means *blah!*
- Reassure your child that you'll serve lots more of the A foods, and no more of the F foods.

Make sure your child understands these concepts and be sure to answer any questions so you can both be working toward the same goal.

## DEFINING HEALTHY FOODS

It's time to discuss the Trim Kids Nutrition Plan. You will learn what types of food are healthier to eat, how much food is healthy, and how to understand what food does to the body.

Sit down together when you have adequate time to explain the information, answer questions, and help your child grasp the concept of portion control.

### Nutrients and Calories

Review what calories are and how they relate to weight loss: calories are the energy produced in your body from the foods you eat. When you eat more food (or calories) than your body needs, the extra calories are stored as fat. That's how you gain weight. When you eat fewer calories than you need, your body breaks down the fat to get the energy it needs. That's how you lose weight. It takes about 3,500 calories to make one pound of body fat. To lose weight, you can eat fewer calories and also burn off extra calories by increasing your activity.

Review where calories come from. There are three kinds of nutrients in food that supply calories:

- Protein is essential for maintaining your child's growth and muscle tissue or lean body mass. One gram of protein yields about 4 calories.
- Carbohydrates help give energy. One gram of carbohydrate yields about 4 calories.
- Smaller amounts of fat are necessary for certain body systems. One gram of fat yields 9 calories.

Each food has its own unique combination of protein, carbohydrate, and fat. Since 1 gram of fat has more than twice the calories of carbohydrates and protein, it's healthiest to eat foods that are lower in fat to reduce the amount of calories you consume and be successful at losing weight.

## Sugar

Explain the need to watch the amount of sugar consumed. Sugar doesn't contain fat, but it has so many calories that if you eat too much of it, you will easily gain weight. More than half of the simple sugar in our diet is found in beverages including sodas, punches, fruit drinks, sport drinks, and fruit juices. Eliminating sugar-containing beverages therefore will significantly reduce your intake of simple sugar (and calories). To lose weight, you need to eat fewer high-sugar foods. You'll still be able to have sweet foods such as sugar-free gelatin, reduced-sugar jam or jelly, low-sugar pancake syrup, and light whipped topping. Fruits are sweet, too, but they contain a lot less sugar than most other desserts—and they're packed with fiber and vitamins! When you want something sweet, you can have an apple, a banana, blueberries, cantaloupe, fruit cocktail, grapefruit, mango, orange, peach, pear, pineapple, strawberries, tangerine, watermelon, or dried fruit (figs, dates, raisins). Yummy!

## CALORIE (PORTION) CONTROL

In addition to eating too much fat and sugar, you can also consume an excessive amount of calories by consuming too large a portion of food, including higher-carbohydrate ("starchy") foods. You will learn how to restrict calories by practicing portion control using the different food groups and food units (see below) as a guide. As your child's activity level increases and weight loss is achieved, his caloric intake may be liberalized.

Growing children need to eat a certain number of calories to stay healthy, but not more than is good for them. As we mentioned in Chapter 3, you'll work with your child's physician to establish your child's goal weight. Current weight will determine which color-coded level of our program he needs to follow. If your child's weight falls into the Green, Yellow, or Red level, one of his objectives may be to lose weight. Use the chart below to determine how many calories he should consume to meet his weight-loss goals.

## DAILY ENERGY NEEDS AND AVERAGE CALORIE REQUIREMENTS

| Age | Average Daily Calorie Needs | Average Calories Needed to Reduce Weight |
| --- | --- | --- |
| 7–10 years (male and female) | 1,600 to 2,200 calories | 1,200 to 1,600 calories |
| 11–14 years (male) | 2,200 to 2,800 calories | 1,500 to 2,000 calories |
| 11–14 years (female) | 1,600 to 2,400 calories | 1,200 to 1,800 calories |
| 15–18 years (male) | 2,400 to 3,400 calories | 1,800 to 2,400 calories |
| 15–18 years (female) | 1,800 to 2,400 calories | 1,200 to 1,800 calories |

## THE FOOD GROUPS

Food groups are based on the food exchange lists of the American Dietetic Association and American Diabetes Association. The calorie assignments of some groups have been modified to offer a general calorie range rather than a specific calorie level.

The Trim Kids Nutrition Plan teaches portion control by using a food unit or portion control system as a guide (see page 117). Foods are grouped into different categories according to their nutrient composition. The food groups are:

- Meat and protein substitutes
- Vegetables
- Carbohydrates, including starches and breads, fruits, and milk and other dairy products
- Fats

Every food falls into at least one of these groups and is assigned a "unit" or a specified portion. Each unit or portion provides a similar amount of calories. It is safe to assume, for instance, that one unit of any fruit has about 60 calories and contains no fat. Or one unit of any lean meat has about 25 to 50 calories and 1 to 3 grams of fat. Knowing this allows you and your child to make informed decisions about what and how much food your child may eat. Let's look a bit more closely at each food group to learn more about portions and nutritional values.

## Meats and Protein Substitutes

This food group includes most animal products and other foods that are good sources of protein. In general, these foods contain mostly protein and few carbohydrates. A unit in this food group generally equals 1 ounce or ¼ cup. One 3-ounce chicken breast, for example, equals three protein units. (We will often refer to this group as "proteins" for short.)

Since some animal products can be very high in fat, we divide this group into three parts based on the fat and calories in each: lean proteins, medium-fat proteins, and high-fat proteins. Take time to review the lower-fat protein choices listed below.

**Lean proteins** are the best choices. These contain no more than 2 or 3 grams of fat and 25 to 50 calories per ounce. Because they are so low in fat—especially seafood, egg substitutes (whites), and vegetable proteins—consuming a few additional units of these foods, especially if you are hungry, is allowed. Some examples of lean proteins include:

- Lean beef (round, sirloin, flank)
- Vegetable proteins (such as veggie or soy burgers), tofu
- Ham or Canadian bacon

### Soy Protein

Eating more soy protein helps lower the level of LDL, or bad cholesterol. Many soy protein–based foods are also good sources of dietary fiber, which means they're really healthy food! They also contain no cholesterol. Replace some animal proteins (meat or poultry and dairy) with soy proteins as desired. Good sources of soy protein include:

- Soy milk
- Soy or vegetable meat and cheese substitutes
- Soy nuts
- Tofu

- Skinless chicken or turkey
- Seafood (the fat in fish and seafood, called omega-3 fatty acids, has been linked to a reduced risk of some diseases, especially heart disease)
- Very low-fat cheeses and cold cuts (containing less than 3 to 5 grams of fat per ounce)
- Egg whites or egg substitutes
- Veal chops or roasts

**Medium-fat proteins** contain no more than 5 to 6 grams of fat and 75 calories per ounce. Eat them less often than lean meats. Examples include:

- Most beef (ground, roasts, or steaks)
- Pork, lamb, and veal cutlets
- Low-fat cheeses and cold cuts (containing about 5 grams or more of fat per ounce)
- Whole eggs (egg yolks are high in cholesterol)

**High-fat proteins** contain 8 to 10 grams of fat and about 100 calories per ounce. Because of their high fat and caloric content, avoid these foods as much as possible. They include:

| | |
|---|---|
| **Peanut Butter**<br><br>Peanut butter is a good protein substitute, although it is fairly high in fat. The good news is that it's a monounsaturated fat and may be eaten in moderation—usually not more than 1 to 2 tablespoons per serving. Choose a peanut butter brand that contains no added hydrogenated vegetable oils. | - Deep-fat fried meat or meat substitute<br>- Prime beef (ribs, corned beef)<br>- Pork sausage or spareribs<br>- Bacon<br>- Regular cheeses<br>- Lunch meats (bologna, salami, liver, cheese)<br>- Regular hot dogs, Vienna sausages |

## Vegetables

The vegetable group includes all nonstarchy vegetables. Members of this group contain on average less than 1 gram of fat and less than 25 calories per serving. These vegetables are also low in carbohydrates (less than 5 grams per serving), and thus low in calories. Therefore, your child may eat as much of them as desired. These include:

- Artichokes, asparagus, green beans
- Bean sprouts, beets, broccoli
- Brussels sprouts, cabbage, carrots
- Cauliflower, eggplant, greens, hearts of palm
- Okra, onions, pea pods
- Peppers, spinach, tomatoes
- Tomato sauce
- Tomato or vegetable juice
- Salad greens
- Summer or zucchini squash
- Vegetable soup

We recommend that your child consume a minimum of five servings per day of fruits and vegetables. Not only are these foods naturally fat-free and packed with vitamins and minerals, but eating an abundance of them may decrease the risk of certain types of cancer, heart disease, and stroke.

## Carbohydrate-Containing Food Groups: Starches and Breads, Fruits, and Milk and Dairy Products

The following food groups contain carbohydrates and will be grouped together as *carbohydrate food units*. These include starches such as breads, fruits, and milk and other dairy foods. These food groups may be mixed and matched as desired, but try not to exceed the Daily Food Prescription (see page 118) for carbohydrate units specified for your calorie level.

*Starches and Breads* In general, one carbohydrate unit of a starch or bread is ½ cup of cereal, grain, or pasta, or a 1-ounce slice of bread, and contains about 80 to 100 calories per unit. Here's a useful hint for portion control: an average nine-inch plate equals about 2 cups or four carbohydrate units. If you choose starches or breads with added fat (oil, butter, etc.) make sure to count the fat portions as part of your daily intake, too. Some items in this food group include:

- Cereals (those containing more than 3 grams of fiber per serving are better choices)
- Pancakes, waffles, muffins
- Grains, pasta
- Beans, peas, lentils
- Corn, potatoes
- Breads, bagels, tortillas (whole-wheat and whole-grain types are better)
- Crackers (wheat), popcorn, pretzels

*Fruits* This group includes fresh fruit and unsweetened canned fruit and fruit juices. (Fresh or canned fruit is a better choice than fruit juice.) One unit is generally equal to one medium-size piece of fresh fruit or ½ cup of canned fruit or fruit juice. Each unit contains less than ½ gram of fat and 60 to 90 calories. Items in this food group include:

- Apple, applesauce (unsweetened), banana, berries (any kind)
- Fruit cocktail, grapes, grapefruit, kiwi
- Mandarin oranges, mango, melons (any kind), nectarines
- Oranges, peaches, pears, pineapple
- Tangerine, watermelon
- Dried fruits such as figs, dates, and raisins
- Fruit juices (in moderation)

*Milk and Dairy Products* This food group includes skim and very low-fat milk and milk products. One unit generally equals 8 ounces (1 cup) of milk or ½ to 1 cup of milk products and averages 90 to 120 calories per unit. Choose milk and dairy products that are lower in fat (containing less than 3 to 5 grams of fat per serving) to keep the calories lower. Items in this food group include:

- Skim and very low-fat (1 to 1½ percent) milk
- Soy milk
- Nonfat and very low-fat yogurt
- Nonfat and very low-fat ice cream, pudding, frozen yogurt

## Fats

Foods in this group contain mainly fat and very little carbohydrate or protein. Fats must be counted in addition to carbohydrate and protein units according to the Trim Kids Nutrition Plan Portion Control Table (see page 117). Each serving in this group averages 50 calories and 5 grams of fat. Items in this food group include:

Better Choices

- Oil (olive, canola, peanut), olives
- Nuts
- Avocado

Other Choices

- Lite margarine (look for liquid vegetable oil as the first ingredient)
- Reduced-fat salad dressings (consume fat-free versions as desired—"free food")
- Reduced-fat mayonnaise (consume fat-free versions as desired—"free food")

Less Healthy Choices (saturated fat)

- Regular margarine (containing hydrogenated or partially hydrogenated vegetable oils)
- Butter
- Bacon
- Sour cream (consume fat-free versions as desired—"free food")
- Cream cheese (consume fat-free versions as desired—"free food")
- Half-and-half

## Free Foods: "Anytime" Foods and Beverages

When your child focuses on what she *can* eat rather than on what she *cannot,* she'll be more apt to want and choose those foods. Below is a list of "free foods"—this term means she can eat them without having to worry about measuring portions. They contain very little fat or no fat and less than 20 calories per serving.

*Sugar-free beverages*

| | | |
|---|---|---|
| Water—the *best* beverage! | Mineral water | Club soda |
| Sugar-free drink mixes★ | Sugar-free sodas★ | Broth, bouillon |

*Condiments*

Fat-free butter substitutes such as butter and olive oil–flavored nonfat, nonstick cooking spray and liquid butter substitutes

Fat-free cream cheese, fat-free mayonnaise, fat-free salad dressings

Fat-free sour cream

Flavoring extracts (vanilla, almond, peppermint, lemon)

Herbs, spices, seasoning blends (any kind)★★

Hot pepper, Tabasco sauce

Powdered salad dressing, soup packets (mixed with fat-free sour cream to make a dip)

Seasoning packets (chili, stir-fry, taco, etc.)

Soy sauce (reduced-sodium preferred)

| | | |
|---|---|---|
| BBQ sauce | Catsup | Horseradish |
| Lemons, limes | Mustard (any kind) | Pickles (any kind) |
| Salsa | Taco sauce | Teriyaki sauce |
| Vinegar (any kind) | Worcestershire sauce | |

*Sweet tooth*★

Low-sugar jelly and jam and fruit spreads

Light whipped topping (2 tablespoons)

All vegetables (see vegetable list above)

| | |
|---|---|
| Sugar-free gum | Diet (sugar-free) Jell-O |
| Sugar-free Popsicles | Low-sugar pancake syrup |

Refer to the Table of Food Portions and Units later in this section (see page 119) for detailed food items and unit portions.

---

★Check with your health-care team before using artificial sweeteners.
★★Although salt contains no calories, don't go overboard. Substitute lower-sodium products when possible.

## YOUR DAILY TRIM KIDS NUTRITION PLAN

To make things easier, we have assigned daily food portion guides for each calorie level. Instead of counting calories, all you have to do is eat a specified number of units (or portions) daily from the carbohydrate, meat and protein substitute, and fat food groups—not exceeding your calorie goal. Refer to Daily Energy Needs and Average Calorie Requirements (page 110) to find the daily portion allowance for your child's calorie goal.

## TRIM KIDS NUTRITION PLAN PORTION CONTROL TABLE

| Daily Weight Loss Calorie Level* (approx.) | Carbohydrate Food Units (OK to mix and match) | | | Total (Starch, fruit, milk) Daily Carbohydrate Units | Total Daily Meat and Protein-Substitute Units | Total Daily Fat Units | Vegetable Group—Lower Carbohydrate Units |
|---|---|---|---|---|---|---|---|
| | Starch Group | Fruit Group | Milk and Dairy Group | | | | |
| 1,200 | 3–4 | 2 | 3 | 8 | 4 to 5 | 4 | Unlimited |
| 1,500 | 5–6 | 2–3 | 3 | 10 | 6 | 5 | Unlimited |
| 1,800 | 7–8 | 2–3 | 3 | 12 | 6 | 6 | Unlimited |
| 2,000 | 9 | 2–3 | 3 | 14 | 6 to 8 | 7 | Unlimited |

*Try to include at least 2 or 3 servings of vegetables per day.

Now it's time to write down your child's own daily food prescription. Based on your child's weight-loss calorie goal, write the number of food units or portions that your child is allowed for each food group below. For example, if the weight-loss calorie goal is 1,500 calories per day, your child will be allowed 10 carbohydrate units, 6 meat or protein sources, and 5 fats per day.

Restricting calories too severely may increase cravings and result in bingeing. If your child is still excessively hungry after adding additional vegetables and calorie-free foods, increase the daily intake by 1 to 2 units, especially from lean protein sources, dairy, or fruits, as needed to prevent excessive hunger.

## Daily Food Prescription

*My Daily Calorie Goal:* _____ *Calories per Day*

*I am allowed to eat:*

_____ *Carbohydrate Units per Day*

*These include:*
- Starches/Breads
- Fruits
- Milk/Dairy

_____ *Meat and Protein Substitute Units per Day*

_____ *Fat Units per Day*

Unlimited Vegetables

# KEEPING TRACK USING THE FOOD CHECKLIST

To help keep track of your child's daily food intake, use the TRIM KIDS AEROBIC ACTIVITY AND FOOD CHECKLIST found in the appendix, "Forms You'll Need," page 386. Each small box on the checklist represents one unit. Check the appropriate box or boxes for every food or drink your child consumes. For example:

Turkey sandwich made with:

| | |
|---|---|
| 2 slices wheat bread | Check 2 carbohydrate boxes. |
| 2 slices of turkey | Check 1 to 2 meat, meat substitute boxes. |
| lettuce and tomato | Check vegetable box. |
| 1 cup skim milk | Check 1 carbohydrate box. |

Checking the boxes will help you practice staying within your child's daily recommended portion intake. Don't worry if you have to "guesstimate" at times, especially if your child is away from home. Following a tight calorie limit is not the goal, but practicing and "reteaching" the body portion control (until it becomes a habit) is.

## FOOD PORTION AND UNIT LISTS

Keeping track of portions ensures that your child is eating the right amounts of foods to achieve the weight-loss calorie goal. Refer to the table below for food group portions and their specific food units.

## TABLE OF FOOD PORTIONS AND UNITS

### Starches

| Common Foods | Portion | Units |
|---|---|---|
| **Breads** | | |
| Bread | 1 slice (1 ounce) | 1 carb |
| "Lite" bread | 2 slices | 1 carb |
| Bagel | Medium (2 ounces) | 2 carbs |
| | Large (4 ounces) | 4 carbs |
| English muffin | Whole | 2 carbs |

| Hamburger or hot dog bun | Whole | 2 carbs |
|---|---|---|
| Dinner roll | Small (1 ounce) | 1 carb |
| Muffin | Small (2 ounces) | 2 carbs |
| | Large (4 ounces) | 4 carbs |
| Waffle/pancake | 1 regular | 1 carb |
| Tortillas | 1 regular | 1 carb |
| **Cereals** | | |
| Dry (breakfast) cereal | 1 cup | 1 carb |
| Hot cereal (oatmeal, Cream of Wheat, grits): | | |
| Plain | ½ cup (1 packet, instant) | 1 carb |
| Fruit, flavored | ⅔ cup (1 packet, instant) | 2 carbs |
| **Grains and Legumes** | | |
| Pasta | ½ cup (cooked) | 1 carb |
| Rice | ½ cup (cooked) | 1 carb |
| Beans (red, navy, lima) | ½ cup (cooked) | 1 carb |
| Lentils | 1 cup (cooked) | 1 carb |
| Stuffing | ¼ cup (cooked) | 1 carb |
| **Snacks** | | |
| Chips (reduced fat) | 1 ounce (1 small bag) | 1 carb |
| Cereal fruit bar | 1 | 2 carbs |

| | | |
|---|---|---|
| Crackers: | | |
| Animal | 15 | 1 carb |
| Graham | 3 squares | 1 carb |
| Wheat or saltine-type | 6 | 1 carb |
| Granola bar | 1 | 2 carbs |
| Popcorn (reduced-fat) | 3 cups (popped) | 1 carb |
| Pretzels | 1 ounce (small bag) | 1 carb |
| Rice cakes: | | |
| Small | 8 | 1 carb |
| Large | 2 | 1 carb |
| **Starchy Vegetables** | | |
| Corn | ½ cup | 1 carb |
| Peas | ½ cup | 1 carb |
| Potatoes (sweet, white) | 1 medium | 2 carbs |
| Squash (acorn, butternut) | ¼ squash | 1 carb |
| **Fruits** | | |
| Fresh fruit | Medium (or about 1 cup) | 1 carb |
| Canned fruit | ½ cup | 1 carb |
| Dried fruit: | | |
| Apricots | 4 | 1 carb |
| Figs | 2 | 1 carb |
| Prunes | 3 | 1 carb |
| Raisins | ¼ cup (small box) | 1 carb |
| Fruit juice: | | |
| Apple | 1 cup (8 ounces) | 2 carbs |
| Cranberry | 1 cup (8 ounces) | 3 carbs |

| | | |
|---|---|---|
| Grape | 1 cup (8 ounces) | 3 carbs |
| Grapefruit | 1 cup (8 ounces) | 2 carbs |

**Dairy\***

| | | |
|---|---|---|
| Milk (skim or reduced fat) | 1 cup (8 ounces) | 1 carb |
| Soy milk | 1 cup (8 ounces) | 1 carb |
| Yogurt: | | |
|   Plain | 1 cup | 1 carb |
|   Fruit, regular sweetened | 1 cup | 2 carbs |
|   Fruit, artificially sweetened | 1 cup | 1 carb |
| Frozen yogurt | ½ cup (4-ounce kiddie-size) | 1 carb |
| Reduced-fat ice cream | ½ cup | 1 carb |
| Reduced-fat cheese | 1-ounce slice | 1 protein (no carbohydrates) |
| Regular cheese | 1-ounce slice | 1 protein + 1 fat |

**Vegetables (lower-carbohydrate)**

| | | |
|---|---|---|
| Unlimited | | |

**Meat, Poultry, Seafood; Protein Substitutes**

| | | |
|---|---|---|
| Beef: | | |
|   Flank, round, sirloin, tenderloin | 1 ounce | 1 protein |
| Poultry (skinless): | | |
|   Chicken | 1 breast (about 4 ounces) | 4 proteins |
| | 1 drumstick (about 2 ounces) | 2 proteins |
|   Turkey | 1 ounce | 1 protein |

\*Choose dairy products containing less than 3 to 5 grams of fat per unit. Choose dairy products containing less than 25 to 30 grams of "sugar" (check the label).

| | | |
|---|---|---|
| Pork:<br>   Canadian bacon, chops (fat trimmed),<br>   ham, loin, tenderloin | 1 ounce | 1 protein |
| Seafood:<br>   Fish (all)<br>   Shellfish (all)<br>   Tuna fish (canned in water) | 1 ounce<br>6 shrimp<br>½ cup | 1 protein<br>1 protein<br>2 proteins |
| Cold cuts (less than 3 to 5 grams<br>of fat per ounce) | 1 ounce | 1 protein |
| Reduced-fat cheese (less than 3 to 5<br>grams of fat per ounce) | 1 ounce | 1 protein |
| Regular cheese | 1 ounce | 1 protein + 1 fat |
| Eggs:<br>   Whole egg with yolk | 1 | 1 protein + 1 fat |
| Egg substitute | ½ cup | 2 proteins |
| Vegetable patties | 1 patty (about 3 ounces) | 2 proteins |
| Peanut butter | 1 tablespoon | 1 protein + 1 fat |
| Tofu | 4 ounces | 2 proteins |
| **Fats**<br>*Better choices | | |
| Avocado* | ¼ avocado | 2 fats |
| Butter or margarine (regular) | 1 tablespoon | 3 fats |
| Margarine, reduced-fat | 1 tablespoon | 1 fat |
| Cream cheese, fat-free* | No limit | 0 |
| Cream cheese, lite or Neufchâtel | 1 tablespoon | 1 fat |

| Margarine, fat-free* | No limit | 0 |
|---|---|---|
| Mayonnaise, regular | 1 tablespoon | 3 fats |
| Mayonnaise, reduced-fat | 1 tablespoon | 1 fat |
| Mayonnaise, fat-free* | No limit | 0 |
| Nuts and seeds:* <br> Peanuts, cashews <br> Almonds <br> Pine nuts, pumpkin seeds, <br> sunflower seeds | About ¼ cup <br> (4 tablespoons) <br> About ¼ cup <br> (4 tablespoons) | 3 fats <br><br> 3 fats |
| Oils: <br> Canola, olive, peanut* <br><br> Corn, safflower, soybean, sunflower | 1 teaspoon <br> 1 tablespoon <br> 1 tablespoon | 1 fat <br> 3 fats <br> 3 fats |
| Olives | About 10 | 1 fat |
| Salad dressing, reduced-fat | 2 tablespoons | 1 fat |
| Salad dressing, fat-free* | No limit | 0 |
| Sour cream, reduced-fat | 2 tablespoons | 1 fat |
| Sour cream, fat-free* | No limit | 0 |
| **Condiments and Seasonings** | | |
| BBQ sauce | 2–3 tablespoons | 0 |
| Catsup | No limit | 0 |
| Herbs and spices | No limit | 0 |
| Horseradish | No limit | 0 |
| Hot sauce | No limit | 0 |

| | | |
|---|---|---|
| Lemon or lime juice | No limit | 0 |
| Mayonnaise (regular) | 1 tablespoon | 3 fats |
| Mayonnaise (reduced-fat) | 1 tablespoon | 1 fat |
| Mayonnaise (fat-free) | No limit | 0 |
| Mustard | No limit | 0 |
| Pickles | No limit | 0 |
| Salsa | No limit | 0 |
| Soy sauce (reduced-sodium is better) | No limit | 0 |
| Taco sauce | No limit | 0 |
| Teriyaki sauce | No limit | 0 |
| Worcestershire sauce | No limit | 0 |
| **Entrees** | | |
| Casseroles: | | |
| Hamburger Helper, lasagna, stew | 1 cup | 2 carbs<br>1 protein<br>2 fats |
| Chili | 1 cup | 2 carbs<br>1 protein<br>3 fats |
| Chinese stir-fry | 1 cup | 2 proteins<br>vegetables<br>1 to 3 fats |
| Italian meat sauce | 1 cup | 2 proteins<br>2 to 3 vegetables |

| Jambalaya | 1 cup | 2 carbs<br>1 protein<br>2 to 3 fats |
| --- | --- | --- |
| Macaroni and cheese | 1 cup | 2 carbs<br>1 protein<br>3 fats |
| Ravioli or Spaghettios™ | 1 cup | 2 carbs<br>1 protein<br>1 vegetable |
| **Fast Food** | | |
| Chicken nuggets or tenders | 6 nuggets or 4 tenders | 2 proteins<br>1 carb<br>3 fats |
| French fries | "Kids" meal-size | 1 carb<br>2 fats |
| | Small | 2 carbs<br>3 fats |
| | Medium | 3 carbs<br>4 fats |
| | Large | 4 carbs<br>5 fats |
| Hamburger | Small—"Kids" meal or "junior" size | 1½ carbs<br>2 proteins<br>2 fats |
| | Regular | 2 carbs<br>3 proteins<br>3 fats |
| Pizza, thin crust | 1 slice, large | 2 carbs<br>2 proteins<br>3 fats |

## SECTION 2: TIME TO GET ACTIVE

# WEEKLY EXERCISE ACTIVITIES

### WEEK 2 AEROBIC ACTIVITY: RECOMMENDED GOALS

At the beginning of the week, be sure to write your exercise goal on the TRIM KIDS AEROBIC ACTIVITY AND FOOD CHECKLIST (page 386). This is the minimum amount of aerobic exercise that you should perform this week. Every day, record what type of physical activity you did and how long you did it. At the end of the week, compare your list with the goals you set at the beginning of the week.

- Red Level: The exercise goal this week is two days per week for twenty minutes each day.
- Yellow Level: The exercise goal this week is two days per week for twenty to twenty-five minutes each day.
- Green Level: The exercise goal this week is three days per week for twenty to thirty-five minutes each day.
- Blue Level: The exercise goal this week is three days per week for thirty to sixty minutes each day.

## Week 2 Aerobic Activity: A Family Biking Trip

Gather the family, some water bottles, and a healthy snack and go on a half-day biking expedition. Don't forget your helmets!

### WEEK 2 STRENGTH AND FLEX EXERCISE

Until he has them memorized, read these instructions aloud to your child as he does these exercises.

### Strength Exercise 2: Leg Curl, Standing

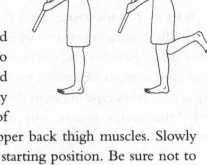

1. Stand up straight and tall with your stomach muscles tight, your hips slightly bent, and your knees slightly bent. Hold on to a bar or other stationary object for support.
2. Slowly raise the heel of one foot toward the back of your hip for a count of two to four seconds. Keep your upper leg and knee stationary. Good job. Now gently squeeze your heel toward the back of your upper leg, fully contracting the upper back thigh muscles. Slowly (over about four seconds) return to the starting position. Be sure not to lock your knees.
3. Repeat sequence eight to twelve times on each leg.

This exercise strengthens your back thigh muscles (hamstrings) and stretches your front thigh muscles (quadriceps).

Common errors your child may make include movement in the upper leg, tensing the upper body, leaning forward onto the hands, and tightening the feet.

### Flex Exercise 2: Chest Stretch

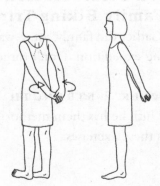

1. Stand with your feet about eighteen inches apart. Slightly bend your knees and push your hips forward as you tighten your stomach.
2. Pull your arms back, pressing your elbows together as you press your shoulders back and squeeze your shoulder blades together. Keep breathing and keep your head, neck, and shoulders relaxed.

3. Slightly tilt your chin upward. Hold this position for fifteen to thirty seconds. Release.
4. Repeat eight to twelve times.

Perform these new strength and flex exercises and also the ones you learned previously in week 1 at least once, but preferably twice this week. Record your progress on the TRIM KIDS STRENGTH AND FLEXIBILITY WORKOUT table in the appendix ("Forms You'll Need"), on page 388. Every week, you will add another exercise to your program.

Don't forget to fill out your TRIM KIDS AEROBIC ACTIVITY AND FOOD CHECKLIST (page 386), and try the aerobic activity of the week with the entire family.

## SECTION 3: TIME TO DINE

# WEEKLY MENU TIPS

- Your child's individual calorie goal may be slightly different from the Daily Food Prescription (page 118). To get this goal, review Daily Energy Needs and Average Calorie Requirements (page 110). This is a chart that will help you to determine your child's individual calorie needs. You will need to alter—decrease or increase—the food units provided in this book to match your child's individual needs, as set out in the Trim Kids Nutrition Plan Portion Control Table (page 117). Using the TRIM KIDS AEROBIC ACTIVITY AND FOOD CHECKLIST (page 386) to keep track of your food intake will help to keep track of your daily intake.
- Very low-calorie beverages, foods, and condiments (those on the free-food list) may be added to your menu plan as desired. Examples include fat-free condiments, any vegetables and salad items, seasonings (we prefer the salt-free and low-sodium versions when available), and sugar-free gelatin and beverages (check with your physician or dietitian regarding the use of sugar-free items).
- You can add vegetables and salads, or increase their amount, as desired. There are no portion limits on vegetables.

## Cooking Healthy: Recipe Substitutions

Substituting ingredients in recipes can significantly reduce the caloric content. Here are some tips.

| Instead of . . . | Use . . . |
|---|---|
| Butter, regular margarine (1,000 calories and 100 grams fat per stick) | Lite margarine (in moderation—first ingredient should be a liquid vegetable oil, not a partially hydrogenated vegetable oil) Nonfat liquid butter substitute Nonfat butter-flavored cooking spray |
| Oil—excessive, as in deep-fat frying (2,000 calories and 200 grams of fat per cup) | Baking or "oven-frying," grilling, pan-sauté, boiling Smaller amounts of olive, canola, or peanut oil |
| Heavy (whipping) cream—found in cream soups and sauces and some desserts (850 calories and 75 grams fat per cup) | Evaporated (undiluted) skim milk Land o'Lakes fat-free half-and-half Skim or low-fat milk thickened with cornstarch |
| Mayonnaise (2,000 calories and 200 grams fat per cup) | Fat-free or very low-fat mayonnaise |

- Most people require a minimum of three to four servings per day of dairy products (milk, yogurt, cheese, pudding) or calcium-fortified foods, or both, to meet calcium requirements. Include these items as snacks if your child's daily meal intake is less than this amount.
- A minimum of five servings per day of vegetables and fruits is recommended. Fruits and vegetables should be the preferred snacks to help meet this requirement.
- Choosing whole-wheat and whole-grain versions of breads and starches will help you meet the daily dietary fiber requirements. Most fruits and vegetables and beans are also good sources of dietary fiber.
- Remember to drink plenty of water during the day!
- The purpose of the portion control meal plans is not to create excessive hunger or "food wars." Encourage liberal intake of vegetables and water to help curb your child's appetite. If excessive hunger persists, increase the daily food units by one to two units as needed.
- Always check with your physician before initiating a calorie-

controlled meal plan. A registered dietitian can be very helpful in providing nutritional counseling and individualized meal planning.

- The recipes and weekly grocery-store shopping lists are for about a four-person household. Make adjustments, as necessary, based on the number of people in your home.

| | |
|---|---|
| Sour cream (400 calories and 40 grams fat per cup) | Fat-free sour cream<br><br>Plain yogurt |
| Cheese (400 calories and 36 grams fat per cup (4-oz.)<br>Cream cheese (800 calories and 75 grams fat per 8-ounce package) | Reduced-fat, part-skim milk, or fat-free cheeses<br>Fat-free cream cheese<br><br>Reduced-fat (Neufchâtel) cream cheese in moderation |

## Week 2 Weekly Menu

*Recipes are given for items in boldface.*

| | Breakfast | Lunch | Dinner | Snacks (1 to 2 choices per day) |
|---|---|---|---|---|
| MONDAY | Whole-grain waffle (1)<br>1 cup strawberries<br>Scrambled egg substitute (optional)<br>Orange juice—calcium fortified (½ cup) | Tuna salad made with reduced-fat mayonnaise (½ cup)<br>Wheat crackers (6)<br>Vegetable soup<br>Milk (1 cup) | **Turkey or BBQ Meat loaf**<br>½ cup mashed potatoes with reduced-fat gravy<br>**Seasoned Green Beans**<br>Milk (1 cup) | Cereal with fiber (1 cup) and skim or soy milk<br>Cereal-fruit bar (1)<br>Reduced-fat chips (15 to 20 chips or 1 ounce) with fat-free dip or salsa<br>Wheat crackers (6) with:<br>Reduced-fat cheese (2 slices) |

|  | **Breakfast** | **Lunch** | **Dinner** | **Snacks** (1 to 2 choices per day) |
|---|---|---|---|---|
| TUESDAY | Cold cereal containing fiber (1 cup)<br><br>1 slice wheat toast with low-sugar jelly<br><br>Banana (1)<br><br>Milk (1 cup) | Peanut butter (1 tablespoon) sandwich on wheat bread<br><br>10 small rice cakes<br><br>Reduced-fat pudding (½ cup)<br><br>Milk (1 cup) | 1 cup beans with ½ cup rice (preferably brown) Cooked or steamed vegetables of choice<br><br>½ cup fruit cocktail<br><br>Green salad with 1 teaspoon olive oil or reduced-fat dressing<br><br>Milk (½ to 1 cup) | Lite cream cheese (2 tablespoons)<br><br>Peanut butter (1 tablespoon)<br><br>Hot cocoa made with skim milk (1 cup)<br><br>English muffin or bagel "pizza" (½ muffin with tomato or pizza sauce and reduced-fat cheese) |
| WEDNESDAY | ½ cup (1 packet) oatmeal with raisins or a banana with 2 tablespoons walnuts (optional)<br><br>Wheat toast (1 slice) with low-sugar jelly<br><br>Milk (1 cup) | Meat loaf sandwich on wheat bread<br><br>Veggie sticks with fat-free dip<br><br>Grapes (½ cup)<br><br>Milk (½ to 1 cup) | Restaurant meal: Pizza—thin crust (2 slices)<br><br>Salad with reduced-fat dressing<br><br>Water or calorie-free beverage | Fruit (1 piece fresh, ½ cup canned, or 3 tablespoons dried)<br>Frozen fruit bar (1)<br><br>Fruit juice "spritzer": 3 ounces fruit juice mixed with 5 ounces club soda or mineral water<br><br>Graham crackers (3 squares)<br><br>Nuts (2 tablespoons)<br><br>Oatmeal (½ cup)<br><br>Oatmeal cookies (2 small)<br><br>Air-popped popcorn (3 to 5 cups) |
| THURSDAY | ½ bagel (preferably whole-wheat or whole-grain) with reduced-fat cream cheese or peanut butter (1 tablespoon)<br><br>Fruit yogurt (4 to 6 ounces)<br><br>Fruit juice—calcium fortified (½ cup) | Whole-wheat pita filled with sliced turkey (2 to 3 slices), vegetables, reduced-fat mayo, and free condiments<br><br>Apple<br><br>Milk (½ to 1 cup) | Baked, grilled fish (1 or 2 fillets) or oven-baked fish sticks (4)<br><br>**Broccoli and Rice *au Gratin*** (½ to 1 cup)<br><br>Salad with 1 teaspoon olive oil or reduced-fat dressing<br><br>Milk (½ to 1 cup) | |

| | Breakfast | Lunch | Dinner | Snacks (1 to 2 choices per day) |
|---|---|---|---|---|
| FRIDAY | Cold cereal containing fiber (1 cup) <br><br> 1 cup strawberries <br><br> Milk (1 cup) | ½ of a reduced-fat cheese sandwich <br><br> Chicken noodle soup (1 to 2 cups) <br><br> Grapes (½ cup) <br><br> Milk (½ to 1 cup) | Grilled or baked veggie burger with bun (preferably wheat) <br><br> **Carrot-Raisin Salad** <br><br> Sliced tomatoes or cherry tomatoes with reduced-fat dressing <br><br> Reduced-fat pudding cup <br><br> Milk (½ to 1 cup) | Reduced-fat pudding or ice cream (½ cup) <br><br> Quesadilla (1 tortilla) with melted, reduced-fat cheese, salsa, and fat-free sour cream <br><br> Rice cakes (10 small or 2 large) <br><br> Sandwich on wheat bread (½) with turkey, tuna with lite mayo, or reduced-fat cheese <br><br> Soup: vegetable or chicken noodle (2 cups) <br><br> Trail mix (4 tablespoons) <br><br> Yogurt, regular or frozen (4 to 6 ounces) |
| SATURDAY | Pancakes (1 or 2 medium), cooked with nonstick, nonfat, butter-flavored spray <br><br> Low-sugar syrup <br><br> Fruit to top the pancakes <br><br> Canadian or turkey bacon (3) <br><br> Milk (1 cup) | McDonald's Salad Shaker™ <br><br> Water or other calorie-free beverage <br><br> "Kiddie"-size frozen yogurt or low-fat ice cream | Spaghetti with ground turkey meat sauce: 1 cup sauce with 1 cup spaghetti noodles or (better) whole-wheat noodles <br><br> Garlic bread, 1-inch slice <br><br> Green salad with 1 teaspoon olive oil or reduced-fat dressing <br><br> Milk (½ to 1 cup) | |
| SUNDAY | Reduced-fat omelet made with egg substitute and reduced-fat cheese and cooked with | Out to eat: Cafeteria <br><br> Meat and vegetable plate with roast chicken or ham | **Leftover Night** <br><br> Food Units <br><br> 1 to 2 starch-bread <br><br> Lean or low-fat protein | |

| | Breakfast | Lunch | Dinner | Snacks (1 to 2 choices per day) |
|---|---|---|---|---|
| SUNDAY (cont.) | nonstick, nonfat, butter-flavored spray (optional ingredients: sautéed veggies, ham, salsa, and fat-free sour cream) 1 slice wheat toast Fresh melon (1/3 melon) Milk (1 cup) | Vegetable dish Potato dish *or* bread serving (1 piece) Salad (unlimited) Cafeteria hints: Skip the butter or margarine pats (1 pat contains about 100 calories and 10 grams of fat). Choose baked or broiled meats instead of fried. Skip the items containing cream or cheese sauces. | 0 to 1 fruit 1 milk-dairy 1 fat Veggies—unlimited! | |

# Week 2 Recipes

## TURKEY MEAT LOAF

2 pounds ground turkey
1 envelope onion soup mix
1 onion, finely chopped
3 tablespoons catsup
1/2 cup egg substitute

Preheat the oven to 350°F. Combine all the ingredients in a bowl, form into a loaf, and place on a rack inside a larger pan. Bake for 1 hour or until turkey is cooked through.

Makes about eight ¾-inch slices.

Nutritional Analysis
⅛ recipe: 3 protein units (150 calories, 6 grams fat)

················································································································

## BBQ MEAT LOAF

1½ pounds ground turkey or very lean ground beef
1 cup bread crumbs (preferably fresh)
1 medium onion, finely chopped
1 egg or ½ cup egg substitute
¼ teaspoon pepper (optional)
½ cup catsup
½ cup water
3 tablespoons vinegar
3 tablespoons dark brown sugar
2 tablespoons mustard
2 tablespoons Worcestershire sauce

Preheat the oven to 375°F. Mix the ground meat, bread crumbs, onion, egg, pepper, and ¼ cup of the catsup in a bowl. Put into a loaf pan. Mix the remaining ¼ cup catsup and other ingredients and pour over the loaf. Bake until cooked through, about 1 hour 15 minutes.

Makes about eight ¾-inch slices.

Nutritional Analysis
⅛ recipe: 2–3 protein units, 1 carbohydrate unit (185 calories, 6 grams fat)

## SEASONED GREEN BEANS

2 teaspoons olive oil
Olive oil–flavored cooking spray
1 onion, finely chopped
6 slices turkey bacon
Three 10-ounce packages frozen green beans
½ cup chicken broth or water
Pepper (optional)
½ teaspoon garlic powder (optional)
¼ teaspoon salt or salt substitute

Put the olive oil into a skillet and sauté the onion (spray if onion sticks), then remove onion. Fry the turkey bacon until crisp, then cut into small bits and return the onion to the skillet along with the green beans, ½ cup chicken broth, and seasonings. Simmer for about 20 minutes.

Makes 4 to 5 cups.

Nutritional Analysis
Vegetable Group: No limit (½ cup = 25 calories, 1 gram fat)

## CARROT-RAISIN SALAD

2 to 3 cups grated carrots
8-ounce can canned crushed pineapple with juice
½ cup raisins
1 cup fat-free mayonnaise or fat-free Miracle Whip™

Combined all the ingredients. Chill if desired.

3 to 4 cups

Nutritional Analysis
Vegetable Group: No limit (½ cup = 55 calories, 0 grams fat)

## BROCCOLI AND RICE *AU GRATIN*

1 onion, finely chopped (optional)
Nonfat butter-flavored spray (optional)
1 can reduced-fat cream of chicken or mushroom soup
½ soup can skim milk
Two 10-ounce packages frozen chopped broccoli, defrosted and drained
2 cups leftover cooked rice, preferably brown
4 ounces reduced-fat shredded Cheddar cheese (about 1 cup)
Bread crumbs (optional)

Preheat the oven to 350°F. In a casserole, sauté the onion, if using, in the nonfat butter spray until tender. Combine the onion and remaining ingredients, except the bread crumbs. Sprinkle with bread crumbs and spray with nonfat butter spray, if desired. Bake for 30 minutes. To make a one-dish meal, this recipe can be doubled for a crowd.

Makes about 6 cups.

Nutritional Analysis
1 cup: 1 carbohydrate unit, 1 protein unit, 1 fat unit (175 calories, 5 grams fat)

# Week 2 Weekly Shopping List

| Fruits | Vegetables | Meat, Deli | Dried, Canned |
|---|---|---|---|
| Apples | Carrots, celery | Turkey bacon | Oatmeal |
| Banana | Salad greens: | Turkey cold-cut slices | Breakfast cereal (fiber content should be more than 2 to 3 grams per serving) |
| Grapes |    Lettuce | Ground turkey (buy a "family pack"—enough for 2 recipes) | |
| Melon (in season) |    Tomatoes | | |
| Strawberries |    Cucumbers, etc. | Fish fillets (your favorite kind) | Brown rice (large bag) |
| Miscellaneous fruits for snacks | Onions | | Spaghetti noodles (preferably whole wheat) |
| | Miscellaneous vegetables for snacks | | Spaghetti sauce (your favorite brand) |
| | | | Beans (dry or canned) |
| | | | Chicken noodle soup |
| | | | Vegetable soup |
| | | | Reduced-fat cream of chicken or mushroom soup |
| | | | Gravy mix |
| | | | Dry onion powdered soup mix |
| | | | Tuna (water-packed) |
| | | | Raisins |
| | | | Pineapple, crushed (8-ounce can) |
| | | | Reduced-fat pudding cups |

| Dairy Case | Frozen Food Section | Breads, Miscellaneous |
|---|---|---|
| Milk (skim, 1½ percent, or soy milk) | Broccoli, chopped,* 2 boxes | Wheat bread |
| Egg substitute or eggs | Green beans,* 3 boxes | French or Italian bread (to make garlic bread during the week) |
| Reduced-fat or part-skim cheese slices (less than 5 grams of fat per ounce or slice) | Mashed potatoes* | Bagels |
| | Pancakes (or can buy the mix) | Whole-wheat pita bread |
| | "Veggie" burgers (vegetable-protein hamburger patties) | Hamburger buns (for the veggie burgers) |
| Reduced-fat shredded cheese | | Rice cakes (any flavor) |
| String cheese (part-skim milk) | | Wheat crackers |
| Fruit yogurt | | |
| Calcium-fortified orange or fruit juice | | |
| Reduced-fat sour cream (to make a fat-free veggie dip with your favorite powdered salad dressing packet) | *Substitute fresh if desired. | |

## Staples

Reduced-fat or very low-fat mayonnaise (less than 3 grams of fat per serving)

Reduced-fat or very low-fat salad dressings (less than 3 to 5 grams of fat per serving)

Catsup, mustard, BBQ sauce, pickles (regular versions OK)

Low-sugar syrup, low-sugar or all-fruit jelly

Peanut butter (no added hydrogenated or partially hydrogenated vegetable oils)

Nuts

Oil (olive, canola, peanut), nonfat cooking spray, nonfat liquid butter substitute (dairy section)

Lite margarine (first ingredient should be *liquid* vegetable oil—not hydrogenated or partially hydrogenated oil)

## WEEK 2 PORTION CONTROL AND FOOD RECORD PRACTICE

Remember to use the TRIM KIDS AEROBIC ACTIVITY AND FOOD CHECKLIST to help keep track of your daily intake. Let's practice portion-control checks for one day:

### Monday

*Breakfast:*

| | |
|---|---|
| Waffle | 1 carbohydrate |
| Strawberries (1 cup) | 1 carbohydrate |
| Scrambled egg substitute | 1–2 very lean proteins |
| Orange juice (½ cup) | 1 carbohydrate |

*Lunch:*

| | |
|---|---|
| Tuna salad | 2 lean proteins (+ 0–2 fats depending on the type of mayonnaise used) |
| Wheat crackers (6) | 1 carbohydrate |
| Vegetable soup | Vegetables—as desired |
| Milk (1 cup) | 1 carbohydrate |

*Dinner:*

| | |
|---|---|
| Turkey meat loaf | 2–3 lean proteins |
| Mashed potatoes (½ cup) | 1 carbohydrate |
| Reduced-fat gravy | 0–2 fats |
| Seasoned green beans | Vegetables—as desired |

*Sample snack:*

| | |
|---|---|
| Apple | 1 carbohydrate |
| Rice cakes (8–10 small) | 1 carbohydrate |
| with 1 tablespoon peanut butter | 1 protein, 1 fat |

| | |
|---|---|
| Total food units for Monday: | 8 carbohydrates |
| | 7 to 8 lean proteins |
| | 2–4 fats |
| | Vegetables—as desired |

## SECTION 4: TIME TO SUM UP

# Trim Kids Weekly Checklist

*Did you remember to:*          *Yes*     *No*     *Will do it by*

Fill out TRIM KIDS WEEKLY REPORT AND GOAL SHEET?

_____   _____   _____

Fill out TRIM KIDS AEROBIC ACTIVITY AND FOOD CHECKLIST?

_____   _____   _____

Fill out TRIM KIDS STRENGTH AND FLEXIBILITY WORKOUT CHART?

_____   _____   _____

Introduce and enforce the three-bite rule?

_____   _____   _____

Review this week's eating guidelines, definition of calories, eating slowly, and the role sugar plays in weight gain?

_____   _____   _____

Establish daily caloric intake?          _____   _____   _____

Study portion control food lists and basic food groups?

_____   _____   _____

Perform the aerobic activity of the week?

_____   _____   _____

Perform the strength and flex exercises of the week?

_____   _____   _____

Parents: After you weigh your child and fill out the weekly report form, be sure to review the past week's goals. Decide whether your child has met or fallen short of the goal for the week. Reward your child for achieving his goal. If he did not achieve it, redirect him to set a new, more achievable goal.

*Never ridicule or punish your child for not meeting his goal.* Also, allow him to "plead the Fifth," meaning that if he knows he did not meet his goal and feels too embarrassed to talk about it, just move on. Don't dwell on the mistakes of the past. Either way, set a new eating and activity goal for the next week.

Now, with a clear grasp on behavior modification, exercise requirements, and nutritional guidance, let's look at how you can be the best role model for your child.

# Week 3

---

# SOLVING PROBLEMS
# FAMILY STYLE

## TRIM KIDS ROAD MAP
## FOR WEEK 3

*This week, after filling out the Trim Kids forms in the appendix (don't forget to weigh your child and set your goals for the week), you will learn the importance of being a good role model for your child. We will discuss how to handle social situations and how to identify the social triggers that cause your child to overeat or be underactive. You'll encourage her to try the MPEP to burn more calories all day. You'll show her how to check her heart rate and breathing and review the homework rule, as well as create some eating rules of your own. There's a Fit Kit to help you plan your family's aerobic activity of the week. You will learn how to select healthy snacks and avoid the top ten food saboteurs. Follow this week's menu plan, try the new recipes, and use the weekly shopping list to get what you'll need.*

## SECTION 1: TIME TO STOP AND THINK

# ROLE MODELING AND STIMULUS CONTROL

One of the greatest surprises of the Trim Kids Program is that it often eliminates household conflicts that have been pressure-cooking your family for years. Your child will know *and choose* what's healthy for him. Family feuds over who gets the most ice cream and which television show to watch frequently give way to grading new foods and vying to play first base. Your child's weekly weight loss, goal check, and accomplishment report session will probably be his greatest motivation for giving up those old, worn-out battles and committing to his new lifestyle. But of course your role modeling matters, too.

This week, let your motto be, "Do as I say, *and* as I do!" Why not consider yourself a student of the program, too? Fill out the forms in the appendix along with your child. Weigh yourself every week—either with or without your child present. Get on the *inside* of the program so you can be your child's best possible role model.

As you experience the challenges and benefits of being both student and mentor, start noticing the things that impel you to choose unhealthy foods and trigger your desire to eat.

### TRIM KIDS TESTIMONIAL

## A Parent's Perspective

"I started getting up early and driving to the local track to walk each morning. I tried to get Kurt and Sam to come along, but they really weren't very interested. Kurt, my younger son, kept running up ahead of us; then he'd do tricks in the middle of the track while we caught up. One day, instead of going to the track, I took them walking along the Bayou side near our home in south Louisiana. Along the way we saw turtles, egrets, and even an owl, and the boys tried to catch dragonflies. Before we knew it we had walked for one hour and still had an hour to get back to the house. The next morning when I said, 'Let's go for a walk,' Kurt was the first one out the door."

Then help your child understand what compels his unhealthy eating habits and how to practice *stimulus control*. Stimulus control means learning to avoid or minimize the situations, foods, or circumstances that sabotage your efforts to reach your goals. Review "cue elimination" (page 39) in Chapter 4. Remove temptation foods from the house if you haven't already done so.

Now that you're probably more aware of what causes you to engage in unhealthy eating or behaviors, it's time to:

- Catch yourself before you make unhealthy choices, and do something healthy instead.
- Think about rewards other than food. Tell yourself how well you've done and how great you look.
- Take the scenic route home instead of going down the main drag with all those tempting fast-food restaurants.
- Mute the television or change channels when commercials laden with high-calorie products appear. Better yet, get up and walk around.

### Stimulus Control

- *Downsize*: From now on, you'll buy smaller portions of less healthy foods such as individually packaged chips, ice cream, etc.
- *Plan*: Before you go to a party or special event, you'll decide what you can eat and how much.
- *Pre-eat*: Eat something satisfying and healthy before going someplace where tempting, unhealthy foods will be served.
- *Bring your own*: When you can, take your own favorite healthy foods to an event and stick with eating them.
- *Schedule holidays:* Remember that it's OK to indulge occasionally in your favorite high-calorie foods. You will not gain unwanted weight from one piece of Grandma's apple pie on Christmas day, but you will gain weight if you snack on her cookies and fudge the week before and the week after Christmas (see Holiday Exercise Strategies on page 158).

## Social Triggers Form

Make a list of the people, places, times, or events that tempt you to overeat or be underactive.

_____

_____

_____

_____

What can you do to change or avoid these situations?

_____

_____

_____

_____

....................... **SECTION 2: TIME TO GET ACTIVE** .......................

## DAILY ENERGY EXPENDITURE AND THE MPEP STEP

Take a moment to observe your child's demeanor. Notice her posture, how quickly or slowly she walks, her overall physique, and how all this makes her look. Many overweight kids move slowly, with hunched shoulders, appearing as though they don't feel confident. If your child improves the way she walks, she can burn considerably more calories and look and feel healthier.

Teach your child that burning calories doesn't happen only when she's doing hard exercise or playing. She burns calories all the time. The following guidelines can help relay this concept and invite her to quicken her pace:

Think about large people. Do they move fast? Usually not, and that may be one reason why they are large. When you move slowly, you don't burn many calories. Also, you don't use many muscles, and those you do use aren't used effectively. Now think of people who walk briskly. They usually appear slimmer, taller, and more energetic. They automatically burn up more calories simply because they move faster and cover more ground in less time. It's amazing how simply walking faster, taking bigger strides, and holding your chin up a little higher can make you look and feel lighter and more effective. And that feels good!

We want you to burn as many calories as you can as often as you can. To do that, you'll have to work your body more effectively on a regular basis. Now, when you hear the term *work,* it will refer to how much energy you expend to burn calories. One way to work more effectively is to walk more briskly, covering as much ground as possible. By walking faster, you automatically increase your daily activity, which will help you lose the weight and keep it off.

One of the first things we do in our local clinic is encourage kids to walk more briskly, with better posture. We call this the MPEP Step, for Moderate-Intensity Progressive Exercise Program (see page 150). We begin by asking children to walk around the room so parents can watch. Most children shuffle slowly with heads and shoulders rolled forward.

"Does this look familiar?" Dr. Melinda asks as she drops her head, rolls her shoulders, and inches slowly forward. "Who do I look like? Do I look very tall? How tall do I look?"

One of the kids snickers, "Four feet tall!" Everyone chuckles, including Dr. Melinda.

"Do I look important and as if I know where I'm going? Can you even see my face? When your head is down and your shoulders are hunched forward, no one can see your pretty face! You appear shorter and more overweight."

Then, Dr. Melinda lifts her head and holds her shoulders back. She walks forward briskly, smiling widely. "Now who do I look like?" she asks. "A supermodel, right?" Again, the kids laugh. "Maybe not, but I do look taller and more important, don't I? Actually, I look about six inches taller just because I lifted my head. And because of that, I also look about 30 pounds lighter."

Demonstrate how to do the MPEP Step, then ask your child to do it. Remind her that when we walk with our chins up and shoulders back, and in a brisk manner, we appear taller, slimmer, and more in control. And walking with the MPEP Step burns about 350 to 450 calories per hour. Ask your child to walk this way every day—no matter where, and no matter what she is doing—for the next week. Better yet, model this behavior for your child from here on.

Melissa was a participant in our program and lost 2 pounds in the first week just by walking with the MPEP Step. She also reported that others reacted differently toward her, she accomplished more, and she felt much more energetic.

# Activity Worksheet

You can calculate how many calories (kcal) you burn in a day.

Take the number of hours in a day:                              24

Subtract sleeping hours:                                       −10

Hours that remain:                                              14

Let's calculate how many calories you would use . . .

Walking casually:

150 kcal/hour × 14 hours/day × 7 days/week = _____

Sitting in a chair:

50 kcal/hour × 14 hours/day × 7 days/week = _____

The difference between sitting in a chair and walking casually

walking calories − sitting calories = _____

Remember! 3,500 kcal = 1 pound of fat!

Just think: if you walk briskly, how many calories you will burn this week?

# Twenty-Four-Hour Activity Diary

Keeping track of everything you do reminds you of how well you're doing. On this page, record your activity for what you are mostly doing during each hour of the day. For example, if you walked to class for ten minutes, sat for forty, and walked for five, your activity would be "sat." List all activities.

| Hour | Activity | Calories Burned |
|------|----------|-----------------|
| 6:00 A.M. | | |
| 7:00 A.M. | | |

8:00 A.M._____

9:00 A.M._____

10:00 A.M._____

11:00 A.M._____

12:00 NOON_____

1:00 P.M._____

2:00 P.M._____

3:00 P.M._____

4:00 P.M._____

5:00 P.M._____

6:00 P.M._____

7:00 P.M._____

8:00 P.M._____

9:00 P.M. [SLEEP]_____

10:00 P.M. [SLEEP]_____

11:00 P.M. [SLEEP]_____

12:00 MIDNIGHT [SLEEP]_____

1:00 A.M. [SLEEP]_____

2:00 A.M. [SLEEP]_____

3:00 A.M. [SLEEP]_____

4:00 A.M. [SLEEP]_____

5:00 A.M. [SLEEP]_____

## STEPPING UP TO MPEP

Read through the following information with your child to understand the exercise strategy we use in the program.

The Trim Kids Program has created the Moderate-Intensity Progressive Exercise Program, MPEP, especially for overweight kids. Remember that moderate—not fast or hard—exercise is best for losing weight. You can do moderate exercise for hours without getting too tired, and this burns the most calories and fat. After about thirty minutes of moderate exercise, your ability to burn fat increases, so the longer you exercise at a moderate pace, the more fat you'll burn.

This program uses moderate workout levels for aerobic, strengthening, endurance, and flexibility exercises. Each color-coded level has its own regimen. It's called progressive because it gradually increases in duration and frequency over time during the twelve weeks.

*Duration* means the amount of time you spend exercising at each session. Some basic rules about duration are:

1. You need to be physically active for at *least* twenty minutes most days per week to gain any health benefits from physical activity (it can be done in two ten-minute sessions).
2. To lose weight and burn calories and fat, you should set a goal and start out slowly and work up to it.

*Frequency* refers to the number of exercise sessions you do in a given week. Basic rules about frequency include:

1. You'll need to exercise a minimum of one or two days per week to prevent losing your current level of fitness.
2. If your goal is to improve your current level of fitness and shed some body fat, you should set a goal to *work up to* exercising three or four days per week.
3. Those who are serious about losing body fat (that's you!) need to gradually work up to exercising four to six days per week. Our aerobic exercise goals for each week automatically do this for you.

*Intensity* means how hard and fast you exercise. The intensity of your workout can change according to the speed, the grade (steepness), the muscles you use, and the force or resistance you apply.

Vigorous intensity = >55–70 percent maximal oxygen uptake ($VO_2$ max)★ or >65–80 percent maximal heart rate (MAXHR)

Moderate intensity = 45–55 percent $VO_2$ max or 55–65 percent MAXHR

Low intensity = <45 percent $VO_2$ max or <55 percent MAXHR

The Trim Kids Program has adopted the guidelines developed by the American College of Sports Medicine (ACSM) for cardiorespiratory fitness, body composition, and muscular strength. We suggest that only children who graduate to the maintenance level of the program should follow these guidelines; other children should work toward them gradually. If your child is in the latter category she soon *won't* feel excluded—the guidelines in our program have been modified for her use, as you're already beginning to see!

- Do *aerobic exercise* three to five times per week for twenty to sixty minutes per session. Go for 60 to 90 percent of your estimated maximum heart rate. Do activities that use large-muscle groups and in which you can continuously maintain a rhythmic beat, such as jogging, biking, cross-country skiing, or swimming.

- *Resistance or strength training* should be done at least one or two times per week, but not more than three times per week. Rest in between days you do it. Perform the exercise at a moderate intensity, but one that can develop and maintain fat-free weight. Shoot for one set of eight to twelve repetitions of eight to ten different exercises which will condition the major muscle groups.

Regardless of the type of exercise you are doing, remember that moderate exercise burns the most fat because you can do it longer.

---

★*Maximal oxygen uptake*, $VO_2$ max, refers to the total amount of oxygen that an individual will consume when exercising at maximum effort. It is well accepted as the best indicator of aerobic fitness.

## Testing Your Child's Heart Rate

When your child is moving, observe her breathing. Is she having difficulty? Is she red in the face? Is she complaining of being hot and tired? These are clues that she may be going too fast, and a good reason to teach your child how to take her heart rate so she'll know the safest speed for her circumstances.

*Resting heart rate:* Get a watch or clock with a second hand. Ask your child to sit quietly for five minutes. Find her pulse by placing the middle three fingers of one hand on the underside of the opposite wrist. If you have difficulty locating her pulse this way, place the same three fingers on either side of her throat just below the point of the jaw, in between the Adam's apple and the neck muscle. There you'll find the pulsing carotid artery. Be careful not to press it too hard. Once you feel her pulse, refer to the second hand of your watch and count the number of pulse beats during a ten-second interval.

Record: _____ Multiply this number by 6: _____
× 6 = _____ (This figure represents your child's resting pulse rate in beats per minute.)
Record the resting pulse rate: _____

*Active heart rate:* After your child has been moving around for ten minutes or more, repeat the process above, but ask her to remain standing and to keep her feet moving from side to side.

Record her active heart rate over ten seconds: _____. Multiply by 6: _____

Use this table to see if she is in the correct range:

| Your child is: | Normal Weight | Overweight | Seriously Overweight |
|---|---|---|---|
| Heart rate in beats per ten seconds | 26–28 | 23–26 | 19–23 |
| Heart rate in beats per minute | 156–168 | 135–156 | 114–135 |

# THE HOMEWORK RULE

Inform your child that since he's supposed to be playing and moving around as much as possible, from now on he will have to burn some calories when he gets home from school. To that end, here are some new house rules:

- Put off homework until after you exercise! When you get home from school, you may feel tired, but it's your brain that's pooped, not your body!

- As soon as you get home from school, drink a big glass of ice water. Maybe you're tired because you're thirsty or dehydrated (not having enough water in your body can cause fatigue).

- If the weather's nice, go outside and play. Ride your bike, skate, walk the dog, play ball or tag, or jump rope. If the weather's bad, come inside to your new play area, turn on some music, and dance! Whatever you do, it has to be active!

- You need to be active for at least thirty minutes before you start your homework. An hour would be even better! This will give your brain a chance to rest from the long school day. After you exercise, do homework. There may be time before dinner for television. You can do your strength and flex exercises while you watch your favorite show.

## WEEKLY EXERCISE ACTIVITIES

### WEEK 3 AEROBIC ACTIVITY: RECOMMENDED GOALS

Write your goal in the TRIM KIDS AEROBIC ACTIVITY AND FOOD CHECKLIST (page 386). This is the minimum amount of aerobic exercise that you should perform this week. Every day, record what type of physical activity you did and how long you did it. At the end of the week, compare your list with the goals you set at the beginning of the week.

- Red Level: The exercise goal this week is two days per week for twenty to twenty-five minutes each day.
- Yellow Level: The exercise goal this week is three days per week for twenty-five to thirty minutes each day.
- Green Level: The exercise goal this week is three days per week for twenty-five to forty minutes each day.
- Blue Level: The exercise goal this week is three days per week for thirty to sixty minutes each day.

WEEK 3 AEROBIC ACTIVITY: THE FIT KIT
(WALKING FOR FUN, HEALTH, AND FITNESS)

Work with your child to develop a walking program that will maintain his goal weight and keep him fit.

The Fit Kit was designed especially for Blue- or Green-Level kids in the Trim Kids Program. (Red- or Yellow-Level kids should choose an alternative activity this week, such as biking or swimming.) By participating in this, you'll burn lots of calories, train your leg and hip muscles, and improve the efficiency of your heart and lungs. Walking is one of the easiest and most convenient ways you can stay active on a daily basis. There may be times when you walk with a friend, but at other times you may prefer to do it alone. Either way is fine as long as you keep on truckin'!

Follow these steps to healthy walking.

STEP 1: Checkup. Check your shoes, clothes, and walking route.

Shoes—Ten Tips for Choosing Walking Shoes

1. Select the lightest-weight walking shoe available.
2. Choose shoes with padding in the tongue, collar, and heel.
3. Make sure the inside is fully lined with light, airy material.
4. Shoes with a leather exterior are best.
5. Don't buy shoes with pointed or tapered toes.
6. Choose shoes that have the best shock absorption in the midsole and foot-bed.
7. Choose shoes that are flexible. Bend the shoe to determine how flexible it is.
8. Check the heel design. It should have a notch that conforms to the Achilles tendon.
9. Velcro straps combined with laces allow a more secure fit.
10. Get a new pair of walking shoes about every six months. Don't try to save money by wearing your shoes longer. These are your precious feet you're walking with!

Clothes

• In summer, choose loose-fitting all-cotton T-shirts and tank tops.
• In winter, dress in layers of warm, soft, loose-fitting clothes, woolen mittens, and a hat.

Walking Route

• Sketch a map of your planned walking route on paper. Make sure to include landmarks, phone locations, water stops, and favorite scenic spots. Post your map on the refrigerator.
• Always tell someone where you'll be walking if it's different from your typical route.

STEP 2: Form a plan of action. Write a one-week walking schedule and put it into your daily calendar.
STEP 3: Get ready. Choose an appropriate warm-up which includes dynamic stretches (stretch while moving). Don't do any static stretches without warming up first. Wait until after your walking to do static stretches.
STEP 4: Put your best foot forward. Walk slowly at first, swinging your arms naturally. Pick up the pace after a few minutes to a comfortable, moderate level. Remember, if you start to breathe too rapidly, slow down until you're going at the pace that's right for you.

Use the chart below to calculate your walking speed. First try to walk one mile (refer to your map) and record how long it took. Then go to the chart. Put one finger on the "1-mile" mark and the other on the time it took you, to the nearest ten minutes. For example, if it took you forty minutes to walk one mile, you were walking at 1.5 mph.

Distance covered     Time it takes
(in miles):_____     (minutes):_____

# YOUR MILES-PER-HOUR CHART

## Time it took (to the nearest 10 minutes)

| Miles walked | 20 | 30 | 40 | 50 | 60 | 70 | 80 | 90 | 100 |
|:---:|:---:|:---:|:---:|:---:|:---:|:---:|:---:|:---:|:---:|
| 1 | 3.0 | 2.0 | 1.5 | 1.2 | 1.0 | .9 | .8 | .7 | .6 |
| 2 | 6.0 | 4.5 | 3.0 | 2.5 | 2.0 | 1.8 | 1.5 | 1.3 | 1.2 |
| 3 | 9.0 | 7.5 | 4.5 | 3.8 | 3.0 | 2.7 | 2.3 | 2.0 | 1.8 |
| 4 | 12.0 | 9.0 | 6.0 | 5.0 | 4.0 | 3.5 | 3.0 | 2.2 | 2.0 |
| 5 | 15.0 | 11.5 | 7.5 | 6.2 | 5.0 | 4.5 | 3.8 | 3.4 | 3.0 |

STEP 5: Cool down and stretch. Reduce your pace during the last five to ten minutes of the walk. Finish up with at least one stretch of each major muscle group. Check the Strength and Flex series in "Week 7" (page 265) for proper technique.

STEP 6: Keep a walking diary. Use the form below to record your experiences.

## My Walking Diary

| Week 1 | Day 1 | Day 2 | Day 3 | Day 4 | Day 5 | Day 6 | Day 7 |
|:---:|:---:|:---:|:---:|:---:|:---:|:---:|:---:|
| Date | | | | | | | |
| Time | | | | | | | |
| Location | | | | | | | |
| Terrain | | | | | | | |
| Weather | | | | | | | |

| | Day 1 | Day 2 | Day 3 | Day 4 | Day 5 | Day 6 | Day 7 |
|---|---|---|---|---|---|---|---|
| Distance | | | | | | | |
| Speed | | | | | | | |
| Conditions | | | | | | | |
| Comments | | | | | | | |
| **Week 2** | **Day 1** | **Day 2** | **Day 3** | **Day 4** | **Day 5** | **Day 6** | **Day 7** |
| Date | | | | | | | |
| Time | | | | | | | |
| Location | | | | | | | |
| Terrain | | | | | | | |
| Weather | | | | | | | |
| Distance | | | | | | | |
| Speed | | | | | | | |
| Conditions | | | | | | | |
| Comments | | | | | | | |

STEP 7: Weigh the outcome of your walk. Determine how many calories you burned during your walk by using the chart below. First, determine the distance you walked. Then figure out your speed (mph) from "Your Miles-Per-Hour Chart" on page 156.

# HOW MANY CALORIES DID I BURN?*

| Speed (in mph) | Distance Covered (in miles) | | | | |
|---|---|---|---|---|---|
| | 1 | 2 | 3 | 4 | 5 |
| 2.0 | 48–63 | 96–126 | 144–189 | 192–252 | 240–315 |
| 2.5 | 50–64 | 100–128 | 150–192 | 200–256 | 250–320 |
| 3.0 | 52–66 | 104–132 | 156–198 | 208–264 | 260–330 |
| 3.5 | 54–67 | 108–134 | 162–201 | 216–268 | 270–335 |
| 4.0 | 58–72 | 116–144 | 174–216 | 232–288 | 290–360 |
| 4.5 | 65–80 | 130–160 | 195–240 | 260–320 | 325–400 |
| 5.0 | 75–90 | 150–180 | 225–270 | 300–360 | 375–450 |

*These figures are based on an average weight of 125 to 150 pounds. If you weigh more than 150 pounds, you will burn more calories. If you weigh less than 125 pounds, you will burn fewer calories.

STEP 8: Take the next step. Many people find walking enjoyable once they get into the habit. If this is true for you, consider joining a local club or enter a fun walk or run. Check with your local recreation, religious, or school organizations for upcoming opportunities. It's a great way to meet new friends who also love to walk and be active.

And there you have it: the "Fit Kit"!

# HOLIDAY EXERCISE STRATEGIES:

Consider organizing a game of flag football (page 181) with the family during Thanksgiving or Christmas instead of watching football on TV. Play baseball at the

Fourth of July Picnic. Or try Aerobic Easter Egg Charades: hide plastic eggs filled with notes (not candy!) telling the kids to dance like their favorite artist, march in place for one minute, or do ten jumping jacks. Also, include some notes with inexpensive game equipment surprises like jump ropes, Frisbees, or balls.

## Week 3 Strength and Flex Exercises

Read the instructions aloud to your child as he does these exercises, until he no longer needs your assistance.

### Strength Exercise 3: Rowing, Low

Sit upright, leaning slightly forward from your hips. Keep your back straight and your shoulders down. Pull your shoulders back.

Now, if you're exercising on a machine or are using an exercise band, pull the handles or end of the band back to your upper abdomen over a period of two to four seconds. (In the first five weeks, you will not use resistance.)

Squeeze your shoulder blades together. That's right. Now take two to four seconds, then return to the starting position, keeping your back stationary.

Do eight to twelve repetitions of this exercise. Be sure to pull back for a full two to four seconds. Then, take another two to four seconds to return to the starting position. This exercise works your upper back muscle (rhomboid) and your middle back muscle (latissimus dorsi).

Common errors that your child may make include moving shoulders upward, leaning back, moving the head forward, and bending the wrists.

### Flex Exercise 3: Upper Back Stretch

Stand with your feet about eighteen inches apart. Bend your knees slightly and push your hips forward as you tighten your stomach muscles.

Bring your arms forward in front of your chest, interlock your fingers, and turn your hands inside out. Round your upper back as you drop your chin down toward your chest.

Now push your hands away from your body, stretching your upper back in between your shoulder blades. Looking good! Hold this position for fifteen to thirty seconds. Repeat this process one more time, holding this position again for fifteen to thirty seconds.

Perform these new strength and flex exercises and also the ones you learned previously in weeks 1 and 2 at least once, but preferably twice this week. Record your progress on the TRIM KIDS STRENGTH AND FLEXIBILITY WORKOUT CHART in the appendix ("Forms You'll Need"), on page 388. Every week, you will add another exercise to your program.

Don't forget to fill out your TRIM KIDS AEROBIC ACTIVITY AND FOOD CHECKLIST on page 386, and try the aerobic activity of the week with the entire family.

## Other Exercise Activity Ideas: Family Fun and Fitness

This week, come up with a list of half-day, weekend activities that the entire family can do together. Gather input from each family member, bring out the calendar, mark what you'll do on which weekend, and stick to it. Here are some of our favorite ways to spend time together burning calories and having fun:

- Water sports: swimming, tubing down the river, fishing, body surfing and playing on the beach, water slide, and water polo
- Ball sports: football, volleyball, tennis, basketball, soccer, croquet, golf, bowling, softball, and playing fetch with your dog
- Mountain sports: cross-country or downhill skiing, snow-shoeing, hiking, caving, horseback riding, and biking
- Around the neighborhood: Frisbee, tag, biking, walking, kick the can, walking the dog, pulling the wagon, and in-line skating

.....................................................
## SECTION 3: TIME TO DINE
.....................................................

*For the Trim Kids Weight Loss Plan to succeed, it is crucial that your child learn how much she should be eating (portion control) by keeping track of her daily food units. Be sure that she is filling in the* TRIM KIDS AEROBIC ACTIVITY AND FOOD CHECKLIST *every day. Review the Food Portion and Unit Lists for "Week 2" (page 119) if you have any questions. Or learn by example: there's a Portion Control Practice Exercise at the end of every week.*

# NUTRITION NUTSHELL: HEALTHY SNACKING

Check your refrigerator, pantry, cabinets, and freezer to be sure you've done what's necessary to eliminate cues (page 39). Make your home a safe food environment by identifying "temptation foods," or "food saboteurs," and begin replacing these with healthy alternatives. The premise behind eliminating cues is "out of sight, out of mind." An even better motto is "smarter food, healthier bodies."

Snacks can be part of a healthy diet if you make wise food choices. The best snacks are those low in fat (less than 5 grams) and calories (less than 100 to 200). Avoid high-fat, high-calorie foods that can make your child feel sluggish and be less active. Foods containing excessive amounts of simple sugars (more than 15 grams per serving) also can cause a dip in energy after the initial boost. Since most people find it difficult to consume five servings per day of fruits and vegetables (as recommended by the U.S. Dietary Guidelines), the majority of snacks should consist of fruits and vegetables.

Help your child learn the differ-

### Top Ten Food Saboteurs

Here are ten foods that "cue" many people to overeat:

1. Candy
2. Chips
3. Ice cream
4. Frosted snack cakes
5. Fruit-flavored drinks
6. Pizza snacks
7. Breakfast pastries
8. Nachos
9. Soda
10. Cookies

ence between cravings and hunger. Permit snacking only if he expresses true hunger, which usually occurs after about two to four hours of not eating. A food craving is stimulated by feelings of boredom or stress, or by the environment. For example, he may see a food advertised on television and suddenly want it. Or he may be in the habit of having a snack just before bed, even though he's not really hungry. So, hand him that big old glass of water again. Or, during the daytime, instruct him to run around outside.

Try to avoid excessive nighttime snacking. Our rule is that if you are not waking up hungry for breakfast, you are probably eating too much at night.

## THE BENEFITS OF FRUITS AND VEGETABLES

At least five servings per day of fruits and vegetables are recommended. A high intake of fruits and vegetables can decrease the risk of cancer, heart disease, and stroke. In addition, most fruits and vegetables are naturally fat-free and are packed with vitamins! Their beneficial effects include these.

- Substances called phytonutrients have been shown to help prevent the development of cancerous cells. These substances are found in soybeans and soybean products such as tofu, soy milk, and soy meat substitutes. They are also found in flaxseed (and flaxseed oil), broccoli, cauliflower, carrots, spinach, soybeans, and berries.
- A substance called lycopene may protect the body against the development of prostate cancer. Tomatoes (and tomato products) are one of the best sources of lycopene.
- Vitamins A, C, and E, known as the antioxidant vitamins, can help rid the body of harmful substances (free radicals) that may cause cell damage, contributing to heart disease and stroke. Foods high in vitamin A include apricots, carrots, cantaloupe, and spinach. Foods high in vitamin C include citrus fruits and juices, broccoli, cabbage, cauliflower, and spinach.
- Folic acid, a B vitamin, is involved in maintaining healthy cells, growth, and a strong immune system. Foods high in folic acid include leafy green vegetables, orange juice, and lentils. For women, an adequate folic acid intake may lower the risk of some birth defects.

## Make Up Your Own Rules for the Week!

Write Your Own Rules for Eating:

This week I will _____ to slow down
my eating speed.

This week I will _____ to decrease the
number of calories I eat.

## Week 3 Weekly Menu

*Recipes are given for items in boldface.*

| | Breakfast | Lunch | Dinner | Snacks (1 to 2 choices per day) |
|---|---|---|---|---|
| MONDAY | Cold cereal containing fiber (1 cup) Wheat toast (1 slice) with low-sugar jelly Banana Milk (1 cup) | Peanut butter (1 tablespoon) sandwich on wheat bread Grapes (½ cup) Milk (1 cup) | Roast beef (2 to 3 slices) Mashed potatoes (½ cup) with reduced-fat gravy (or 1 baked potato) **Low-Fat Broccoli and Cheese** Tossed salad as desired (with 1 or 2 teaspoons olive oil or reduced-fat salad dressing) Water or calorie-free beverage | Celery sticks with reduced-fat cream cheese (2 tablespoons) or peanut butter (1 tablespoon) Cereal containing fiber (1 cup) and skim milk Cereal-fruit bar (1) Reduced-fat chips (about 15 chips or 1 ounce) with fat-free dip or salsa Wheat crackers (6) with: |
| TUESDAY | ½ English muffin with reduced-fat cream cheese or 1 tablespoon peanut | Fast-food meal: 6-inch submarine sandwich (turkey, ham, chicken | **Oven-Fried Chicken** (about 1 breast) | Reduced-fat cheese (2 slices) Lite cream cheese (2 tablespoons) |

| | Breakfast | Lunch | Dinner | Snacks (1 to 2 choices per day) |
|---|---|---|---|---|
| TUESDAY (cont.) | butter and/or low-sugar jam or jelly<br><br>Scrambled egg substitute scrambled in nonstick cooking spray (optional)<br><br>Strawberries (1 cup)<br><br>Milk (1 cup) | breast, or tuna with lite mayo)<br><br>Baked chips (1 single-serving bag)<br><br>Water or calorie-free beverage | Brown rice (½ cup) with nonfat liquid butter substitute<br><br>Mixed vegetables<br><br>Fruit cocktail (½ cup)<br><br>Milk (1 cup) | Peanut butter (1 tablespoon)<br><br>Hot cocoa made with skim milk (1 cup)<br><br>English muffin or bagel "pizza" (½ muffin with tomato or pizza sauce and reduced-fat cheese) |
| WEDNESDAY | Oatmeal (1 cup) with raisins and walnuts (2 tablespoons each) and 1 teaspoon brown sugar or honey (or low-sugar pancake syrup) if desired<br><br>Milk (1 cup) | ½ whole-wheat pita with tuna or chicken salad (made with reduced-fat mayo) and vegetables<br><br>Carrot and celery sticks with fat-free dip<br><br>Fresh fruit of choice<br><br>Milk (1 cup) | Open roast beef sandwich (leftover roast) made with 1 or 2 slices of wheat bread and 2 or 3 slices of roast beef with reduced-fat gravy<br><br>Cooked or steamed vegetables of choice<br><br>Tossed salad with 1–2 teaspoons olive oil or reduced-fat dressing<br><br>Milk (½ to 1 cup) | Fruit (1 piece fresh, ½ cup canned, or 3 tablespoons dried)<br><br>Frozen fruit bar (1)<br><br>Fruit juice "spritzer": 3 ounces fruit juice mixed with 5 ounces club soda or sparkling water<br><br>Graham crackers (3 squares)<br><br>Teddy grahams (½ cup)<br><br>Nuts (2 tablespoons)<br><br>Oatmeal (½ cup) |
| THURSDAY | Cheese toast: 1–2 slices wheat bread with reduced-fat cheese, melted | Chef salad with ham and/or turkey slices or cubes and reduced-fat dressing (2 tablespoons) | Restaurant:<br><br>Mexican meal—Soft tacos or fajitas, chicken or beef (2) with salsa | Oatmeal cookies (2 small)<br><br>Air-popped popcorn (3 to 5 cups) |

| | **Breakfast** | **Lunch** | **Dinner** | **Snacks (1 to 2 choices per day)** |
|---|---|---|---|---|
| THURSDAY *(cont.)* | Fruit yogurt (½ cup)<br><br>Orange juice—calcium-fortified (½ cup) | Small rice cakes (8)<br><br>Milk (1 cup) | Black beans (½ cup) or Mexican rice (½ cup)<br><br>Tortilla chips (15) with salsa<br><br>Water or calorie-free beverage | Reduced-fat pudding or ice cream (½ cup)<br><br>Quesadilla (1 tortilla) with melted reduced-fat cheese, salsa, and fat-free sour cream |
| FRIDAY | Wheat toast (1 to 2 slices) with nonfat liquid butter substitute and low-sugar jelly<br><br>Egg substitute scrambled with nonfat butter-flavored cooking spray<br><br>Turkey bacon (3) or "veggie" breakfast sausage links (2)<br><br>Sliced fresh tomato<br><br>Milk (1 cup) | Wheat crackers (12) with reduced-fat sliced cheese<br><br>Vegetable soup<br><br>Fat-free pudding (½ cup)<br><br>Water or calorie-free beverage | **Tuna-Noodle Bake** (1 cup)<br><br>Carrots (cooked with nonfat liquid butter substitute)<br><br>Tossed salad with 1 or 2 teaspoons olive oil or reduced-fat dressing<br><br>Fruit salad (1 cup)<br><br>Milk (½ to 1 cup) | Rice cakes (10 small or 2 large)<br><br>Sandwich on wheat bread (½) with turkey, tuna with lite mayo, or reduced-fat cheese<br><br>Soup: vegetable or chicken noodle (2 cups)<br><br>Trail mix (4 tablespoons)<br><br>Yogurt, regular or frozen (4 to 6 ounces)<br><br>Raw vegetables with fat-free dip (unlimited) |
| SATURDAY | Whole-grain waffle (1) with low-sugar syrup<br><br>Cottage cheese (½ cup) and canned pineapple or peaches (½ cup) | English muffin "pizza": whole English muffin with tomato sauce (any kind) and reduced-fat cheese<br><br>Popcorn (about 3 cups popped) | **Sesoned Lentils** (1 cup)<br><br>Brown rice (½ cup)<br><br>**Creamed Spinach**<br><br>Green salad with 1 or 2 teaspoons olive oil or reduced-fat salad dressing | |

|  | **Breakfast** | **Lunch** | **Dinner** | **Snacks** (1 to 2 choices per day) |
|---|---|---|---|---|
| SATURDAY (cont.) | Orange juice—calcium-fortified (½ cup) | Strawberries (1 cup) or grapes (½ cup) Milk (½ to 1 cup) | Water or calorie-free beverage | |
| SUNDAY | Yogurt shake: 1 cup yogurt 1 cup frozen or fresh strawberries ½ banana (optional) Ice Skim or soy milk as needed if a "thinner" shake is desired | **Low-Fat Chicken Parmesan** (about 1 breast) Noodles (½ cup cooked) Garlic bread (1 slice) Steamed or cooked vegetables of choice Green salad with 1 to 2 teaspoons olive oil or reduced-fat dressing Water or calorie-free beverage | **Leftover Night** Food Units 1 to 2 starch-bread Lean or low-fat protein 0 to 1 fruit 1 milk-dairy 1 fat Veggies—unlimited! | |

# Week 3 Recipes

## LOW-FAT BROCCOLI AND CHEESE

1 large bunch broccoli, cut into bite-size pieces
1 can reduced-fat cream of mushroom soup
½ soup can skim milk or chicken broth
6 ounces reduced-fat shredded Cheddar or American cheese (1½ cups)

Salt and pepper to taste
½ cup bread crumbs (optional)
Nonfat butter-flavored spray (optional)

Preheat the oven to 375°F. Combine all ingredients except bread crumbs and nonfat butter-flavored spray in a casserole. Top with crumbs and spray, if desired. Bake uncovered for 30 to 40 minutes.

To microwave: Microwave the broccoli until just tender, 3 to 5 minutes. Add remaining ingredients and microwave on medium-high for another 5 minutes.

Makes about 4 cups.

Nutritional Analysis
Vegetable Group: ½ cup = 45 calories, 1–3 grams fat + 1 protein

....................................................................................................................................

## OVEN-FRIED CHICKEN

Chicken breasts, skin removed
Salt or salt substitute (optional) and pepper to taste
1 cup egg substitute
Italian-style bread crumbs
Nonfat butter-flavored spray

Preheat the oven to 375°F. Salt and pepper the chicken breasts, dip into the egg substitute, and roll in the bread crumbs (re-dip and roll in the crumbs again for a thicker crust). Spray and place on a baking sheet. Bake for 45 to 50 minutes.

Nutritional Analysis
1 breast: 3–4 protein units, ½ carbohydrate unit (145 calories, 5 grams fat)

....................................................................................................................................

## TUNA-NOODLE BAKE

4 cups cooked macaroni or other noodles (preferably whole wheat)
1 can reduced-fat cream of mushroom or celery soup
½ soup can skim milk
¼ cup fat-free mayonnaise
2 teaspoons mustard
4 ounces reduced-fat shredded American or Cheddar cheese (about 1 cup)
Two 6-ounce cans water-packed tuna, drained
1 cup bread crumbs
Nonfat butter-flavored spray (optional)

Preheat the oven to 375°F. Mix all of the ingredients except the bread crumbs in a casserole. Sprinkle with the bread crumbs and spray lightly if desired. Bake uncovered for 40 to 45 minutes.

Makes 6 cups.
Nutritional Analysis 1 cup: 2 carbohydrate units, 1 protein unit, 1 fat unit (200 calories, 7 grams fat)

····································································································

## SEASONED LENTILS

1 pound dried lentils, picked over and rinsed
4 to 5 cups water
2 chicken, beef, or vegetable bouillon cubes
2 bay leaves (optional)
Hot pepper sauce to taste
Nonfat butter-flavored spray (optional)

Combine the lentils, water, bouillon cubes, and bay leaves in a saucepan. Bring to a boil and simmer uncovered for 15 to 20 minutes, until lentils are just tender. (Be careful not to overcook the lentils, or they will become mushy.) Drain, and remove the bay leaves. Season with a little hot sauce. Spray if desired. As an option, mix with the Mushroom-Onion Sauté or make Cheesy Tomato Lentils (recipes follow).

Makes 4 to 5 cups.

## MUSHROOM-ONION SAUTÉ

2 teaspoons olive oil
Nonfat butter-flavored spray
½ pound fresh mushrooms, washed and sliced
1 medium onion, chopped

Put the olive oil into a skillet with enough spray to coat the bottom, add the mushrooms and onions, and sauté over medium heat until tender, about 15 minutes. (Cook the onions for about 5 minutes before adding the mushrooms, as the onions take a bit longer to soften.) Toss with the seasoned lentils.

## CHEESY TOMATO LENTILS

14½-ounce can diced tomatoes, drained
2 cups shredded, reduced-fat Cheddar or American cheese
½ cup lentil broth

Combine the ingredients with the seasoned lentils in a saucepan and heat through.

Nutritional Analysis
1 cup: 2 carbohydrate units (160–180 calories)
+ 1½ protein units + 1 fat unit for the Cheesy Tomato Lentils

## CREAMED SPINACH

Nonfat butter-flavored spray
2 teaspons olive oil
Two 10-ounce packages frozen spinach, defrosted and drained
1 cup fat-free sour cream, or more to taste
2 tablespoons fat-free mayonnaise
¼ teaspoon salt or salt substitute (optional)
¼ teaspoon hot pepper sauce (optional)
1 teaspoon finely chopped jalapeño pepper, or more to taste (optional)

Spray the bottom of a saucepan, add the olive oil, and heat the spinach. Add the remaining ingredients and heat through.

To make a cheesy creamed spinach, add ½ to 1 cup reduced-fat shredded American, Cheddar, or mozzarella cheese.

Makes about 2 cups.

Nutritional Analysis
Vegetable Group: No limit (½ cup = 40 calories, 0 grams fat)
+ ½ protein and 1 fat if adding the cheese

---

## LOW-FAT CHICKEN PARMESAN

Olive oil spray or nonfat butter-flavored spray
6 skinless, boneless chicken breasts
1 cup egg substitute
Italian-style bread crumbs
6 slices part-skim mozzarella cheese
One 26-ounce jar spaghetti sauce
½ cup grated Parmesan cheese

Preheat the oven to 375°F. Spray the bottom of a baking pan. Dip the chicken breasts in the egg and roll in the bread crumbs. Put the breast in the pan and bake uncovered for 20 to 25 minutes. Remove from the oven and top each chicken breast with one slice of mozzarella cheese. Cover with the spaghetti sauce and sprinkle with the Parmesan. Bake for another 15 to 20 minutes or until heated through.

Makes 6 portions.

Nutritional Analysis
1 breast: 4 protein, ½ carbohydrate (180 calories, 7–8 grams fat)

# Week 3 Weekly Shopping List

| Fruits | Vegetables | Meat, Deli | Dried, Canned |
|---|---|---|---|
| Apples | Broccoli (2 bunches) | Roast beef slices | Oatmeal |
| Banana | Carrots, celery | Chicken breasts, skinless, boneless (buy a "family pack"—enough to make 2 recipes during the week) | Breakfast cereal (fiber content should be more than 2 to 3 grams per serving) |
| Grapes | Salad greens: | | Bread crumbs, Italian-style |
| Strawberries | Lettuce | | Macaroni (or other) noodles for the tuna-noodle casserole |
| Miscellaneous fruits for snacks | Tomato | Ham (or other) cold-cuts | |
| | Cucumbers, etc. | Turkey bacon | Brown rice |
| | Miscellaneous vegetables for snacks | | Lentils (1 bag, dried) |
| | | | Beef gravy mix (package) |
| | | | Reduced-fat cream of mushroom soup |
| | | | Tuna (water-packed)—extra cans |
| | | | Reduced-fat pudding, diet Jell-O |
| | | | Pineapple, fruit cocktail, or other (canned) |
| | | | Raisins |

| Dairy Case | Frozen Food Section | Breads, Miscellaneous |
|---|---|---|
| Milk (skim, 1½% or soy milk) | Mixed vegetables | Wheat bread |
| Egg substitute, eggs | Spinach, chopped (2 boxes) | English muffins |
| Reduced-fat or part-skim cheese slices (less than 5 grams of fat per ounce or slice) | Mashed potatoes | Whole-wheat pita bread |
| | Waffles (preferably whole-grain) | French or Italian bread (to make garlic bread during the week) |
| | Frozen strawberries | |
| Reduced-fat shredded cheese (extra) | | Air-popped popcorn |
| Fruit yogurt | | Baked chips (less than 3 grams of fat) |
| Calcium-fortified orange or fruit juice | | |
| Cottage cheese | | |
| Fat-free sour cream | | |

## Staples

Reduced-fat or very low-fat mayonnaise (less than 3 grams fat per serving)

Reduced-fat or very low-fat salad dressings (less than 3–5 grams fat per serving)

Catsup, mustard, BBQ sauce, pickles (regular versions OK)

Low-sugar syrup, low-sugar or all-fruit jelly

Peanut butter (no added hydrogenated or partially hydrogenated vegetable oils)

Nuts

Oil (olive, canola, peanut), nonfat cooking spray, nonfat liquid butter (dairy section)

Lite margarine (first ingredient should be *liquid* vegetable oil—not hydrogenated or partially hydrogenated oil)

# WEEK 3 PORTION CONTROL AND FOOD RECORD PRACTICE

Don't forget to use TRIM KIDS AEROBIC ACTIVITY AND FOOD CHECKLIST (page 386) to help keep track of your daily intake. Let's practice portion control checks for one day:

## Thursday

*Breakfast:*

| | |
|---|---|
| Cheese toast (1–2 slices): | 1–2 carbohydrates (bread) |
| | 2 proteins, 1–2 fats (low-fat cheese, 0 fats if cheese is fat-free) |
| Yogurt (½ cup or 4 ounces) | 1 carbohydrate |
| Orange juice (½ cup) | 1 carbohydrate |

*Lunch:*

| | |
|---|---|
| Chef salad | 2–3 proteins (ham, turkey, reduced-fat cheese), 1–2 fats Vegetables—as desired |
| Reduced-fat dressing (2 tablespoons) | 1–2 fats (0 if fat-free) |
| Rice cakes (8–10 small) | 1 carbohydrate |
| Milk (1 cup) | 1 carbohydrate |

*Dinner:*

| | |
|---|---|
| Soft taco or fajitas (2) | 2 carbohydrates (tortillas) 2–3 proteins (meat or chicken) Vegetables—as desired |
| Black beans (½ cup) | 1 carbohydrate + 0–2 fats if oil is used |
| Tortilla chips (15) | 1 carbohydrate + 2 fats |
| Salsa | Vegetables—as desired |
| Sample snacks: | |
| Cherry tomatoes | Vegetable—as desired |
| Reduced-fat pudding cup | 1 carbohydrate |

TOTAL food units for Thursday:      10 carbohydrates

7–8 proteins

6 fats

Vegetables—as desired

··················································································
## SECTION 4: TIME TO SUM UP
··················································································

# ONGOING SUPPORT AND FAMILY MATTERS

It's been only a few weeks since you began the program, and your child may not yet be inspired and energized by the results of these efforts. This transition can be a difficult time.

Lending your ear and pouring on praise for small successes are the best things you can do to help him through the transition. Let your child know that it is difficult to be a leader or on the cutting edge, and that "Rome was not built in a day." Acknowledge that there are probably people who may not care if he succeeds, but you do—and he definitely does. And that's the most important thing. Discuss how this process can be difficult for the entire family, since everyone is making the same sacrifices and changes. Most important, let your child know that you are there, that you're willing to work things out when they become too tough. Reassure your child that if he is teased at school, you will help in whatever ways are necessary.

Giving your family praise is another good way to support your child and unify efforts among family members. Each week, rave about the new healthy foods and activities in which your child and the entire family are engaged. Remember to give your child credit for being the impetus for your family's change. Never mind if your child blushes and tells you to stop. We all thrive on attention, especially when it's positive attention.

# Trim Kids Weekly Checklist

*Did you remember to:*        *Yes*     *No*     *Will do it by*

Fill out TRIM KIDS WEEKLY REPORT AND GOAL SHEET?

\_\_\_\_    \_\_\_\_    _____

Fill out TRIM KIDS AEROBIC ACTIVITY AND FOOD CHECKLIST?

\_\_\_\_    \_\_\_\_    _____

Fill out TRIM KIDS STRENGTH AND FLEXIBILITY WORKOUT CHART?

\_\_\_\_    \_\_\_\_    _____

Model healthy eating and activity for your child?

\_\_\_\_    \_\_\_\_    _____

Have your child fill out Social Triggers form?

\_\_\_\_    \_\_\_\_    _____

Help your child understand stimulus control?

\_\_\_\_    \_\_\_\_    _____

Downsize the food portions in your house?

\_\_\_\_    \_\_\_\_    _____

Walk with the MPEP Step?    \_\_\_\_    \_\_\_\_    _____

Increase daily energy expenditure?    \_\_\_\_    \_\_\_\_    _____

Introduce and enforce the homework rule?

\_\_\_\_    \_\_\_\_    _____

Make a list of half-day family weekend activities, and do one?

\_\_\_\_    \_\_\_\_    _____

| *Did you remember to:* | *Yes* | *No* | *Will do it by* |
|---|---|---|---|
| Have your child make up his own rules for eating? | ___ | ___ | _____ |
| Conduct a kitchen inventory and make sure you've eliminated tempting foods from your child's sight and reach? | ___ | ___ | _____ |
| Perform the aerobic activity of the week? | ___ | ___ | _____ |
| Perform the strength and flex exercises of the week? | ___ | ___ | _____ |

Parents: After you weigh your child and fill out your weekly report forms, be sure to review the past weeks' goals. Decide whether your child has met or fallen short of the goal for the week. Reward your child for achieving his goal. If he did not achieve it, redirect him to set a new, more achievable goal. *Never ridicule or punish your child for not meeting his goal.* Also, allow him to "plead the Fifth," meaning that if he knows he did not meet his goal and feels too embarrassed to talk about it, just move on. Don't dwell on the mistakes of the past. Either way, set a new eating and activity goal for the next week.

You're three weeks into the program—which means you've done the toughest part of all by simply beginning and sticking to the program. In week 4, we'll provide more tools for success by going one step further with your child's goals.

# Week 4

# MONITORING YOUR
# MOMENTUM

## TRIM KIDS ROAD MAP FOR WEEK 4

*This week, after you have filled out the Trim Kids forms in the appendix (remember to weigh your child and list your goals for the week), we will show you how to use positive attention—redirecting and other techniques—to help your child begin new healthy behaviors. We'll give you ideas on how to create adventure areas in your home to encourage active play. Your family will continue to increase physical activity and fitness by trying the aerobic, strength, and flexibility activities of the week. You will learn how to use portion control to reduce your child's food intake. Follow this week's menu plan, try the new recipes, and use the weekly shopping list to get what you'll need. Fill out the TRIM KIDS AEROBIC ACTIVITY AND FOOD CHECKLIST. Check your child's progress with the Trim Kids Weekly Checklist at the end of the chapter.*

## SECTION 1: TIME TO STOP AND THINK

As you work with your child to implement healthier behaviors, remind her that old habits can be difficult to change or modify. Like other learned behaviors that involve motor responses (such as learning to swim or ride a bike) learning new habits takes time, practice, and patience. Slipups will occur, just as falls are inevitable in learning to ride a bike. Remind her that you will be there to help her get back on track, and that eventually, she will master the new behaviors.

We've mentioned that positive reinforcement works more effectively than negative reinforcement to change behaviors. Positive reinforcement includes verbally acknowledging *every* healthy choice your child makes. "I noticed you came home after school and went straight to riding your bike. And you lost 2 pounds this week—that's awesome!" Or, "I'm so proud that you had dessert only two times this week."

Another way to give positive reinforcement is to provide social or material rewards and incentives. Your child's personal preferences will determine what rewards or incentives will be the most effective motivators. Most kids love new exercise clothes or equipment, and trips to theme parks, pools, or activity centers. Give acknowledgments, rewards, and incentives for attaining both short and long-term goals.

The most constructive responses to unhealthy behavior are to ignore it, redirect the child's attention elsewhere, or solve the problem. So, for example, if your child is watching television when she shouldn't be, instead of arguing with or shaming her simply turn off the set and tell her it's time for a bike ride. Or, if walking is part of her fitness routine but she just doesn't like it, turn to problem solving. Offer a Walkman and her favorite tape so she can listen to music or a story while walking.

If, on the other hand, your child lies about sneaking a treat or simply refuses to participate in the prescribed exercises, you may want to impose consequences—for example, remove phone privileges. A consequence like having to go to bed early

---

### TRIM KIDS TESTIMONIAL

## A Parent's Perspective

"My son Jeremy was in the Trim Kids Program eight years ago, when he was eleven. He lost 43 pounds and now, at nineteen, he's still at his goal weight. Not only that, he is a complete health and fitness advocate. He never misses an opportunity to tell people what food is healthy and how they should be more active. He doesn't smoke or drink and never did even during those tough teenage years. Last year, when we saw Dr. Melinda in the lab for his annual evaluation (we never missed one), I asked her, 'Do you even know how much this program means to these kids? Just look at him!' She just beamed and asked, 'Do you know what you have given your son through your commitment to his health?'"

or getting less allowance for a week is more effective than nagging, arguing, or degrading her. Your child will be more likely to respond with increased energy and commitment to the program, rather than sullenly obeying your orders.

## SECTION 2: TIME TO GET ACTIVE

# INSIDE ADVENTURE: WHEN THE WEATHER'S BAD

Have you refurbished your house so that your child can stay active during rainy, cold, and snowy months?

There are plenty of places to take your child when cabin fever sets in. Sign her up for weekly indoor activities or just go for a one-day visit when the mood strikes.

- Gyms and fitness centers: These offer a variety of calorie-burning fun including gymnastics, tumbling, indoor basketball, wrestling, kick-boxing or other martial arts, wall-climbing, track, badminton, volleyball, table tennis, and swimming. Don't forget indoor tennis.
- Dance studios: Kids are welcome in all kinds of classes including ballet, tap, modern, jazz, hip-hop, line dancing, ballroom dancing, yoga, free movement, and other music-dance combination classes.
- Indoor rinks: Ice skating and roller skating can provide hours of fun on a rainy day.
- Children's museums: These exist in most cities and provide interesting, educational, and fun activities that keep your kid on the move!
- Indoor nature centers or aquariums offer similar opportunities for movement.
- Restaurants with games: They're popping up all over. Choose those that offer the best energy burners, including laser tag and other fast-paced activities. Most have salad bars, so plan on light meals.

Another great option is to create an "imagination station" (page 46). You can create one in a room in your house, where you set up areas for your child to try different activities. Here are some ideas for older children:

- A plastic tub filled with costumes, dress-up clothes, and accessories like crowns, wands, toy shields, armor, masks, vests, belts, shoes, hats, grass skirts, scarves, play jewelry, wigs, and so forth
- Boom box with various dance music tapes or CDs
- Microphone, drums, toy musical instruments, stage curtains
- Puppets, marionettes, magician kits, various stuffed animals
- Batons, small flags, pom-poms, streamers, hula hoops
- Foam mats and wedges, indoor tents, large building blocks or cardboard boxes, beanbag chairs, soft pillows, old blankets, sheets
- Hopscotch mat, action games like Twister, Charades, Simon Says, follow-the-leader, paddle balls, indoor ball-toss games, beanbags, juggling balls, hacky sack
- Kid-safe dartboards or other target games
- Indoor basketball hoop and soft foam balls
- Jump ropes, skip-it, small kid-safe hand weights, exercise stretch bands

For younger children, try:

- Small pull-push toys or plastic wagons
- Toy household cleaning items such as brooms, mops, vacuum cleaners, and feather dusters
- Toy kitchen, restaurant, and accessories
- Indoor riding toys

Meanwhile, when you're gathered in front of the television watching your favorite show, don't forget to stand up and do the "TV commercial boogie" whenever the ads come on. You'll be amazed at how much moving you'll do to the soundtracks of those endless commercials! And be sure to engage in collective boo-ing when junk-food ads fill the screen.

## WEEKLY EXERCISE ACTIVITIES

### WEEK 4 AEROBIC ACTIVITY: RECOMMENDED GOALS

Write your goal in the TRIM KIDS AEROBIC ACTIVITY AND FOOD CHECKLIST (page 386). This is the minimum amount of aerobic exercise that you should perform this week. Every day, record what type of physical activity you did and how long you did it. At the end of the week, compare your list with the goals you set at the beginning of the week.

- Red Level: The exercise goal this week is two days per week for twenty to twenty-five minutes each day.
- Yellow Level: The exercise goal this week is three days per week for twenty-five to thirty minutes each day.
- Green Level: The exercise goal this week is three days per week for twenty-five to forty minutes each day.
- Blue Level: The exercise goal this week is three days per week for thirty to sixty minutes each day.

### WEEK 4 AEROBIC ACTIVITY: FLAG FOOTBALL

Buy inexpensive table napkins in two different colors. Divide your family into two teams and ask everyone to tuck one of the colored napkins into his or her waistband.

Play a game of football with these aerobic rules: Allow only twenty seconds to prepare for the kick-off. Allow only ten seconds for the huddle. The ball must be snapped for the next play no more than ten seconds after it is down. Switch players' positions: If you were quarterback and your child was running back, switch every fifteen minutes. These rules keep the game moving and the calories burning.

### WEEK 4 STRENGTH AND FLEX EXERCISES

Read the instructions aloud to your child as he does these exercises, until he no longer needs your assistance.

## Strength Exercise 4: Overhead Press

Stand tall and erect with your stomach and hips tight. Make a fist with both hands and hold them at shoulder level with your thumbs turned slightly backward.

Slowly, over two to four seconds, raise your fists over your head just in front of your ears, extending your arms fully. Then stretch up and lift your shoulders. Lower your shoulders, then bend your elbows out to the side and slowly lower to the starting position over four seconds. It's very important to *keep your back*

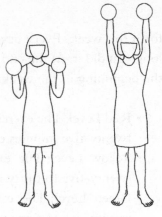

*straight and tummy tight throughout this entire movement.*

Do eight to twelve repetitions of this exercise. As you do them, be sure to lift for two to four seconds, and lower for two to four seconds. This exercise works your shoulder muscles (deltoids) and the backs of your upper arms (triceps).

Common errors that your child may make include arching the back and improper position of thumbs.

## Flex Exercise 4: Single Rear Shoulder Stretch

Stand with your feet about eighteen inches apart. Tighten your hips and push them slightly forward.

Now tighten your tummy and slightly bend your knees. Raise your right arm straight up above your head just to the side of your right ear.

Bend your elbow and drop your hand down in between your shoulder blades. Good. Now, reach up with your left arm. Bring it over your head to grab your right elbow. That's it. Gently pull your right elbow toward your left side.

Hold this position for fifteen to thirty seconds. Gently release. Now it's time to repeat this exercise with your left arm.

Repeat this process one more time, holding this position for each arm again for fifteen to thirty seconds.

Perform these new strength and flex exercises and also the ones you learned previously in weeks 1–3 at least once, but preferably twice this week. Record your progress on the TRIM KIDS STRENGTH AND FLEXIBILITY WORKOUT CHART in the appendix ("Forms You'll Need"), on page 388. Every week, you will add another exercise to your program.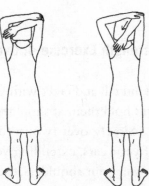

Don't forget to fill out your TRIM KIDS AEROBIC ACTIVITY AND FOOD CHECKLIST on page 386, and try the aerobic activity of the week with the entire family.

# EXERCISE ACTIVITY IDEAS: PULL YOUR OWN WEIGHT SERIES

Let's say you're out of town visiting relatives or on a family vacation. By now, you love your new, toned, beautiful body and you're aching to do some strengthening exercises.

The exercises below work the major muscle groups, and you don't need a gym or special equipment to do them. Instead you'll use your own body weight to tone and strengthen your muscles. Be sure to do them slowly, and be sure to fully extend and contract your muscles to get full strengthening and toning benefit.

## Modified Standing Push-Up

Stand two to three feet from a wall, sturdy table, or chair, with your feet together and your hands extended forward. Place your hands on the wall or grasp the table or chair as you lean your body forward at a forty-five-degree angle to the floor. Slowly, bend your elbows and lower your chest until it touches the edge of the table, chair, or wall. Now, push with your hands, extending your arms, and return to the original position. Keep your head in line with your body. Keep your legs straight and extended throughout the exercise. Repeat eight to twelve times.

You are training the chest muscles (pectorals).

### Modified Lunge

Stand with your feet about six to eight inches apart and grasp the back of a sturdy chair with both hands. Arms should be fully extended. Step forward with your right leg approximately eighteen inches. Keep your head, shoulders, and hips in a straight line. Bend your knees and lower the left knee onto the floor. Do not allow the right knee to move in front of your right foot. Push the heel of the right foot into the floor as you lift and return to the starting position. Repeat with your left leg forward. Repeat eight to twelve times on each leg.

You are working the buttocks muscles (gluteus), the back of the upper leg (hamstrings), and the front upper leg (quads).

### Triceps Dip

Sit in a sturdy chair or on a step with your legs extended in front of you, heels on the floor, toes up and relaxed. Place your hands on either side of your hips, grasping either side of the chair seat. Slowly slide your hips forward slightly in front of the chair, and lower them six to eight inches. Your elbows will bend as you lower your hips. Then, lift your hips by slowly straightening your elbows (without snap-

ping or locking) and extending your arms to a full, straight position. Repeat this move eight to twelve times.

You are working the back of the upper arm (triceps).

## SECTION 3: TIME TO DINE

*For the Trim Kids Weight Loss Plan to succeed, it is crucial that your child learns how much she should be eating (portion control) by keeping track of her daily food units. Be sure that she is filling in the* TRIM KIDS AEROBIC ACTIVITY *and* FOOD CHECKLIST *every day. Review the Food Portion and Unit Lists for "Week 2" (page 119) if you have any questions. Or learn by example: there's a Portion Control Practice Exercise at the end of every week.*

# NUTRITION NUTSHELL: TIPS FOR ADDING MORE FRUITS AND VEGETABLES TO YOUR DAILY FOOD PLAN

- Use more fruits and vegetables as snacks. Serve raw vegetables with a reduced-fat ranch dip and fruit with a low-fat yogurt dip to enhance appeal.
- Add fruit (raisins, banana chunks, sliced strawberries) to cereals, oatmeal, and yogurt.
- Keep raisins or grapes in the freezer for a quick "frozen snack."
- Add extra vegetables to soup.
- Enhance salads with reduced-fat cheese and artificial bacon bits to increase acceptance and intake.
- Toss fresh spinach leaves in a salad.
- Make a "yogurt shake" with fresh fruit such as bananas and strawberries, yogurt, and milk.
- Keep packaged frozen fruit in the freezer for "last-minute" use in muffins, quick breads, and shakes.
- Stir-fry vegetables with a little low-sodium soy sauce for a quick different flavor.

- Melt a little reduced-fat cheese over steamed or cooked vegetables to increase acceptance.
- Add extra canned tomatoes or tomato paste to sauces and soups.
- Mix unsweetened fruit juice with carbonated water for a "natural soda."

## Week 4 Weekly Menu
*Recipes are given for items in boldface.*

| | Breakfast | Lunch | Dinner | Snacks (1 to 2 choices per day) |
|---|---|---|---|---|
| MONDAY | Pancakes (1–2) with low-sugar syrup<br>Berries (½ to 1 cup)<br>Scrambled egg substitute (optional)<br>Milk (1 cup) | Turkey and reduced-fat cheese sandwich—preferably whole wheat<br>Vegetable soup<br>Raisins (small box)<br>Milk (1 cup) | Baked ham<br>Baked sweet potato (½ medium) or canned yams (½ cup)<br>Seasoned green beans<br>Applesauce (½ cup)<br>Water or calorie-free beverage | Cereal with fiber (1 cup) and skim or soy milk<br>Cereal-fruit bar (1)<br>Reduced-fat chips (about 15 chips or 1 ounce) with fat-free dip or salsa<br>Wheat crackers (6) with:<br>Reduced-fat cheese (2 slices) |
| TUESDAY | Oatmeal (1 cup) with chopped apple or banana and walnuts (2 tablespoons) and brown sugar (1 teaspoon) or low-sugar syrup<br>Milk (1 cup) | Peanut butter bagel—whole bagel with 1 tablespoon peanut butter<br>Low-sugar jam or jelly<br>Carrot or celery sticks with fat-free dip<br>Milk (1 cup) | Out to eat:<br>Chinese wonton or egg drop soup<br>Stir-fry dinner such as chicken with vegetables or beef and broccoli (no deep-fat or breaded, fried dinners) with white rice (not fried rice) | Lite cream cheese (2 tablespoons)<br>Peanut butter (1 tablespoon)<br>Hot cocoa made with skim milk (1 cup) |

| | Breakfast | Lunch | Dinner | Snacks (1 to 2 choices per day) |
|---|---|---|---|---|
| TUESDAY (cont.) | | | Fortune cookie<br><br>Water or calorie-free beverage | English muffin or bagel "pizza" (½ muffin with tomato or pizza sauce and reduced-fat cheese)<br><br>Fruit (1 piece fresh, ½ cup canned, or 3 tablespoons dried)<br><br>Frozen fruit bar (1)<br><br>Fruit juice "spritzer": 3 ounces fruit juice mixed with 5 ounces club soda or sparkling water<br><br>Graham crackers (3 squares)<br><br>Teddy grahams (½ cup)<br><br>Nuts (2 tablespoons)<br><br>Oatmeal (½ cup)<br><br>Oatmeal cookies (2 small)<br><br>Air-popped popcorn (3 to 5 cups)<br><br>Reduced-fat pudding or ice cream (½ cup) |
| WEDNESDAY | Cinnamon whole-wheat toast (1–2 slices) with 2 teaspoons lite margarine and a sprinkle of cinnamon sugar<br><br>Cottage cheese (½ cup) with applesauce or pineapple (½ cup)<br><br>Milk (1 cup) | Wheat crackers (6) with reduced-fat cheese slices<br><br>Chicken noodle soup<br><br>Fruit cup (½ cup)<br><br>Milk (½ to 1 cup) | Grilled skinless chicken (marinate in your favorite brand of marinade mix)<br><br>**Grilled Vegetables**<br><br>Tossed salad as desired with 1 to 2 teaspoons olive oil or reduced-fat salad dressing<br><br>Bread or dinner roll—preferably whole wheat (1)<br><br>Milk (½ to 1 cup) | |
| THURSDAY | Fried egg sandwich (1 egg fried in nonfat butter-flavored spray) with 2 slices wheat toast and reduced-fat cheese (optional)<br><br>Sliced tomato<br>½ cup orange juice—calcium-fortified | Tuna salad made with fat-free mayo and chopped apples and celery if desired<br><br>½ whole-wheat pita<br><br>Rice cakes—any flavor (8 to 10 small)<br><br>Milk (1 cup) | **Split Pea Soup** (1 cup)<br><br>Steamed or cooked vegetables of choice<br><br>Tossed salad with 1 to 2 teaspoons olive oil or reduced-fat dressing<br><br>Frozen yogurt with fruit topping | |

| | Breakfast | Lunch | Dinner | Snacks (1 to 2 choices per day) |
|---|---|---|---|---|
| THURSDAY *(cont.)* | | | ("kiddie" size, 4-ounce) Water or calorie-free beverage | Quesadilla (1 tortilla) with melted, reduced-fat cheese, salsa, and fat-free sour cream |
| FRIDAY | Cold cereal with fiber (1½ cups) Banana Milk (1 cup) | Fast-food meal: Kid's meal-size hamburger (no mayonnaise) and fries (kid's meal-size) Water or calorie-free beverage | **Shrimp Scampi** (1 cup) over spaghetti, fettuccine, or noodles (½ to 1 cup) **Zucchini Italian Style** Fruit cup (½ cup) Milk (1 cup) | Rice cakes (10 small or 2 large) Sandwich on wheat bread (½) with turkey, tuna with lite mayo, or reduced-fat cheese Soup: vegetable or chicken noodle (2 cups) Trail mix (4 tablespoons) Yogurt, regular or frozen (4 to 6 ounces) |
| SATURDAY | Scrambled egg substitute with reduced-fat cheese and salsa Bagel (½) or wheat toast (1 slice) Berries (1 cup) or melon (⅓ melon) Milk (1 cup) | Split pea soup, leftover (1 cup) Tossed salad as desired with 1 to 2 teaspoons olive or reduced-fat salad dressing Fresh fruit of choice Milk (1 cup) | **Oven Chicken Nuggets** (4–6) Oven french fries or tater tots (½ cup) Green beans **Waldorf Salad** (1 cup) Water or calorie-free beverage | |
| SUNDAY | Cold cereal with fiber (1 cup) 1 slice wheat toast Banana (1) or berries (1 cup) Milk (1 cup) | Out to eat, cafeteria: Meat and vegetable plate with roast chicken, beef, or ham Vegetable dish | **Leftover Night** Food Units 1 to 2 starch-bread Lean or low-fat protein 0 to 1 fruit 1 milk-dairy | |

|  | **Breakfast** | **Lunch** | **Dinner** | **Snacks** <br> **(1 to 2** <br> **choices per day)** |
| --- | --- | --- | --- | --- |
| SUNDAY <br> *(cont.)* |  | Potato or pasta dish (½ cup) <br><br> Salad (unlimited) <br><br> Water or calorie-free beverage | 1 fat <br> Veggies—unlimited! |  |

# Week 4 Recipes

## SPLIT PEA SOUP

2 teaspoons olive oil

1 onion, chopped, or 1 envelope onion soup mix

Ham bone from leftover baked ham (optional)

2 to 3 cups diced ham or 6 to 8 slices leftover cooked turkey bacon or vegegtable sausage (optional)

1-pound package of dried split peas

4 celery stalks, chopped

2 garlic cloves, minced

¼ teaspoon salt or salt substitute (optional) and pepper to taste

2 bay leaves

6 to 7 cups water

A few dashes Tabasco sauce (optional)

Put the oil in a large pot and sauté the onion. Add the remaining ingredients and simmer for 2 hours. Remove the bay leaves and serve. (The soup can also be cooked in a crock pot on a low setting for 10 to 12 hours.)

Makes about 6 cups.

Nutritional Analysis

1 cup: 2 carbohydrates (180 calories, 1–2 grams fat) + 1 to 2 protein units if ham is added

## SHRIMP SCAMPI

2 pounds large raw shrimp, peeled
2 teaspoons olive oil
¼ cup nonfat liquid butter substitute
Juice of 2 lemons
¼ cup white wine or chicken broth
1 teaspoon Italian seasoning
2 garlic cloves, minced
½ teaspoon salt or salt substitute (optional)
3 to 4 cups cooked noodles

Combine the ingredients except the noodles and simmer in a nonstick frying pan for 5 to 10 minutes, until shrimp is cooked through. Toss with your favorite noodles.

Makes about 4 cups.

Nutritional Analysis

1 cup: 3 proteins (90 calories, 4 grams fat). The noodles will add 1 carbohydrate per ½ cup.

## ZUCCHINI ITALIAN STYLE

Nonfat butter or olive oil–flavored cooking spray
2 teaspoons olive oil
1 onion, thinly sliced (optional)
4 fresh zucchini, diced
One 14½-ounce can diced tomatoes, drained
1 garlic clove, minced (optional)
1 tablespoon dried oregano

½ teaspoon pepper
¼ teaspoon salt or salt substitute (optional)
½ cup finely shredded Parmesan cheese

Spray the bottom of a skillet with nonfat cooking spray, add the olive oil, and sauté the onion, if using, and the zucchini. Add the tomatoes, garlic, and seasonings and simmer uncovered for about 10 minutes, until the zucchini is crisp-tender. Sprinkle with a generous amount of Parmesan just before serving.

Makes about 5 cups.

Nutritional Analysis
Vegetable Group: No limit (½ cup = 30 calories, 1 gram fat)

........................................................................................................................................

## GRILLED VEGETABLES

*For the marinade*
2 to 3 tablespoons olive oil
Juice of 1 large lemon
1 tablespoon water
2 garlic cloves, minced (optional)
Salt or salt substitute (optional)
Seasoning of choice, such as Italian or Creole (optional)

Raw vegetables such as eggplant, sliced in 1-inch rounds; zucchini or yellow squash, sliced "lengthwise" in ½-inch strips; tomatoes sliced in half; red or yellow peppers, sliced in half; corn on the cob; onions, sliced thick; Portobello mushrooms (add 2 tablespoons balsamic vinegar when marinating mushrooms).

Put the marinade ingredients into a large zippered bag. (If using mushrooms, add the balsamic vinegar.) Add the vegetables, zip bag closed, and shake well. Marinate for 1 to 3 hours.

Grill the vegetables on medium coals until tender, 5 to 10 minutes each side. Vegetables may be seasoned while grilling if desired.

LEFTOVERS HINT: Dice the leftover grilled vegetables for vegetarian chili. Add 14½-ounce can diced tomatoes, one 15-ounce can tomato sauce (regular or no salt added), one 15-ounce can pinto beans, and your favorite chili seasoning packet. Simmer chili according to the seasoning packet directions. Or, put the vegetables in a pita bread pocket for a sandwich.

Nutritional Analysis
Vegetable Group: No limit + 1 to 2 fats depending on the amount of olive oil used
(30–70 calories, 2 to 8 grams fat)

## OVEN CHICKEN NUGGETS

1 cup flour
¼ teaspoon each paprika, salt substitute, and garlic powder
4 skinless, boneless chicken breasts sliced into strips or nuggets
1 cup liquid egg substitute
4 tablespoons fat-free mayonnaise or Miracle Whip (optional)
1 tablespoon Dijon mustard (optional)
Cornflakes, crushed
Nonfat butter-flavored spray

Preheat the oven to 375°F. Combine the flour and seasonings in a plastic or paper bag. Shake the chicken in the bag to coat with the flour mixture. Dip the chicken in the egg substitute. (For a thicker coating add fat-free mayonnaise to the egg substitute and add the mustard for a zestier flavor.) Roll in the cornflakes. Spray the baking dish and place chicken in it. Bake uncovered for about 30 minutes, until chicken is cooked through.

Nutritional Analysis
About 4 tenders (1 breast): 3 protein units, ½ carbohydrate unit (145 calories, 5 grams fat)

## WALDORF SALAD

4 to 5 apples, left unpeeled, cored, and diced
1 to 1½ cups low-fat yogurt or fat-free mayonnaise
¼ cup raisins
1 to 2 tablespoons lemon juice
2 to 3 celery stalks, sliced
¼ cup walnuts (optional)

Combine and mix ingredients. Serve chilled.

Makes 4 to 5 cups.

Nutritional Analysis
1 cup: 1 carbohydrate (90 calories, 0–2 grams fat)

## Week 4 Weekly Shopping List

| Fruits | Vegetables | Meat, Deli | Dried, Canned |
| --- | --- | --- | --- |
| Apples | Carrots, celery | Chicken breasts— boneless, skinless (buy a "family pack," enough for 2 recipes) | Oatmeal |
| Bananas | Salad greens: | | Split peas, dry (1-pound bag) |
| Lemons |    Lettuce | | Spaghetti, fettuccine, or noodles |
| Miscellaneous fruits for snacks |    Tomatoes | Baked ham | Cornflake crumbs (or cornflake cereal to crush |
| |    Cucumbers, etc. | Shrimp (fresh or frozen) | Flour |
| | Onions | Turkey cold-cut slices | Chicken marinade mix or packet (your favorite brand) |
| | Sweet potatoes | | Diced tomatoes (14½-ounce can) |
| | Zucchini squash | | Vegetable soup, chicken noodle soup |
| | Miscellaneous grilled vegetables and vegetables for snacks | | |

# Week 4 Weekly Shopping List *(cont.)*

| Fruits | Vegetables | Meat, Deli | Dried, Canned |
|--------|-----------|------------|---------------|
| | | | Tuna (water-packed) |
| | | | Reduced-fat pudding pack |
| | | | Applesauce, fruit cup |
| | | | Raisins |

| Dairy Case | Frozen Food Section | Breads, Miscellaneous |
|-----------|--------------------|-----------------------|
| Milk (skim, 1½%, or soy milk) | Frozen french fries or tater tots | Wheat bread |
| Egg substitute, eggs | Green beans,* 3 boxes | Bagels |
| Reduced-fat or part-skim cheese slices (less than 5 grams of fat per ounces or slice) | *Can substitute fresh if desired | Whole-wheat pita bread |
| Reduced-fat shredded cheese | | Wheat crackers |
| String cheese (part-skim milk) | | |
| Fruit yogurt | | |
| Orange or other fruit juice—calcium-fortified | | |
| Cottage cheese | | |
| Parmesan cheese | | |

## Staples

Reduced-fat or very low-fat mayonnaise (less than 3 grams fat per serving)

Reduced-fat or very low-fat salad dressings (less than 3–5 grams fat per serving)

Catsup, mustard, BBQ sauce, pickles (regular versions OK)

Low-sugar syrup, low-sugar or all-fruit jelly

Peanut butter (no added hydrogenated or partially hydrogenated vegetable oils)

Nuts

Oil (olive, canola, peanut), nonfat cooking spray, nonfat liquid butter (dairy section)

Lite margarine (first ingredient should be *liquid* vegetable oil—not hydrogenated or partially hydrogenated oil)

# WEEK 4 PORTION CONTROL AND FOOD RECORD PRACTICE

Don't forget to use TRIM KIDS AEROBIC ACTIVITY AND FOOD CHECKLIST to help keep track of your daily intake. Let's practice portion-control checks for one day.

## Tuesday:

*Breakfast:*

| | |
|---|---|
| Oatmeal (1 cup) | 2 carbohydrates |
|   with banana or apple pieces | ½ carbohydrate |
|   with walnuts (2 tablespoons) | 2 fats, some protein |
|   with low-sugar syrup | Free |
| Milk (1 cup) | 1 carbohydrate |

*Lunch:*

| | |
|---|---|
| Bagel (whole) | 2 carbohydrates |
|   with peanut butter (1 tablespoon) | 1–2 fats, 1 protein |
|   with low-sugar jelly | Free |
| Carrot or celery sticks | Vegetables as desired |
| Fat-free dip | Free |
| Milk (1 cup) | 1 carbohydrate |

*Dinner:*

| | |
|---|---|
| Wonton soup | ½ carbohydrate |
| Stir-fry (meat or chicken and vegetables) | 3 proteins, 3–4 fats, vegetables |
| White rice, ½ restaurant portion is | |
|   1 to 1½ cups | 3 carbohydrates |
| Fortune cookie | Free |

*Sample snacks:*

| | |
|---|---|
| Grapes (½ cup) | 1 carbohydrate |
| Sugar-free Jell-O | Free |

Total food units for Tuesday:          11 carbohydrates
                                        5–6 proteins
                                        6 fats
                                        Vegetables

## SECTION 4: TIME TO SUM UP

# Trim Kids Weekly Checklist

*Did you remember to:*                    Yes      No      *Will do it by*

Fill out TRIM KIDS WEEKLY REPORT AND GOAL SHEET?

——  ——  ————

Fill out TRIM KIDS AEROBIC ACTIVITY AND FOOD CHECKLIST?

——  ——  ————

Fill out TRIM KIDS STRENGTH AND FLEXIBILITY WORKOUT CHART?

——  ——  ————

Praise your child when you observed healthy behaviors?

——  ——  ————

Ignore, redirect, or solve the problem when unhealthy behaviors emerged?

——  ——  ————

Enroll your child in an indoor activity?    ——  ——  ————

Finish an imagination station inside your home?

——  ——  ————

Perform the aerobic activity of the week?

——  ——  ————

*Did you remember to:*            Yes          No          *Will do it by*

Perform the strength and flex exercises of the week?

_____          _____          _____


The Trim Kids Program is rooted in both physical and cognitive research. In "Week 5," we'll explain how we *know* that our techniques are effective in supporting success for overweight children and their families.

# Week 5

# BODY BASICS

## TRIM KIDS ROAD MAP FOR WEEK 5

*Begin this week by weighing your child on the same day and at the same time as you did last week, and record her weight on the* TRIM KIDS WEEKLY REPORT AND GOAL SHEET. *Refer to the exercise recommendations in Week 5 for your child's color level and goal for this week's number of minutes and number of days per week on the* TRIM KIDS AEROBIC ACTIVITY AND FOOD CHECKLIST. *Review these with your child and help her to select appropriate, enjoyable activities. Review last week's goals and have your child record accomplishments. Reward her for meeting her goals. Discuss any problems or questions with your child. You can refer to last week's Trim Kids Aerobic Activity and Food Checklist to praise your child for healthy selections or to see why she may be having problems.*

*This week, we will explain how kids learn new behaviors. You will learn the ABCs of behavior change. You will read about the difference between hunger and craving, and take a short quiz. You and your child will learn how the body's metabolic engine works, and this will help you to identify the best type of physical activity for your child. You will fill out a chart to determine your child's target heart rate range. Your family will continue to increase physical activity and improve fitness by trying the aerobic, strength, and flexibility activities of the week. We will give you tips about how to prepare quick, healthy, and tasty breakfasts.*

## SECTION 1: TIME TO STOP AND THINK

# MOTOR AND MENTAL LEARNING

Replacing old habits with new ones requires practice, practice, and more practice! Because of that—and the fact that many overweight kids don't believe in themselves or have the confidence to try new things—your child's behavior won't change overnight. Neither will yours. But years of studying overweight children have given us valuable insight into the most efficient and effective ways to motivate positive behavioral changes.

## Social Learning Theories: The Backbone of Behavioral Change

According to social learning theories, children who can grasp the concepts behind specific behavioral changes and who are physically able to make them will do so willingly if they believe they will *benefit* from the new behaviors. This is why we are so adamant that parents provide positive reinforcement, rewards, and incentives. What's more, kids will partici-pate in new behavior *if they believe they can do it*. This is why we set up easy-to-attain goals—ones kids absolutely will reach. Also, when kids learn to *listen to their bodies* (to slow down if they're exercising too hard, to speed up if an exercise isn't challenging enough, and to distinguish between hunger and cravings, for example), they acquire a new mastery or understanding of the body as well as how to carry out a healthier lifestyle. These elements, coupled with your role modeling,

> **TRIM KIDS TESTIMONIAL**
>
> ### A Child's Perspective
>
> "My mom and dad are divorced. I live with my mom, but I see my dad almost every day. My dad is really fit, and he kept bugging me about my weight. He'd make me go jogging with him and he'd get mad if I couldn't keep up. I started the Trim Kids Program. I was really happy when Dr. Melinda said that I didn't have to keep up with my dad anymore. Now my dad and I do fun things like basketball and bike riding. Sometimes I even beat him in bike races—I think he lets me win, but that's OK. I've already lost 12 pounds! Dad is so proud of me."
>
> —Carolyn, age ten

add up to the strongest probability that your child will indeed participate and succeed in the program.

If you read Part One of this book, you're already in tune with these concepts. But since anchoring behavioral changes in everyday life takes practice, we'll review them here as you approach the midway point of the program. Remember: we're not operating on hunches. Research shows that if these guidelines are followed, your child's behavior *will* change over time.

- Provide positive reinforcement. Kids will do *anything* for attention, and the type of attention you give (positive or negative) is thought to drive and maintain the child's behavior. So, for example, if you give attention for positive actions, chances are your child will repeat them in the future. Likewise, if you respond to an unhealthy action, chances are your child will repeat *that* behavior in the future. It's essential to focus on positive behaviors that reinforce weight-loss goals while ignoring or redirecting negative behaviors or consciously solving problems.

- Be a strong and consistent role model. Children—especially young children—imitate the behavior of significant role models in their lives. Children look primarily to their parents as role models. Studies show that groups in which both parents and children participated in weight-management programs had significantly better long-term maintenance of weight loss than groups made up of children only. The parent-child groups also reported more satisfaction with the program.

- Have your cake and eat it too—but less often. Instead of vowing that you'll never eat high-calorie or high-fat foods again, take a more gradual approach to developing new habits. For instance, if your family ordinarily eats fast foods four out of seven nights a week, don't quit cold turkey; cut it down to only once a week. After several weeks of that, adjust it to once every other week, then to once a month. This approach gives you a stronger sense of control over your new habits and heightens feelings of accomplishment, while also facilitating long-term maintenance of weight-loss goals.

- Say what you mean and mean what you say. In the beginning of the program, parents of overweight children sometimes have a hard time setting limits on eating and activities for their children. Implementing the Trim Kids rules is a built-in way to achieve success in setting and sticking to limits. For example, the three-bite rule encourages family members to try new foods they otherwise wouldn't eat. Reward those who adhere to the rule, and ignore those who don't—or remind them that there will be another chance for rewards at the next meal.

Ultimately, the best way to train yourself to develop and maintain new habits (such as catching your child at being good and commenting on it) is to practice. When you slip up, take a deep breath, regroup, and direct your attention to the healthy changes your child has been making. Recommit to the program as many times as it takes. If it helps, use Mark Twain's words of wisdom as a mantra whenever you feel yourself falling, fumbling, or frustrated: "Habit is habit and not to be flung out the window by any man, but coaxed down stairs a step at a time."

## THE CHAIN OF BEHAVIOR: EASY AS ABC

An excellent way to practice new behaviors is to understand how unhealthy behaviors play out and catch them before they sweep you away. Read the following with your child and explain how his old chain of behaviors creates unhealthy habits, and how new chains of behavior can create new, healthy habits.

Start noticing what makes you want to overeat or be underactive. Then you can break the old habit and replace it with a new one. Let's look at an example of chains of behaviors to understand how to do this.

Jerry came home from school feeling very bored and sad. Since he was feeling sad, he sat down and watched television. Then he went to the refrigerator and pulled out the whole milk. He grabbed a bag of chocolate chip cookies and ate in front of the TV, which he loves to do.

When his mother saw him, she asked Jerry why he was eating high-calorie snacks instead of the lower-calorie foods allowed on his diet. He said that he was sad and didn't feel like staying on the diet any longer.

In this story, Jerry's old habits of eating high-calorie snacks and using TV to make himself feel better resulted in negative consequences. They prevented him from meeting his weight-loss goals and ultimately made him feel worse, not better. This is an example of the ABCs of a chain of behaviors:

A. When Jerry feels bored and sad, he doesn't want to do anything. He has felt this way before in prior situations, **A**ntecedents. They lead to:

B. **B**ehavior associated with high-calorie eating. Jerry likes to watch TV and eat high-calorie snacks. That leads to:

C. Negative **C**onsequences. These behaviors make Jerry gain weight and feel even worse, so he decides that he is a failure and can't stay on the diet.

Once Jerry began the Trim Kids Program and realized what his habits were, he was able to break the chain of behavior. When he came home feeling bored or sad, he either ate a low-calorie snack or did something fun and active. You can break the chain of behavior, too. Instead of playing out your old chain of behaviors, do something new. When you come home feeling bored or sad, you could:

- Talk with Mom or Dad, another relative, or a friend about why.
- Talk to yourself in a positive way.
- Choose an alternative activity (ride your bike, walk to a friend's house, go swimming).
- When you watch TV, don't allow yourself to eat.
- If you catch yourself thinking that you aren't able to follow the diet, tell yourself positive things such as:

    "I know I can do this, but maybe I should talk to Mom."
    "Breaking the diet once doesn't mean I can't stay on the diet."
    "I'll just have *one*."
    "I think I'll do _____ instead."

Let's practice together, using the following story.

## The ABCs of Behavior

Shelly is trying to lose weight by making healthier food choices and becoming more active. On her way to play softball, she meets three friends. She follows them to the "Snack Shack," where they all sit at a picnic table gossiping and munching on chips and candy bars and drinking sodas. As she finishes a can of soda and a chocolate bar, Shelly realizes that she has slipped off her diet. She begins to feel down and defeated as her friends gossip away.

Antecedent: What happened first?

_____

_____

Behavior: Did Shelly and her friends choose a healthy or unhealthy food?

_____

_____

Consequence: How did Shelly feel?

_____

_____

Think of a time when you had a tough decision to make about what to eat. Write about it by using the ABCs of behavior chain.

Antecedent: What happened first?

_____

Behavior: Did you choose a healthy or an unhealthy food?

_____

Consequence: How did you feel afterward?

_____

This week, focus on practicing alternative behaviors from the list of behavior substitutions you made in week 1 (pages 89 and 94). Remember: these attitudes will help you in many situations and in other aspects of your life.

## Cravings and Hunger

When you are developing new chains of behavior, it's useful to pinpoint what motivates unhealthy behavior. There's a difference between being hungry and craving a food, but your child may not yet know how to distinguish between the two. Help her recognize when she's responding to a true physical need (hunger) or if she's acting on internal feelings, habit, or something in the external environment (craving).

- Train yourself to eat only when you are hungry. You'll get hungry after about three to four hours of not eating. When you're truly hungry, you may feel:

  Emptiness or "grumbling" in your stomach

  A decrease in your energy level

  Tired

- Craving food is different from hunger. Cravings occur even when you're not hungry. Cravings are stimulated by all kinds of things, including these:

  You see food that you like—and you want it!

  Someone offers you food, and even though you're not hungry—you want it!

  You smell food as you pass a restaurant or bakery—and you want it!

  You see food advertised on television or in a magazine—and you want it!

  You eat just before bed simply because you're in the habit of doing it.

  You have a large dessert after a large meal because it's customary.

Eating because you crave something rather than because you are hungry is one of the easiest ways to consume too many calories and put on extra weight. Your job is to learn to distinguish between hunger and craving.

## Pop Quiz: Identifying Hunger Versus Craving

Read the list below and decide which situation is hunger, and which is craving. Check the box below that better describes your feeling.

|  | Hunger | Craving |
|---|:---:|:---:|
| 1. After eating a large meal, you still want dessert. | ❒ | ❒ |
| 2. You feel grumbling in your stomach after hours of not eating. | ❒ | ❒ |
| 3. When someone mentions cake, you feel like eating. | ❒ | ❒ |

4. You feel hungry after not eating for several hours. ☐ ☐

5. When you pass a bakery, you want to eat sweets. ☐ ☐

6. You are always hungry just before bed. ☐ ☐

7. You feel like eating after you see a
   commercial on TV. ☐ ☐

(See page 206 for answer key.)

## "Distractibles"

For some people, it happens in the winter when playing inside gets boring. Others experience it during summer months when they get bored with too much downtime. Boredom often triggers the desire to eat. Here is a list of "distractibles" to refer to during those times to keep your child from eating in response to boredom. Ask your child to add his own suggestions at the bottom of the list. Then, post a copy where he can easily see it.

(Do this instead of eating!)
Go for a walk.
Go sledding.
Walk around while talking to a
   friend on a portable phone.
Go to the park.
Listen to your favorite music.
Read a book or magazine.
Fly a kite.
Make a snowman.
Work on a crossword puzzle.

### The Satiety Mechanism

When your stomach is full, it sends a message to the brain saying that you are full, or satiated. But it takes about twenty minutes to get this message through to the brain. That's one good reason to eat slowly—so your brain can catch up with what's happening in your stomach. So that you won't overeat, learn also to recognize cues, such as eating from cravings or out of habit, or eating while you are doing something such as studying, watching television, or talking on the phone.

Plan your next meal.
List your own ideas:

_____

_____

_____

_____

_____

Answer Key for Pop Quiz: Craving Versus Hunger
1, craving; 2, hunger; 3, craving; 4, hunger; 5, craving; 6, craving; 7, craving

·············· **SECTION 2: TIME TO GET ACTIVE** ··············

# THE FOUR COMPONENTS OF FITNESS

Because your child's body and brain work together during the process of losing weight and becoming healthy, it's important to teach your child about the four components of fitness that define physical well-being. Review the following with your child:

1. *Cardiorespiratory endurance*: This type of workout demands that your large muscles move at moderate or high intensity for long stretches of time. It is also called *aerobic exercise*. Examples include walking, jogging, dancing, and swimming. Aerobic training can strengthen your heart and lungs, improve your stamina, keep your body in good, toned shape, and improve your outlook on life.

2. *Body composition*: Our bodies are made up of many different tissues. Body composition refers to the percentage of your body weight composed of fat, and the percentage composed of lean tissue and bone. Fat is a soft tissue primarily found underneath your skin. The rest of our tissues—muscles and bones—are classified as lean body mass. Exercise burns fat tissue and helps to maintain or improve lean muscle tissue. Your body

composition changes after you begin exercising regularly and engaging in different types of exercise. Your doctor helped you recognize what percentage of body fat you had before you started the Trim Kids Program (page 20). Take another look at the percentage of body fat you had then and compare the number with the chart below to find out whether you were lean, optimal, healthy, overweight, or obese. You'll check again with the doctor in another three months to see how your percentage of body fat classification has changed.

Use the following chart, which works for all ages, to help you determine your body fat percent classification:

| Classification | Male percent fat | Female percent fat |
|---|---|---|
| Lean | <6–8 | <14–16 |
| Optimal | 8–15 | 16–22 |
| Healthy | 16–20 | 23–28 |
| Overweight | 21–25 | 29–35 |
| Obese | >25 | >35 |

Athletes (because they're avid exercisers, they have low fat percent levels):

| | | |
|---|---|---|
| Long-distance runners | 4–9 | 10–15 |
| Wrestlers | 4–10 | 10–17 |
| Gymnasts | 4–10 | 10–17 |
| Bodybuilders (elite) | 6–10 | 10–17 |
| Swimmers | 5–11 | 18–24 |
| Basketball athletes | 7–11 | 18–24 |

| Canoers/kayakers | 11–15 | 18–24 |
| --- | --- | --- |
| Tennis players | 14–17 | 19–22 |

3. *Muscular strength and endurance*: Strength is defined as the maximum force that a muscle or group of muscles can generate. Endurance is the ability of that muscle or group of muscles to repeat contractions over time. Strength training, sometimes called weight lifting, increases both muscular strength and endurance. Strength training can improve blood pressure, body composition, and bones. An added benefit: once a muscle is *trained*, or toned, it will burn calories even when you are not moving! Strength training actually increases your metabolic rate, since it takes 20 to 30 calories per hour to maintain a trained muscle. Fat tissue just hangs around, burning only 3 to 10 calories per hour.

4. *Flexibility*: This is the maximum ability to move a joint through its full range of motion. Flexibility keeps your body in balance. If you neglect flexibility in your training, you may injure your muscles or joints or develop chronic disorders. Stretching will help you improve and maintain flexibility.

As you've probably noticed, the Trim Kids Program incorporates aerobic activity, exercise for muscular strength and endurance, and flexibility exercise for each color-coded level.

## METABOLIC ENGINES: WHAT PROPELS YOUR BODY

Explaining the metabolic system to children is easy when you use engines as a metaphor and music as a motivator. Select three pieces of music with varying tempos: one slow, one medium-fast, and one very fast. After several minutes of playing music with a slower beat, change to a song with a faster beat and then to one with a very fast tempo. Vary the pace of your movement to match the beat of the music and encourage your child to do the same. During this activity discuss and do the following with your child:

- When you exercise, your body depends on three different engines to move. Engine 3 is the slowest engine; it's the best one for getting rid of fat because you can do it for longer periods of time. Engine 2 is faster than Engine 3, and it works well for becoming stronger and more powerful. Engine 1 is the superfast engine and is used by very powerful athletes such as Olympic weight lifters and jumpers.
- Tell your child, "I'm going to put on some music, and we'll dance around to it."
- After several minutes of dancing to one kind of music, change to another, and so on. As the child moves to each tempo, ask the following questions:

  What type of engine are you using now?

  How long do you think you can use this engine?
- If you are using Engine 2, the fast engine, you will be able to keep moving for only up to about five minutes. If it is Engine 1, the superfast engine, you can keep this up for only about ten seconds. But if you are using Engine 3, the slow engine, you can go on for hours because all this engine needs for fuel to make it run is your breathing (oxygen, stored fat, and some of what you've eaten). This is the engine you use when exercising at a moderate intensity.

## AEROBICS AND ANAEROBIC EXERCISES

Explain to your child that when doing aerobic exercises, he should use Engine 3 to burn the most calories. When he kicks into Engine 1 or 2, he's engaging in *anaerobic exercise,* which won't burn as many calories simply because he won't be able to sustain the pace for long enough time periods. Review the following information so he'll grasp the difference between the two types of exercise.

The word *aerobic* means "with oxygen." *Anaerobic* means "without oxygen." When you do aerobic activities, you send oxygen to the muscles. There, the oxygen mixes with glucose, a sugar that your body produces from carbohydrates and fats. Together, they produce fuel so your body can continue to participate in the aerobic activity. The stronger and better-trained your cardiorespiratory system becomes from doing aerobic exercise, the more oxygen is delivered to your exercising muscles, and the more exercise you can do with more ease. The more trained your muscles are, the more they can accept and use that oxygen to make you go.

When you move into Engine 2 or an anaerobic pace, your body uses only the glucose—not oxygen—for fuel. You can do this for only between three and five minutes because when you burn glucose, a substance called lactic acid builds up in your muscles. That's what creates a burning sensation in your muscles and, after a short time, causes your muscles to lose energy. The more intensely you exercise, the sooner muscle fatigue occurs. At that point, you have to slow down so that the oxygen demand is lower and the lactic acid is absorbed, or your body will be *physically* unable to continue.

The point at which your body shifts from aerobic to anaerobic exercise is called the *anaerobic threshold*. When you exercise hard enough to activate the anaerobic metabolism, your muscles will burn, you'll be out of breath, and you'll feel tired all over.

This doesn't mean that anaerobic exercise is bad for you. In fact, to become stronger and more fit, you will have to use your anaerobic system to do quite a few activities. See the chart below to know when you are doing aerobics, and when you kick into anaerobic activity.

## AEROBIC VERSUS ANAEROBIC ACTIVITIES

| Aerobic | Anaerobic |
|---|---|
| Walking | Running, high-speed |
| Jogging | Body toning |
| Cycling | Weight lifting |
| Stair climber | Gymnastic stunts |
| Swimming laps | Interval training |
| Aerobic dance | Power lifting |
| Step aerobics | Sprints |

# RATE THE AEROBIC ACTIVITY*

### Best Calorie Burners

**Swimming**
30 yards/minute = 375 calories/hour
45 yards/minute = 615 calories/hour

**Cross-country skiing**
850–1200 calories/hour

**Low-impact aerobics**
360–480 calories/hour

**Jumping rope**
50–60 skips/minute = 455 calories/hour

**Karate or martial arts**
750 calories/hour

### Second-Best Calorie Burners

**Brisk walking or jogging**
5.5 miles/hour = 550–600 calories/hour

**Handball, squash, racquetball**
600–660 calories/hour

**Cycling**
12 miles/hour = 480–600 calories/hour

**Soccer and long-distance field sports**
525–575 calories/hour

**Roller or ice skating**
360–420 calories/hour

### Third-Best Calorie Burners

**Football, basketball, hockey**
5.5 miles/hour = 585 calories/hour

**Tennis singles**
380–420 calories/hour

**Volleyball**
300–330 calories/hour

**Windsurfing**
280–400 calories/hour

*This chart is based on a person weighing 150 pounds. Your child will burn fewer calories if he is smaller, and more if he is larger.

| Fourth-Best Calorie Burners | |
|---|---|
| **Golf without a cart**<br>240–300 calories/hour | **Softball**<br>300–360 calories/hour |
| **Water skiing**<br>240–300 calories/hour | **Sailing**<br>180–240 calories/hour |
| **Bowling**<br>240–300 calories/hour | |

# KEEPING THE BEST PACE

Working out at the most efficient and safest pace requires that you monitor your breathing, temperature, and heart rate. While exercising, find a pace at which you can talk without difficulty, your breathing is not too labored, and you don't get overheated—meaning very hot, light-headed, and weak.

You can monitor your heart rate during an aerobic activity by determining your own individual *target heart range* (THR) beforehand. Here's how:

1. Subtract your age from 220. 220–_____ = _____
2. To get the low end of your range, multiply your answer by 55 percent. _____ × 0.55 = _____
3. To figure the high end of your range, multiply your answer by 65 percent. _____ × 0.65 = _____
4. Review how to take your heart rate, and the recommended heart rate ranges, on page 152 in week 3.

Aim for the low end of your THR when you first begin exercising, and gradually work up to the higher range. If you have an existing medical condition, work with your doctor to determine the best THR.

# WEEKLY EXERCISE ACTIVITIES

### WEEK 5 AEROBIC ACTIVITY: RECOMMENDED GOALS

Write your goal in the TRIM KIDS AEROBIC ACTIVITY AND FOOD CHECKLIST (page 386). This is the minimum amount of aerobic exercise that you should perform this week. Every day, record what type of physical activity you did and how long you did it. At the end of the week, compare your list with the goals you set at the beginning of the week.

- Red Level: The exercise goal this week is three days per week for twenty-five to thirty minutes each day.
- Yellow Level: The exercise goal this week is three days per week for twenty-five to thirty-five minutes each day.
- Green Level: The exercise goal this week is four days per week for twenty-five to forty-five minutes each day.
- Blue Level: The exercise goal this week is three days per week for thirty to sixty minutes each day.

### WEEK 5 AEROBIC ACTIVITY: ROCKIN' TO THE OLDIES AEROBICS

Put on your favorite old rock 'n' roll music and teach your child the twist, the mashed potato, the hustle, the monkey, the skate, the pony, and the jitterbug.

### WEEK 5 STRENGTH AND FLEX EXERCISES

Read the instructions aloud to your child as he does these exercises, until he no longer needs your assistance.

## Strength Exercise 5: Sitting Bicep Curl

Sit upright and clench your fists (beginning in week 6 you'll hold hand weights) with your arms extended toward the ground, wrists facing outward. Your elbows should be at the sides of your ribs.

Slowly bend your elbows, bringing your fists (the weights) up to your chest as

you count to four. Good. Now slowly return to the starting position over a count of four, making sure to extend your arms completely.

Do eight to twelve repetitions of this exercise. Be sure to lift for four seconds and lower for four seconds. This exercise strengthens the front upper arm muscles (biceps).

Common errors your child may make include moving the upper arm, or gripping the weight too tightly.

## Flex Exercise 5: Lying Quad Stretch

Lie on the floor on your right side. Support your head with your right hand. Bend both your knees, but bend your left leg back further and grab the left ankle with your left hand.

Pull your left heel into the back of your left hip as you move your knee back. Hold this stretch for fifteen to thirty seconds.

Feels good? Great. Gently release your ankle. Now repeat this move while lying on your left side, holding your right ankle.

Repeat this process for each leg one more time, holding this position again for fifteen to thirty seconds.

Perform these new strength and flex exercises and also the ones you learned previously in weeks 1–4 at least once, but preferably twice this

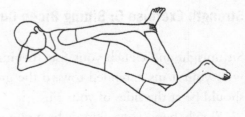

week. Record your progress on the TRIM KIDS STRENGTH AND FLEXIBILITY WORK-OUT CHART in the appendix ("Forms You'll Need"), on page 388. Every week, you will add another exercise to your program.

Don't forget to fill out your TRIM KIDS AEROBIC ACTIVITY AND FOOD CHECKLIST on page 386, and try the aerobic activity of the week with the entire family.

## SECTION 3: TIME TO DINE

*For the Trim Kids Weight Loss Plan to succeed, it is crucial that your child learn how much she should be eating (portion control) by keeping track of her daily food units. Be sure that she is filling in the TRIM KIDS AEROBIC ACTIVITY AND FOOD CHECKLIST every day. Review the Food Portion and Unit List for "Week 2" (page 386) if you have any questions. Or learn by example: there's a Portion Control Practice Exercise at the end of every week.*

# NUTRITION NUTSHELL: HEALTHY BREAKFASTS

Many overweight kids don't eat a healthy breakfast—or any breakfast at all. That's all changing now that you're buying healthy foods and all the right choices are within arm's reach.

Be sure your child's breakfast contains a complex carbohydrate (such as whole-grain bread or cereal) and protein (low-fat dairy, egg substitute, or peanut butter). Compare old breakfast ideas with new ones, and see how delicious a healthy breakfast can be!

Remember, if you're not waking up hungry, you're probably eating too much and too late at night!

# Week 5 Weekly Menu

*Recipes are given for items in boldface.*

|  | Breakfast | Lunch | Dinner | Snacks (1 to 2 choices per day) |
|---|---|---|---|---|
| MONDAY | Whole-grain waffle (1) with low-sugar syrup<br><br>Fruit yogurt (4 ounces) with added sliced fruit (berries or a banana)<br><br>Orange juice—calcium-fortified (½ cup) | Cheese sandwich made with reduced-fat cheese and wheat bread (½ sandwich)<br><br>Chicken noodle soup (1 cup)<br><br>Grapes (½ cup)<br><br>Milk (½ to 1 cup) | **Turkey Burger** with bun (preferably whole wheat)<br><br>**Broccoli Salad**<br><br>Water or calorie-free beverage | Cereal containing fiber (1 cup) and skim or soy milk<br><br>Cereal-fruit bar (1)<br><br>Reduced-fat chips (about 15 chips or 1 ounce) with fat-free dip or salsa<br><br>Wheat crackers (6) with:<br><br>Reduced-fat cheese (2 slices)<br><br>Lite cream cheese (2 tablespoons)<br><br>Peanut butter (1 tablespoon)<br><br>Hot cocoa made with skim milk (1 cup)<br><br>English muffin or bagel "pizza" (½ muffin with tomato or pizza sauce and reduced-fat cheese)<br><br>Fruit (1 piece fresh, ½ cup canned, or 3 tablespoons dried)<br><br>Frozen fruit bar (1) |
| TUESDAY | Sandwich: egg fried in nonstick cooking spray, on bagel or wheat toast with reduced-fat cheese if desired<br><br>Berries (1 cup)<br><br>Milk (1 cup) | Fast-food lunch: Thin-crust pizza (1 to 2 medium slices)<br><br>Tossed salad with 1–2 teaspoons olive oil or reduced-fat dressing<br><br>Water or calorie-free beverage | BBQ (oven-baked or grilled) skinless chicken breast or 2 skinless legs<br><br>Baked beans (½ cup)<br><br>Coleslaw (limit to ½ cup if not made with fat-free mayonnaise)<br><br>Tossed salad as desired<br><br>Fruit cup (½ cup)<br><br>Water or sugar-free beverage | |

|  | **Breakfast** | **Lunch** | **Dinner** | **Snacks** (1 to 2 choices per day) |
|---|---|---|---|---|
| WEDNESDAY | Yogurt shake made with 1 cup yogurt, frozen strawberries (½ to 1 cup), banana, and ice blended together (add some skim or soy milk if you like a thinner shake) | ½ bagel with peanut butter (1 tablespoon)<br>Popcorn (3 cups, about a small "sandwich" bag-full)<br>Raisins (small box— about 3 tablespoons)<br>Milk (½ to 1 cup) | Sandwich: grilled tuna salad (made with fat-free mayonnaise) with reduced-fat melted cheese (cook with nonstick cooking spray)<br>Carrot or celery sticks with fat-free dip<br>Popcorn (3–5 cups)<br>Milk (½ to 1 cup) | Fruit juice "spritzer": 3 ounces fruit juice mixed with 5 ounces club soda or sparkling water<br>Graham crackers (3 squares)<br>Teddy grahams (½ cup)<br>Nuts (2 tablespoons)<br>Oatmeal (½ cup) |
| THURSDAY | Cold cereal with fiber (1 cup)<br>Wheat toast (1 slice) with reduced-sugar jelly (1 teaspoon) and lite margarine (1 teaspoon)<br>Banana (1) or strawberries (1 cup)<br>Milk (1 cup) | Sliced (leftover) BBQ chicken wrapped in a tortilla or ½ pita bread with extra BBQ sauce or reduced-fat ranch dressing and reduced-fat cheese and preferred vegetables (optional)<br>Fresh fruit in season<br>Milk (½ to 1 cup) | **Sweet-and-Sour Pork Chops**<br>Brown rice (½ cup)<br>Steamed or cooked vegetable of choice<br>Tossed salad with reduced-fat dressing<br>Milk (½ to 1 cup) | Oatmeal cookies (2 small)<br>Air-popped popcorn (3 to 5 cups)<br>Reduced-fat pudding or ice cream (½ cup)<br>Quesadilla (1 tortilla) with melted, reduced-fat cheese, salsa, and fat-free sour cream<br>Rice cakes (10 small or 2 large) |
| FRIDAY | Cheese toast made with melted reduced-fat cheese (1 or 2 pieces)<br>Turkey bacon (2) or "veggie" sausage links (2), optional | Turkey or ham sandwich— preferably whole wheat<br>Rice cakes—any flavor (8 to 10 small) | Restaurant meal, American:<br>Grilled chicken breast<br>Double vegetable of the day (substitute |  |

| | Breakfast | Lunch | Dinner | Snacks (1 to 2 choices per day) |
|---|---|---|---|---|
| FRIDAY (cont.) | Sliced tomato<br><br>Orange juice—calcium-fortified (½ cup) | Milk (1 cup) | an extra vegetable for the potato)<br><br>Fruit cup—½ cup<br><br>Water or calorie-free beverage | Sandwich on wheat bread (½) with turkey or tuna with fat-free mayonnaise or reduced-fat cheese |
| SATURDAY | Whole-grain waffle (1) topped with 2 tablespoons nuts, cut banana, 2 tablespoons lite whipped topping, and low-sugar syrup<br><br>"Veggie" breakfast sausage (2), optional<br><br>Milk (1 cup) | Grilled cheese sandwich, preferably on whole wheat with reduced-fat cheese<br><br>Sliced cucumber with fat-free mayo or dip<br><br>Apple (1) or grapes (½ cup)<br><br>Water or calorie-free beverage | Turkey chili, made with ground turkey and your favorite turkey seasoning packet (1 cup)<br><br>Corn on the cob or cooked corn (½ cup)<br><br>Tossed salad with 1 to 2 teaspoons olive oil or reduced-fat dressing<br><br>Water or calorie-free beverage | Soup: vegetable or chicken noodle (2 cups)<br><br>Trail mix (4 tablespoons)<br><br>Yogurt, regular or frozen (4 to 6 ounces) |
| SUNDAY | Breakfast "soft taco": Wrap 1 heated tortilla sprayed with nonfat liquid butter substitute over—Scrambled egg substitute with reduced-fat cheese (if desired)<br><br>Turkey bacon (3 slices) | Baked or grilled fish (your favorite kind) with lemon juice, garlic (if desired), and nonfat liquid butter substitute<br><br>Brown rice (½ cup)<br><br>**Zucchini Parmesan**<br>Tossed salad as desired<br><br>Milk (½ to 1 cup) | **Leftover Night**<br>Food Units<br><br>1 to 2 starch-bread<br><br>Lean or low-fat protein<br><br>0 to 1 fruit<br><br>1 milk-dairy<br><br>1 fat<br><br>Veggies—unlimited! | |

| | Breakfast | Lunch | Dinner | Snacks (1 to 2 choices per day) |
|---|---|---|---|---|
| SUNDAY (cont.) | Salsa or sliced tomato<br>Orange juice—calcium-fortified (½ cup) | | | |

# Week 5 Recipes

## GRILLED TURKEY BURGERS

1 pound ground turkey
½ cup cornflake crumbs (optional)
1 teaspoon Worcestershire sauce
¼ cup barbecue sauce
1 tablespoon grated Parmesan cheese
¼ teaspoon ground pepper
Hamburger buns

Combine the ingredients except the buns and form into patties. Grill on medium to high heat for about 10 minutes on each side or until cooked through.

Makes about four 4-ounce patties.

Variation: Make the burgers with 1 pound ground turkey, 1 package powdered ranch salad dressing mix, and 2 tablespoons water.

Nutritional Analysis
1 turkey burger (cooked): 3 protein units (135 calories). The hamburger bun will add 2 carbohydrate units.

## BROCCOLI SALAD

1 cup fat-free mayonnaise
4 tablespoons milk
¼ cup red wine vinegar
¼ cup sugar
2 bunches broccoli, cut into small pieces
6 to 8 strips turkey bacon, crisply fried, well drained, and cut into bite-size pieces
1 medium onion, finely chopped
½ cup raisins (optional)

Mix the mayonnaise, milk, vinegar, and sugar in a bowl. Add the remaining ingredients and toss well. Serve chilled (refrigerate overnight if possible).

Makes 6 to 7 cups.

Nutritional Analysis
Vegetable Group: No limit (½ cup = 35 calories, 1–2 grams fat)

........................................................................................................................

## SWEET-AND-SOUR PORK CHOPS

2 teaspoons olive or peanut oil plus any kind of nonstick cooking spray
4 to 5 rib or loin pork chops, fat trimmed
¼ teaspoon salt or salt substitute (optional)
One 8-ounce can pineapple chunks, with juice
¼ cup chicken broth or water
2 green peppers, cut into strips
3 tablespoons dark brown sugar or low-sugar pancake syrup
3 tablespoons white vinegar
1 tablespoon cornstarch
1 tablespoon reduced-sodium soy sauce
⅛ teaspoon red pepper flakes

Spray the bottom of a skillet, add the oil, and fry the pork chops about 10 minutes on each side or until lightly browned. Remove the chops and keep warm. Put the remaining ingredients in the skillet and boil gently until the sauce thickens. Add the pork chops and simmer, covered, for an additional 5 minutes.

Nutritional Analysis

1 pork chop with sauce: 3–4 protein units, ½ carbohydrate unit (235 calories, 12 grams fat)

........................................................................................................................................

## ZUCCHINI PARMESAN

Olive oil–flavored nonfat spray
4 to 6 zucchini, thinly sliced in rounds
1 cup grated Parmesan cheese
2 teaspoons olive oil
1 teaspoon minced garlic, or more to taste, or ½ teaspoon garlic powder
1 teaspoon dried oregano, or more to taste
Salt or salt substitute and pepper to taste
2 fresh tomatoes, thinly sliced (optional)

Makes 4 to 5 cups.

Preheat the oven to 375°F. Spray the bottom of a baking dish with the olive oil–flavored spray. Line the dish with the zucchini slices, sprinkle with some Parmesan, the oil, garlic, oregano, and salt and pepper. Top with tomatoes, if desired, and sprinkle with the cheese and seasonings again. Repeat the layering and seasoning. Top with extra Parmesan. Bake, uncovered, for about 30 minutes, depending on how crispy you like your vegetables.

Nutritional Analysis
Vegetable Group: No limit (½ cup = 30 calories, 0 grams fat)

# Week 5 Weekly Shopping List

| Fruits | Vegetables | Meat, Deli | Dried, Canned |
|---|---|---|---|
| Banana | Broccoli (2 bunches) | Chicken pieces (for the BBQ chicken) | Breakfast cereal (fiber content should be more than 2–3 grams per serving) |
| Grapes | Carrots, celery | Fish fillets—your favorite kind (fresh or frozen) | Brown rice |
| Miscellaneous fruits for snacks | Corn on the cob (or frozen or canned corn) | Pork chops (rib or loin) | Baked beans |
| | Green peppers (2 or 3) | Ground turkey (buy a "family pack"—enough for 2 meals) | Tomato sauce (for the chili) |
| | Salad greens:<br>    Lettuce<br>    Tomato<br>    Cucumbers, etc. | Turkey bacon | Canned beans (for the chili) |
| | Zucchini squash | Turkey or ham cold-cuts | Chili seasoning packet |
| | Miscellaneous vegetables for snacks | Coleslaw (deli) | BBQ sauce (your favorite brand) |
| | | | Red wine vinegar |
| | | | Soy sauce—reduced-sodium |
| | | | Vinegar—regular |
| | | | Cornstarch |
| | | | Chicken broth (or bouillon cubes) |
| | | | Salsa |
| | | | Tuna (water-packed) |
| | | | Pineapple chunks |
| | | | Fruit cup or fruit cocktail |
| | | | Raisins |
| | | | Graham crackers |

| Dairy Case | Frozen Food Section | Breads, Miscellaneous |
|---|---|---|
| Milk (skim, 1½% or soy milk) | Waffles | Whole-wheat bread |
| Egg substitute, eggs | Frozen strawberries | Bagels |
| Reduced-fat or part-skim cheese slices (less than 5 grams of fat per ounce or slice) | "Veggie" vegetable protein sausage links | Hamburger buns |
| | | Tortillas |
| Fruit yogurt | | Reduced-fat popcorn |
| Orange or fruit juice—calcium-fortified | | Rice cakes (any flavor) |
| Parmesan cheese | | |

**Staples**

Reduced-fat or very low-fat mayonnaise (less than 3 grams fat per serving)

Reduced-fat or very low-fat salad dressings (less than 3 to 5 grams fat per serving)

Catsup, mustard, pickles, BBQ sauce (regular versions OK)

Low-sugar syrup, low-sugar or all-fruit jelly

Peanut butter (no added hydrogenated or partially hydrogenated vegetable oils)

Nuts

Oil (olive, canola, peanut), nonfat cooking spray, nonfat liquid butter (dairy section)

Lite margarine (first ingredient should be *liquid* vegetable oil, not hydrogenated or partially hydrogenated oil)

# WEEK 5 PORTION CONTROL AND FOOD RECORD PRACTICE

Use the TRIM KIDS AEROBIC ACTIVITY AND FOOD CHECKLIST (page 386) to help keep track of your daily intake. Let's practice portion-control checks for one day:

## Thursday:

*Breakfast:*

| | |
|---|---|
| Cold cereal (1 cup) | 1 carbohydrate |
| Wheat toast (1 slice) | 1 carbohydrate |
| with low-sugar jelly | Free |
| with 1 teaspoon lite margarine | 1 fat |
| Milk (1 cup) | 1 carbohydrate |
| 1 banana or 1 cup strawberries | 1 carbohydrate |

*Lunch:*

| | |
|---|---|
| BBQ chicken breast | 2–3 proteins |
| with extra BBQ sauce | Free |
| Tortilla | 1 carbohydrate |
| Fresh fruit | 1 carbohydrate |
| Milk (½–1 cup) | ½–1 carbohydrate |

*Dinner:*

| | |
|---|---|
| Sweet-and-sour pork chop (1) with sauce | 3–4 proteins, ½ carbohydrate |
| Brown rice (½ cup) | 1 carbohydrate |
| Cooked vegetable of choice | Vegetables, as desired |
| Salad | Vegetables, as desired + 1–2 fats (if olive oil or reduced-fat dressing is used) |
| Milk (½ to 1 cup) | ½–1 carbohydrate |

*Sample Snacks:*

| | |
|---|---|
| Fruit yogurt (½ cup) | 1 carbohydrate |
| Graham crackers (3 squares) | 1 carbohydrate |
| Nuts (2 tablespoons) | 1–2 fats, some protein |

| | |
|---|---|
| Total food units for Thursday: | 10½ carbohydrates |
| | 6–7 proteins |
| | 4–6 fats |
| | Vegetables |

## SECTION 4: TIME TO SUM UP

## Trim Kids Weekly Checklist

*Did you remember to:*       *Yes*    *No*    *Will do it by*

Fill out TRIM KIDS WEEKLY REPORT AND GOAL SHEET?

——   ——   —————

Fill out TRIM KIDS AEROBIC ACTIVITY AND FOOD CHECKLIST?

——   ——   —————

Fill out TRIM KIDS STRENGTH AND FLEXIBILITY WORKOUT CHART?

——   ——   —————

Review social learning theories?   ——   ——   —————

Review ABCs of the behavior chain?   ——   ——   —————

Distinguish between hunger and cravings?

——   ——   —————

Make a list of distractibles?   ——   ——   —————

Review four components of fitness, and metabolic engines?

——   ——   —————

Figure out your child's target heart rate?   ——   ——   —————

Perform the aerobic activity of the week?

——   ——   —————

Perform the strength and flex exercises of the week?

——   ——   —————

The social learning theories you learned this week illustrate that your child's mind and body work together. That's why it's important for your child to have an upbeat attitude and a positive perception of herself. In week 6, we'll show how your child can maintain good self-esteem, which can greatly improve her chances for long-term healthy living.

# Week 6

# ESTEEM BUILDERS

......................................................................................

## TRIM KIDS ROAD MAP FOR WEEK 6

*This week, after filling out the Trim Kids Forms in the appendix (remember to weigh your child and list your goals for the week), you and your child will do some written and verbal exercises that help your child improve how she feels about herself. You will fill out the Self-Image Assessment chart. There are also guidelines for safe strength training, and tips on reading food labels.*

## SECTION 1: TIME TO STOP AND THINK

## SELF-TALK: TURNING NEGATIVE INTO POSITIVE

Henry Ford knew a lot about cars. He also knew something about human nature. One of the things he's famous for saying is "Whether you think you can or think you can't, you'll be right."

It's easy to translate that into Trim Kids terms: If your child believes he will be able to stay on the program and lose weight, he will most likely succeed. If he believes he won't be able to, then he will most likely not succeed.

One of the behavioral changes we ask of you and your kids is to reinvent how you talk to yourself. Review the following scenarios with your child, and discuss ways in which he can speak to himself in a positive, upbeat fashion that will reinforce his goals.

- When something unpleasant happens to you, stop and notice how you respond. Do you think something positive about yourself, or something negative? Telling yourself negative things can make you believe that you are incapable and unpopular. On the other hand, talking positively to yourself can make you feel that you can do anything, and that people like you. Review the following negative feelings and beliefs, and see if any of them apply to you.

| If you think that . . . | You will come to believe that . . . |
| --- | --- |
| You have an unpleasant appearance. | "No one likes me, because I'm fat." |
| You need to avoid classmates. | "No one wants to be with me." |
| You can't compete with other children. | "I can't play ball because I'm not fast enough." |
| You are unable to do things well. | "I can't succeed at anything." |
| You cannot handle stressful situations. | "I can't deal with life's hardships." |

Turning negative self-talk into positive self-talk takes practice. But it's very important to learn this skill, since it will influence how well you do in just about everything.

- What you say to yourself *conditions* or trains you to believe things about yourself. Those thoughts contribute to how you behave.

    After he began the Trim Kids Program, Billy started refusing high-calorie snacks offered by friends. On his way to school one day, he met a friend who offered him some chocolate candy. Billy told himself that he likes chocolate candy and that he couldn't say no. "I don't think she'll understand that I'm ashamed to be fat and that I'm trying to lose weight. OK, so I'll take just one piece."

But Billy didn't feel good about himself for taking the candy, so the negative self-talk continued. "Now I've broken my diet. I knew I couldn't do it. I might as well eat some more candy. I'm no good at anything."

One way to prevent yourself from falling into the habit of saying negative things to yourself is to anticipate the temptations you might encounter. Then, tell yourself what you *want* to do and say when temptations occur. Take time now to prepare positive responses to difficult situations like the one Billy was in. What could you say if you were offered chocolate candy on the way to school? Look at the comments below. Did you come up with any of them on your own?

- "No, thanks. I've already had breakfast."
- "I'm not hungry now. Besides, I'll eat my sandwich at lunch."
- "I love chocolate, but it's full of calories. I think I'll pass."

After refusing a temptation that has lots of calories, it's always good to say something positive to yourself.

- I'm proud of myself; it was hard to say no.
- I'm strong enough to say no.
- I like the idea of losing weight more than I like chocolate.
- I feel great about myself.
- This diet is making me feel better about my body and myself.

Thinking positive thoughts builds your self-esteem and helps you develop a strong self-image. Gaining confidence

### TRIM KIDS TESTIMONIAL

## A Parent's Perspective

"When Tim started the program, he did really great, but in no time we were back to where we started—eating fast food almost every night and totally vegging out on weekends. Then one day we had a long family talk and decided to recommit to a healthier lifestyle. It was easier to get back on track than we thought. We were most aware of our strengths and weaknesses as individuals and as a family. We just picked up where we left off, and we've been losing—or, rather, *winning*—ever since."

is one of the benefits of the Trim Kids Program, and believing in yourself contributes to a healthier lifestyle.

## IMPROVING SELF-IMAGE

Have your child fill out the self-assessment below to recognize negative thoughts he may have, and learn how to replace them with positive ones.

## Self-Image Assessment

Do you believe that you do not look attractive?                    Yes         No

Make a list of your positive physical characteristics. Work with your parents to develop your list.

_____

_____

_____

_____

Do you believe that you have fewer favorable                    Yes         No
qualities and abilities than other kids?

List your favorable qualities and abilities. Work with your parents to develop your list.

_____

_____

_____

_____

_____

Do you believe that you don't have any interests?          Yes          No

Make a list of your hobbies and interests.

_____

_____

_____

_____

Do you fear being rejected or avoided by classmates?          Yes          No

Make a list of your friends:

_____

_____

_____

_____

_____

What have been the positive reactions of your friends and of adults since you started the Trim Kids Program?

_____

_____

_____

_____

_____

## HOMEWORK FOR PARENTS

- Help your child recognize positive aspects of his appearance, qualities, abilities, interests, and social relationships.
- Make a diligent effort to point out these attributes to your child.
- Try to stimulate the interests, qualities, and social relationships of your child and of other family members.

## ESTEEM BOOSTERS

It may take time for your child to grasp the concept of becoming his own best friend. But it's a powerful concept, and one that will help him stay true to his new weight-loss goals. Take time to explain what it means to esteem oneself. Point out that patting yourself on the back when you do well, or giving yourself a break by accepting that you're not perfect when things don't go well, is another way to live a healthier life—just as important as choosing healthy foods.

Make a copy of the following esteem boosters so your child can read them on a regular basis and practice feeling better about himself.

### Trim Kids Self-Esteem Boosters
- I can do anything if I want to do it badly enough.
- I do anything when I want to badly enough.
- Yes, I can stay on my eating and activity plan.

- Yes, I do stay on my eating and activity plan.
- I look great since I lost all this weight.
- I look and feel so much better.
- One slip is *not* the end of the world.
- I slipped, but I will make up for it by _____ (riding my bike, taking a long walk, not eating dessert at my next meal).
- I can resist tempting situations during _____ (school parties, holidays, spending the night at a friend's house).
- I resist tempting situations all the time.
- I like being active.
- I am much more active and physically fit.
- My parents, my friends, and other people who know I'm on the Trim Kids Program are proud of my success.
- I am proud of my accomplishments in the program.
- I look great.
- I feel great.
- I am great!

## SECTION 2: TIME TO GET ACTIVE

## STRENGTH TRAINING

Running around the yard and burning calories aerobically is an important component of your child's fitness program—but not the only one. It's now time to focus on strength training. Remember: the exercises we've developed are made just for your child, and he should be able to accomplish them without much difficulty. To help gear him up, review the points on strength training in this chapter, then elaborate:

If you exercise muscles with some kind of weight (either a hand weight or your own body weight) at least twice a week, they become and stay *toned* or *trained*. Working with weights forces resistance against the muscle, which trains and strengthens the muscle. Trained muscles are metabolically active and actually burn more calories than they burned before they were trained. Muscles that have been exercised over a period of weeks or months burn about 20 to 30 calories an hour even when you are not moving! As we noted in week 5, fat just hangs around, burning only 3 to 10 calories per hour.

## INTRODUCING . . . RESISTANCE WEIGHT TRAINING!

Resistance weight training has a lot of different names and forms (weight training, strength training, circuit weight training, isometrics, and isokinetics). Generally it means that you exercise your muscles against moderate to heavy loads, with few repetitions. Depending on what you do, this is the method for building muscle size, increasing lean body mass, and increasing your strength and power.

## EQUIPMENT YOU'LL NEED

Your child will begin using a 1-pound weight in each hand, and a 2.5-pound weight around each ankle. Your child will use this amount of weight until he can do 12 reps in perfect form. These weights are inexpensive and can be purchased at most department stores.

You will also need a resistance or "stretchy" band. (Fitness Wholesale, Inc., in Stow, Ohio, makes the Dynaband™, but other brands are also readily available. Visit your local department store or athletic equipment store.)

Researchers find a significant improvement in body composition and strength performance in people—even kids—who engage in this type of exercise. Here are some guidelines for planning your resistance weight-training program:

- Allow enough time to adequately warm up and cool down before and after strength training.

### A Few of the Many Benefits Your Child Will Get from Weight Training

- Improves strength and endurance
- Helps prevent disease
- Decreases blood pressure
- Increases lean muscle
- Prevents musculoskeletal disorders (especially back problems)
- Improves self-image

## Guidelines for Strength Training:

- Begin the program using weight at about 60 percent of what you can lift in one try (this is called your 1 rep max).
- Lift the same amount of weight at each workout until you can perform twelve repetitions in perfect form with little effort.
- When you are able to do a strength exercise perfectly twelve times, increase the weight by 1 to 2 pounds.
- Use a two- to four-second count to lift and lower the weight.
- Begin doing strength exercises once per week, gradually working up to twice per week. Never do strength exercises more than three times per week. ALWAYS REST AT LEAST ONE DAY BETWEEN STRENGTH WORKOUTS.
- Rest one to two minutes after each set of eight to twelve repetitions.*
- Follow the instructions and the diagrams in this book to ensure a safe and effective workout.
- Isolate and focus on the muscles you are working by keeping all the other parts of the body stationary and relaxed (abdominals should always be pulled in, also glutes for standing exercises).
- Fully extend and contract the muscles without locking the joints when you are performing each strength exercise.
- Grip the weight handles lightly to prevent an increase in blood pressure.
- Breathe normally throughout the exercises.

*One set of each strength exercise is recommended for children under age fourteen. One or two sets are recommended for older children.

- Start with your large-muscle groups, preferably your leg muscles.
- Next, work your upper-body muscles in unison.
- Now exercise another large-muscle group such as abdominals or oblique (waistline) muscles. Abdominals are typically performed near the end of the routine.
- Finally, exercise the calf muscles.
- If you feel pain during any of the strengthening exercises, stop immediately. The pain may indicate an existing injury, a structural problem, or an improper technique.
- Be sure to monitor your results. Use the TRIM KIDS STRENGTH AND FLEXIBILITY WORKOUT CHART (page 388) to track how much weight you lift, how many times you lift it, and how often you do your exercise. This

is the only way to determine if the duration and intensity of each exercise are right for you.

- Genetic factors come into play, and they will affect your results. Respect your own limitations and avoid comparing yourself with others.

## DEVELOPING HEALTHY MUSCLES

Review the following information with your child so he knows what to expect from his strength training exercises.

When you first begin strength training, your body will experience a *learning effect* due to adaptations that your nervous system undergoes as a result of the training. At this stage, your brain is actually doing most of the work, since it must learn to communicate with your muscles more effectively. As your muscles learn new movements and you become stronger, your brain, essentially, has to record it all. During these initial stages of training, you'll notice substantial strength gains from your workout. But those gains will level out, or reach a *plateau*, once your body is accustomed to the training, and you will have to use different methods to develop more muscles.

The key to greater muscle development when you reach a plateau is to:

- Change your training exercises
- Change your training frequency
- Change the relationship between resistance and repetitions

Increase either your training intensity or the amount of weight you are lifting. Make sure you can do the exercise in perfect form for at least twelve repetitions before you increase the weight. Increase by one to two pounds at a time.

If you remain on a plateau even after taking these steps, make sure you're getting enough sleep (between nine and eleven hours per night), drinking enough water (muscles are 75 percent water), and eating a nutritious, well-balanced diet.

Keep in mind that your muscles get stronger after your workout, during the rebuilding period. This is when proteins are resynthesized and connective tissue is rebuilt. You may need to rest more between workout days.

Your goal is to exercise the greatest number of muscle fibers per movement, and to exercise those fibers in different movement patterns.

Always breathe normally throughout your strength training.

By explaining what happens when muscles are worked, parents can help improve children's self-concept and their belief in their ability to perform exercises. By using a technique called *physiologic feedback*, you demonstrate how the muscles move the limbs while the child feels, sees, and hears what you're doing. Simply tell your child to make a muscle in his arm. He will probably bend his elbow and try to get his upper arm muscle (biceps) to bulge. Show him how the muscle changes from long (when the arm is straight) to short (when it is bent) to move the lower arm up and down. Ask him to place the hand of

> ## Muscle Fibers
>
> Strength training ultimately changes the muscle fibers:
>
> 1. The muscle fibers lengthen and widen, and more fibers may be produced.
> 2. The muscle undergoes increased *vascularization*, or blood flow and capillary development.
> 3. Fluid retention or *edema* can occur in the muscle area (this usually happens during protein rebuilding). This is normal and temporary.
>
> These changes may increase muscle size (hypertrophy). They result in muscles that are more metabolically active and therefore denser and more toned.

the other arm on the muscle, so he can feel the muscle shortening as the elbow bends. This technique will help your child remember the concept of muscle "contracting."

By the end of this twelve-week program, your child will have learned a total of twelve strength exercises. The combination of these exercises will provide your child with a well-balanced workout that targets all the major muscle groups. It is extremely important that your child perform all of the exercises each week, to avoid developing strength imbalances that can lead to injury. Spot training is strictly prohibited. One of the biggest predictors of back pain later in life is unbalanced workouts attempted early in childhood or adolescence. It is especially common to see adolescent boys performing strength exercises—typically the bench press—only for the chest, because they equate strength with how much they can "press." If the chest is all that's trained, however, the back will become more vulnerable, especially later in life. Also, refer to the list in Chapter 5 of activities and classes that promote strength gains—like martial arts, gymnastics, and monkey bars—especially for younger children.

# WEEKLY EXERCISE ACTIVITIES

### WEEK 6 AEROBIC ACTIVITY: RECOMMENDED GOALS

Write your goal in the TRIM KIDS AEROBIC ACTIVITY AND FOOD CHECKLIST (page 386). This is the minimum amount of aerobic exercise that you should perform this week. Every day, record what type of physical activity you did and how long you did it. At the end of the week, compare your list with the goals you set at the beginning of the week.

- Red Level: The exercise goal this week is three days per week for twenty-five to thirty minutes each day.
- Yellow Level: The exercise goal this week is three days per week for twenty-five to thirty-five minutes each day.
- Green Level: The exercise goal this week is four days per week for twenty-five to forty-five minutes each day.
- Blue Level: The exercise goal this week is three days per week for thirty to sixty minutes each day.

### WEEK 6 AEROBIC ACTIVITY: THE AEROBIC EXERCISE GRAB BAG

Write down different aerobic activities on small pieces of paper. Fold them up and put them in a bag, box, hat, or jar. Every day, pick an activity out of your grab bag, and do it nonstop for the appointed time listed for your level (above).

### WEEK 6 STRENGTH AND FLEX EXERCISES

Read the instructions aloud to your child as he does these exercises, until he no longer needs your assistance.

## Strength Exercise 6: Triceps Extension

Lie on the floor with your knees bent and your stomach muscles tight. Holding your hand weights, extend your arms straight above your body. Keep your thumbs turned back. Good.

Keeping your upper arms still, on a count of four, slowly bend your elbows and

 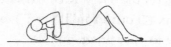

bring your hands down toward your head. Keep those upper arms still, and slowly extend your arms on a count of four until they are, once again, straight above your body. Looks good!

Do eight to twelve repetitions of this move. Be sure to lower for four seconds and lift for four seconds. This exercise trains and tones the rear upper arm muscles (triceps).

Common errors your child may make include moving the upper arm and failing to fully extend (straighten but not lock) the elbow.

## Flex Exercise 6: Seated Hamstring Stretch

Sit on the floor with both of your legs extended and your tummy held tight. Relax your head, neck, and shoulders. Great.

Now slightly bend the knee of your right leg out to the side until your right heel rests between the ankle and knee of your left leg. Make sure your left knee and left foot are pointed toward the ceiling. Nice job.

Now place both of your hands on your left knee. Keeping your upper body straight and your head up, bend forward from the hip as you slide your hands down your left leg. Hold this stretch for fifteen to thirty seconds. Good job. Now let's repeat this move with the right leg straight and the left leg bent.

Repeat this process one more time for each leg, holding this position again for fifteen to thirty seconds.

Perform these new strength and flex exercises and also the ones you learned

previously in weeks 1–5 at least once this week, and preferably twice. Record your progress on the TRIM KIDS STRENGTH AND FLEXIBILITY WORKOUT CHART in the appendix ("Forms You'll Need"), on page 388. Every week, you will add another exercise to your program.

Don't forget to fill out your TRIM KIDS AEROBIC ACTIVITY AND FOOD CHECKLIST on page 386, and try the aerobic activity of the week with the entire family.

······················································
## SECTION 3: TIME TO DINE
······················································

*For the Trim Kids Weight Loss Plan to succeed, it is crucial that your child learns how much she should be eating (portion control) by keeping track of her daily food units. Be sure that she is filling in the* TRIM KIDS AEROBIC ACTIVITY AND FOOD CHECKLIST *every day. Review the Food Portion and Unit Lists for Week 2 (page 119) if you have any questions. Or learn by example: there's a Portion Control Practice Exercise at the end of every week.*

## NUTRITION NUTSHELL: UNDERSTANDING FOOD LABELS

The new food label offers a lot of helpful information to assist you with your nutrition plan. Let's look at the food label for some tips:

### About the Food Label

**Serving size:** The serving size is the portion on which the nutrition facts and values are based.

**Servings per container:** The number of servings or portions per container. For example, if the serving size is 1 cup and there are 3 servings per container, the container holds 3 cups.

**Calories:** The amount of calories in *one serving.*

**% Daily Value:** This represents how much of the nutrient one serving of the product contains in relation to the average daily requirements. The "average" is based on a 2,000-calorie-per-day diet. Recommendations for a 2,000-calorie-per-day diet are:

| Total fat: | 65 grams |
| --- | --- |
| Saturated fat: | 18 grams |
| Cholesterol: | 300 milligrams |
| Total carbohydrate: | 270 grams |
| Dietary fiber: | 20 grams |
| Protein: | 46 grams |
| Sodium: | 2,400 milligrams |

The daily values can be a quick guide to determine if a particular product contains more or less of a given nutrient above. Because the caloric and nutritional needs of each individual vary, however, focus on the specific gram values rather than on the percentages, and relate them to your own dietary goals.

**Total fat:** The amount of fat in *one serving*. Here is a simple rule that even kids can follow: if total fat grams exceed 5 grams, especially for smaller portions, the product is probably a higher-fat food.

**Saturated fat:** The amount of saturated fat in *one serving*. Keep in mind that the total daily saturated fat intake for an *average* child should be about 20 grams.

**Cholesterol:** The amount of cholesterol in *one serving*.

**Total carbohydrate:** The amount of carbohydrate in *one serving*. Tip: One carbohydrate food unit contains about 15 grams carbohydrate.

| **Nutrition Facts** | |
| --- | --- |
| Serving Size: | |
| Servings Per Container: | |
| **Amount Per Serving** | |
| **Calories** | Calories from Fat |
| **% Daily Value** | |
| **Total Fat** | % |
| Saturated Fat | % |
| **Cholesterol** | % |
| **Sodium** | % |
| **Total Carbohydrate** | % |
| Dietary Fiber | % |
| Sugars | |
| **Protein** | |
| **Ingredients:** | |

**Dietary fiber:** The amount of fiber in *one serving*. Fiber is part of the product's total carbohydrate. Kids need to consume at least 10 to 20 grams of fiber per day on average (5 grams + the child's age).

**Sugars:** The amount of simple sugars in *one serving*. Sugars are part of total carbohydrate and include natural (fruit and milk sugars) and added sugars.

**Protein:** The amount of protein in *one serving*.

**Sodium:** The amount of sodium in *one serving*.

**Ingredients:** These are listed from most to least. Be careful if these ingredients appear early on in the ingredient list:

- Added sugars: high-fructose corn syrup (the most common sweetener), corn syrup, sugar, and dextrose.
- Unhealthy fats: hydrogenated or partially hydrogenated vegetable oils, lard, and coconut or palm oils.

# Week 6 Weekly Menu

*Recipes are given for items in boldface.*

| | Breakfast | Lunch | Dinner | Snacks (1 to 2 choices per day) |
|---|---|---|---|---|
| MONDAY | Fast-food option: Egg, ham, cheese, and English muffin sandwich<br><br>Orange juice (4 to 6 ounces) or low-fat milk (8 ounces) | Peanut butter sandwich—preferably whole wheat<br><br>Carrot sticks with reduced-fat ranch dressing<br><br>Milk (½ to 1 cup) | Baked chicken (1 breast or 2 legs)*<br><br>**Spinach Casserole**<br><br>Sliced or cherry tomatoes with 1–2 teaspoons olive oil or reduced-fat dressing<br><br>Fruit cup or Waldorf salad (½ cup)<br><br>Milk (½ to 1 cup) | Cereal containing fiber (1 cup) and skim or soy milk<br><br>Cereal-fruit bar (1)<br><br>Reduced-fat chips (about 15 chips or 1 ounce) with fat-free dip or salsa<br><br>Wheat crackers (6) with:<br><br>Reduced-fat cheese (2 slices) |

| | Breakfast | Lunch | Dinner | Snacks (1 to 2 choices per day) |
|---|---|---|---|---|
| **MONDAY** *(cont.)* | | | *Save some of the baked chicken for the Thursday Chicken and Noodle Alfredo | Lite cream cheese (2 tablespoons)<br><br>Peanut butter (1 tablespoon)<br><br>Hot cocoa made with skim milk (1 cup)<br><br>English muffin or bagel "pizza" (½ muffin with tomato or pizza sauce and reduced-fat cheese)<br><br>Fruit (1 piece fresh, ½ cup canned, or 3 tablespoons dried)<br><br>Frozen fruit bar (1) |
| **TUESDAY** | Oatmeal (1 cup) with 1 teaspoon brown sugar or low-sugar syrup, 1 tablespoon walnuts or pecans, and 2 tablespoons raisins<br><br>Milk (1 cup) | Turkey or ham in a pita with lettuce, tomato, and allowed condiments<br><br>Popcorn (3 to 4 cups—about a small "sandwich" bag-full)<br><br>Fruit cup (½ cup)<br><br>Milk (½ to 1 cup) | **Bean Casserole** (1 cup)<br><br>Cooked carrots with nonfat liquid butter substitute<br><br>Tossed salad with 1 teaspoon olive oil or reduced-fat salad dressing<br><br>Milk (½ to 1 cup) | |
| **WEDNESDAY** | Cinnamon toast (1–2 slices) made with 2 teaspoons lite margarine and a sprinkle of cinnamon sugar<br><br>Fruit yogurt (small, 4 to 6 ounces)<br><br>Orange juice—calcium-fortified (½ cup) | Tuna or chicken salad (made with fat-free mayonnaise) in a tomato cup<br><br>Celery sticks (fill with reduced-fat cream cheese or peanut butter (if desired)<br><br>Grapes (½ cup)<br><br>Milk (1 cup) | Tacos (2) made with ground turkey and your favorite taco seasoning mix<br><br>Black beans (½ cup)<br><br>Salsa, fat-free sour cream, and reduced-fat cheese<br><br>Fruit cup (½ cup)<br><br>Water or calorie-free beverage | Fruit juice "spritzer": 3 ounces fruit juice mixed with 5 ounces club soda or sparkling water<br><br>Graham crackers (3 squares)<br><br>Teddy grahams (½ cup)<br><br>Nuts (2 tablespoons)<br><br>Oatmeal (½ cup)<br><br>Oatmeal cookies (2 small) |

| | Breakfast | Lunch | Dinner | Snacks (1 to 2 choices per day) |
|---|---|---|---|---|
| THURSDAY | Bagel "sandwich" with scrambled egg substitute, reduced-fat cheese, and salsa or sliced tomato if desired<br><br>Orange juice—calcium-fortified (½ cup) | Leftover bean casserole (½ cup)<br><br>Wheat crackers (6)<br><br>Apple (1)<br><br>Skim or soy milk (1 cup) | **Chicken and Noodle Alfredo** (1 cup)<br><br>Seasoned green beans or leftover carrots<br><br>Tossed salad if desired<br><br>Water or calorie-free beverage | Air-popped popcorn (5 cups)<br><br>Reduced-fat pudding (½ cup)<br><br>Quesadilla (1 tortilla) with melted, reduced-fat cheese, salsa, and fat-free sour cream<br><br>Rice cakes (10 small or 2 large) |
| FRIDAY | Cold cereal containing fiber (1 cup)<br><br>Banana (1) or berries (1 cup)<br><br>Whole-wheat toast (1 slice), optional<br><br>Skim or soy milk (1 cup) | Grilled cheese sandwich (1) made with reduced-fat cheese and nonstick cooking spray<br><br>Raisins (small box)<br><br>Vegetable soup<br><br>Milk (½ to 1 cup) | Dining-out meal: Sushi, 10–12 pieces<br><br>Miso soup<br><br>Edamame (soybeans)<br><br>Water or calorie-free beverage | ½ sandwich on whole-wheat bread with turkey, tuna with lite mayo, or reduced-fat cheese<br><br>Soup: vegetable or chicken noodle (2 cups)<br><br>Trail mix (4 tablespoons)<br><br>Yogurt, regular or frozen (4 to 6 ounces) |
| SATURDAY | Pancakes (1–2) with low-sugar syrup<br><br>Egg substitute, scrambled in nonfat butter-flavored cooking spray (optional)<br><br>Berries (1 cup)<br><br>Skim or soy milk (½ to 1 cup) | Bagel "pizza": ½ bagel with pizza sauce, melted reduced-fat cheese, and low-fat topping<br><br>Small rice cakes—any flavor (8 to 10)<br><br>Grapes (½ cup)<br><br>Milk (½ to 1 cup) | Reduced-fat hot dog (less than 3 grams fat per hot dog), 1 bun and 1 to 2 hot dogs<br><br>Baked beans (½ cup)<br><br>Carrot and celery sticks with reduced-fat ranch dip<br><br>Skim or soy milk (½ to 1 cup) | |

|  | **Breakfast** | **Lunch** | **Dinner** | **Snacks** (1 to 2 choices per day) |
|---|---|---|---|---|
| SUNDAY | Oatmeal (½ to 1 cup) Banana (1) or berries (1 cup) Skim or soy milk (1 cup) | Roast turkey Dressing (½ cup) Seasoned green beans Tossed salad if desired Milk (½ to 1 cup) | **Leftover Night** Food Units 1 to 2 starch-bread Lean or low-fat protein 0 to 1 fruit 1 milk-dairy 1 fat Veggies—unlimited! | |

# Week 6 Recipes

## SPINACH CASSEROLE

2 teaspoons reduced-fat margarine or olive oil
½ onion, finely chopped
Two 10-ounce packages frozen chopped spinach, thawed and drained
2 eggs or ½ cup egg substitute
8 ounces fat-free sour cream
8 ounces reduced-fat or fat-free cream cheese
½ cup grated Parmesan cheese
Salt or salt substitute (optional) and pepper to taste

Preheat the oven to 375°F. In a skillet, heat the margarine or olive oil and sauté the onion. Add the remaining ingredients and mix well. Transfer to a casserole and bake, uncovered, for about 30 minutes, until firm.

Makes about 6 cups (twelve 1½-inch squares).

Nutritional Analysis
Vegetable Group: ½ cup = 55 calories, 1–2 grams fat, and ½ carbohydrate

## BEAN CASSEROLE

2 teaspoons olive oil, plus olive oil–flavored cooking spray as needed
8 ounces reduced-fat sausage, "veggie" sausage substitute, ham, or cooked chicken or turkey, cut into bite-size pieces (about 1½ cups) (optional)
1 onion, chopped
1 garlic clove, minced
2 tablespoons fresh minced parsley
2 bay leaves
Two 15-ounce cans navy beans
¼ to ½ cup chicken broth
¼ teaspoon hot pepper sauce (optional)

Preheat the oven to 350°F. Heat the olive oil in a skillet and spray as needed. Sauté the meat, if using, and onion until the onion is tender. Add the remaining ingredients (use less broth for a thicker dish), mix well, and transfer to a casserole. Bake, covered, for about 1 hour. Uncover and bake for another 15 to 20 minutes.

Nutritional Analysis
1 cup: 2 carbohydrate units, 2 protein units (230 calories, 6–9 grams fat)

## CHICKEN AND NOODLE ALFREDO

Nonfat butter-flavored spray
2 tablespoons reduced-fat margarine plus 1 tablespoon olive oil
¼ cup onion, finely chopped
3 tablespoons flour
¼ teaspoon salt or salt substitute (optional)
½ teaspoon white pepper (optional)
½ teaspoon garlic powder, or more to taste
2 cups skim milk
3 cups cooked macaroni or spaghetti, preferably whole wheat
2 cups cooked, diced leftover chicken or shrimp
2 cups cooked, diced carrot or broccoli (optional)
½ cup grated Parmesan cheese

Spray the bottom of a saucepan, heat the margarine and oil, and sauté the onion until tender. Stir in the flour and seasonings. Add the milk and simmer, stirring constantly, over medium heat until thick (do not let boil). Stir in the noodles, chicken, vegetables, if using, and Parmesan and heat through. Serve with extra Parmesan if desired.

Makes 7 to 8 cups.

Nutritional Analysis
1 cup: 2 carbohydrate units, 2 protein units, 1 fat unit (240 calories, 7–8 grams fat)

# Week 6 Weekly Shopping List

| Fruits | Vegetables | Meat, Deli | Dried, Canned |
|---|---|---|---|
| Apple | Carrots, celery | Chicken pieces (enough for leftovers) | Oatmeal |
| Banana | Salad greens: | Ham cold cuts | Spaghetti noodles |
| Berries (in season) |    Lettuce | Reduced-fat hot dogs (less than 3 grams fat) | Stuffing mix |
| Grapes |    Tomato | Reduced-fat sausage (less than 3 to 5 grams fat, optional) or "veggie" sausage links, found in the frozen food section | Turkey gravy mix |
| Miscellaneous fruits for snacks |    Cucumber, etc. | | Pizza sauce (your favorite brand) |
| | Onions | | Taco shells, taco seasoning mix |
| | Miscellaneous vegetables for snacks | | Salsa |
| | | Turkey or turkey breast (for roasting) | Black beans, canned |
| | | Ground turkey | Baked beans, canned |
| | | | Navy beans, 2 (15-ounce) cans |
| | | | Ranch seasoning packet |
| | | | Chicken broth or bouillon cube |
| | | | Vegetable soup |
| | | | Tuna (water-packed) |
| | | | Fruit cup |
| | | | Raisins |

| Dairy Case | Frozen Food Section | Breads, Miscellaneous |
|---|---|---|
| Milk (skim, 1½% or soy milk) | Pancakes (or buy a mix) | Wheat bread |
| Egg substitute, eggs | Spinach, chopped (2 boxes) | Bagels |
| Reduced-fat or part-skim cheese slices (less than 5 grams of fat per ounce or slice) | Green beans* | Hot dog buns |
| | Frozen fruit bars | Whole-wheat pita bread |
| Reduced-fat shredded cheese | | Wheat crackers |
| String cheese (made with part-skim mozzarella cheese) | *Substitute fresh if desired. | Air-popped popcorn |
| Fruit yogurt | | |
| Orange or other fruit juice—calcium-fortified | | |
| Neufchâtel or fat-free cream cheese (2) | | |
| Fat-free sour cream (2) | | |
| Parmesan cheese | | |

## Staples

Reduced-fat or very low-fat mayonnaise (less than 3 grams per serving)

Reduced-fat or very low-fat salad dressings (less than 3–5 grams per serving)

Catsup, mustard, pickles, BBQ sauce (regular versions OK)

Low-sugar syrup, low-sugar or all-fruit jelly

Peanut butter (no added hydrogenated or partially hydrogenated vegetable oils)

Nuts

Oil (olive, canola, peanut), nonfat cooking spray, nonfat liquid butter (dairy section)

Lite margarine (first ingredient should be *liquid* vegetable oil—not hydrogenated or partially hydrogenated oil)

# WEEK 6 PORTION CONTROL/FOOD RECORD PRACTICE

Don't forget to use TRIM KIDS AEROBIC ACTIVITY AND FOOD CHECKLIST to help keep track of your daily intake. Let's practice portion-control checks for one day.

## Wednesday:

*Breakfast:*

| | |
|---|---|
| Cinnamon toast (1–2 slices) | 1–2 carbohydrates (wheat toast) |
|    with 2 teaspoons lite margarine | 1 fat (0 fats if nonfat butter-flavored spray is used) |
|    with cinnamon sugar (small amount) | Free |
| Fruit yogurt (½ cup) | 1 carbohydrate |
| Orange juice (½ cup) | 1 carbohydrate |

*Lunch:*

| | |
|---|---|
| Tuna or chicken salad (made with fat-free mayonnaise) | 2–3 proteins |
| Tomato cup | Vegetable—as desired |
| Celery sticks | Vegetable—as desired |
|    with reduced-fat cream cheese or peanut butter | 1 fat, 0–1 protein |
| Grapes (½ cup) | 1 carbohydrate |
| Milk (1 cup) | 1 carbohydrate |

*Dinner:*

| | |
|---|---|
| Tacos (2) | 2 carbohydrates, 2–3 proteins, 3–4 fats |
| Black beans (½ cup) | 1 carbohydrate |
| Salsa | Vegetable—as desired |
| Fat-free sour cream | Free |
| Fruit cup (½ cup) | 1 carbohydrate |

*Sample snacks:*

| | |
|---|---|
| String cheese, part-skim milk (4) | 2 proteins, 1–2 fats |
| Frozen fruit bar | 1 carbohydrate |

| | |
|---|---|
| Total food units for Wednesday: | 9–10 carbohydrates |
| | 6–7 proteins |
| | 6–7 fats |
| | Vegetables |

## SECTION 4: TIME TO SUM UP

## Trim Kids Weekly Checklist

*Did you remember to:*       *Yes*    *No*    *Will do it by*

Fill out TRIM KIDS WEEKLY REPORT AND GOAL SHEET?

_____    _____    _____

Fill out TRIM KIDS AEROBIC ACTIVITY AND FOOD CHECKLIST?

_____    _____    _____

Fill out TRIM KIDS STRENGTH AND FLEXIBILITY WORKOUT CHART?

_____    _____    _____

Have your child fill out the Self-Image Assessment chart?

_____    _____    _____

Review and discern the difference between negative and positive self-talk?

_____    _____    _____

Copy "Esteem Builders" and post it in a visible place?

_____    _____    _____

| Did you remember to: | Yes | No | Will do it by |
|---|---|---|---|
| Study the material about strengthen exercises and participate in those appropriate for you? | ___ | ___ | _____ |
| Review food labels? | ___ | ___ | _____ |
| Complete the Aerobic Grab Bag and perform the aerobic activity of the week? | ___ | ___ | _____ |
| Perform the strength and flex exercises of the week? | ___ | ___ | _____ |

Congratulations! You're halfway through the program. But even the most confident Trim Kids participants can get stressed out. Managing stress is another key to managing good health. In "Week 7," we'll show you how.

# Week 7

# SUCCESS
# OVER STRESS

## TRIM KIDS ROAD MAP
## FOR WEEK 7

*As usual, you'll begin this week by weighing your child on the same day and at the same time as you did last week. Review last week's goals and have your child record her accomplishments. Reward her for meeting her goals. You can refer to last week's Trim Kids Aerobic Activity and Food Checklist to praise your child for making healthy selections or to see why she may be having problems.*

*This week you and your child will learn how to combat stress with relaxation and stretching, practicing the relaxation exercises together. You'll help your child take the Trim Kids Flex Test. You will reassess your child's goal-setting techniques and fill out the Goal Check form. Read the section on vitamins and minerals and learn which foods are the best sources of calcium. Follow this week's menu plan, try the new recipes, and use the weekly shopping list to get what you'll need.*

## RELAXATION ROTATION: HOW, WHEN, AND WHY TO RELAX

By now, as a committed member of the Trim Kids Program, your child is eating well, engaging in more activity, and learning to change his own behavior. That adds up to the heartening fact that he is gradually but steadily reversing the vicious circle of overweight. That's all good news, but even so, along the way, he (and you!) may experience some unexpected stress.

Learning to relax can be of great benefit to those seeking behavioral changes. Once you and your child learn the techniques in this section, the key then becomes to recognize precursors of stress and apply the relaxation technique before the stress plays out through overeating or underactivity.

Many relaxation techniques have stood the test of time, developed and practiced as inspirational healing traditions for centuries around the world. These techniques are often based on breathing slowly and deeply until a sense of calm and well-being takes over.

Relaxing deeply enough so that the relaxation can be influential requires some initial dedication. Practicing for a couple of weeks will get you off to a good start. Follow these guidelines, and feel yourself become lighter!

- Get comfortable on a floor mat or bed with no environmental distractions such as TV, radio, or other noise. Set a timer to go off in ten to fifteen minutes.
- Focus on something—anything will do—a picture on the wall, the corner of the room, or a ceiling fan. As you focus, begin to notice your breathing. Try breathing a little more deeply—but don't fill your lungs to capacity.
- Inhale to the count of one. Exhale to the count of two. Proceed slowly as you count with each breath.
- Your goal during the first week is to count to twenty without allowing extraneous thoughts to intrude. When thoughts do enter—and they will—simply begin counting over. Don't be distressed. Eventually you will make it to the count of twenty without interruption. At

that point, you will experience a new sense of calm, well-being, and relaxation.

Some experts recommend trying visualization, soothing music, or positive self-talk to assist with the process and to keep from being distracted. The theory is that if you visualize a calm, serene scene, you can't worry about daily stress and conflict. This can be difficult, however, if you don't yet know how to breathe slowly and deeply. Experiment with these tools only after you and your child feel comfortable and confident with the breathing response.

Once you are proficient at this exercise, use it when you feel stress coming on. For example, if your child complains about having to eat vegetables, or if you feel annoyed by having to cook, take a moment, go into the other room, and practice relaxing. Afterward, you'll feel renewed and more able to begin the process of problem solving. Suggest that your child take a few minutes to do the same.

Positive self-talk is very effective for children once they learn the breathing technique. Teach your child to repeat phrases such as, "I can do anything I want," or "I'm looking better all the time," or "This will get easier." These phrases will sink in more when your child has reached a state of relaxation after doing the breathing exercise. Practice these exercises with your child for ten to fifteen minutes one to two times per week.

> **TRIM KIDS TESTIMONIAL**
>
> ### A Parent's Perspective
>
> "I got into the habit of giving in to my daughter when we'd fight about her eating too much or not being active enough. I took Dr. Kris's advice and started establishing new household rules each week with my daughter's and my family's input. When the arguments began to escalate again, I would call an immediate halt. Everyone would take a ten-minute break. I'd spend mine reassuring myself that as the parent I would negotiate a reasonable solution to the problem. When we got back together, I would reiterate the rules, choices, and consequences we'd been talking about—and it started working. It took a few weeks, but things are much easier now for everyone."

## REASSESSING GOALS

If your child has been consistently reaching his short-term and weekly goals, then it's a good indication that his long-term goals are attainable. If his progress is more hit-and-miss, you may have set unrealistic goals. Review the points below with your child to make sure the goals you're working to attain are within reach. If not, change them. As you go through this process, don't forget to focus on what he's done *well*. If he's fallen short of his goals, be matter-of-fact without passing judgment, and stay solution-oriented.

Let's talk about your goals. Which ones have you met? Which ones seem impossible, and why? Fill out the self-assessment below so we can clearly understand your progress.

## Your Goals

List the goals you have set for yourself since you started the Trim Kids Program.

1. _____

2. _____

3. _____

4. _____

Which have been easy, and why?

1. _____

2. _____

3. _____

4. _____

Which have not been easy, and why?

1. _____

2. _____

3. _____

4. _____

List the goals you have achieved:

1. _____

2. _____

3. _____

4. _____

List the goals you still want to achieve:

1. _____

2. _____

3. _____

4. _____

It's up to parents to determine how reasonable and attainable the child's goals really are. If goals seem too difficult, don't hesitate to regroup and set more realistic and attainable goals. Remember: your child's success and willingness to participate in the program depend on his being able to reach his goals. Don't feel bad if you need to create new goals—this is an ongoing process of discovering how to make things work.

# FLEXIBILITY: THE BODY'S BALANCING ACT

Stretching and flexibility are important to your child's exercise routine to maintain good posture and overall balance. Using a car as a metaphor helps kids understand the value of good posture and a balanced body.

We can't drive a car that has a flat tire—it's unbalanced. And we can't drive on the road to health if we don't have a balanced body. When you were born, your body was a perfectly designed machine—just like a brand-new car. It was symmetrical, meaning that the left side was identical to the right, and the front was in balance with the rear. But after years of using one part of your body more than other parts, you can get out of balance. Although we don't have flat tires to show us that we're out of balance, we do have poor posture or, worse, an injury or pain in our bones and joints.

If you overtrain or neglect to stretch your chest muscles or undertrain your back area, you could walk around looking like a gorilla! (Parents demonstrate.) What's more, your back could begin to hunch over and you'll start to look like a very old alien from outer space! (Parents demonstrate.) But if your chest is flexible and your back is strong, you'll appear taller, thinner, and stronger. This is why you've been doing stretch and flex exercises since week 1. Do these exercises whenever and wherever you can. It's easy to do them while you're watching television or playing outside or in your room.

The Flex Test is a way of checking to see if you have any of these imbalances. Flex exercises can help correct those imbalances and prevent others from occurring.

Take the Flex Test now. Then continue with the information that follows.

## Flex Test

*Examine the figures below and answer the question beneath each. If your answer is "Yes," note which side (left or right) is particularly problematic. Then try the exercises suggested as indicated. These will help balance the body and improve posture.*

Do you look like this?

Then try these.

Yes _____ no _____

Rowing, low:
Do 8–12 repetitions 2–3 times per week.

Chest stretch:
Do this 3 times a day.

Do you look like this?

Yes _____ no _____

Then try these.

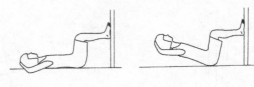

Stomach crunch, pelvic tilt:
Do 8–20 repetitions 2–3 times per week.

---

Do you look like this?

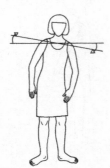

Yes _____ no _____ side _____

Then try this:

Shoulder stretch:
Do this 3 times a day.

Do you look like this?

Yes _____ no _____ side _____

Then try these.

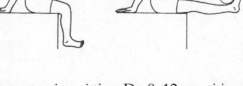

Leg extension, sitting: Do 8–12 repetitions 2–3 times per week.

Leg curl, standing: Do 8–12 repetitions 2–3 times per week.

Then try these *(continued)*.

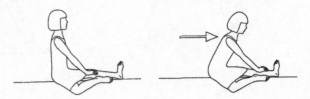

Seated hamstring stretch:
Do this 3 times a day.

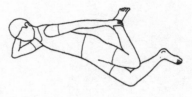

Lying quad stretch: Do this 3 times a day.

Important: Keep knees "soft" or slightly bent when standing (don't lock or hyper-extend the knees). This automatically takes stress off the knee joints and the lower back.

·············································································

Do you look like this?          Do you look like this?

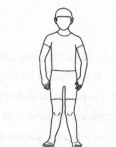                 

Yes _____ no _____ side _____     Yes _____ no _____ side _____

Do you look like this?

Yes _____ no _____ side _____

    Then see your pediatrician or family physician. He or she may refer you to an orthopedic specialist.

# EXERCISE ACTIVITY IDEAS: FLEXIBILITY IN MOTION

If your child enjoys how flexibility exercises make him feel, consider enrolling him in a class in which stretching and flexibility are at the core of the discipline. These days, schools, academies, and various organizations offer a wide range of kid-friendly karate and dance classes, as well as yoga and gymnastics. Your options include tap, ballet, jazz dancing, rhythm gymnastics, tumbling, cheerleading, dance teams, swimming, synchronized swimming (water ballet), springboard diving, martial arts (karate, judo, self-defense, tai bo), tai chi, and ice skating.

Most classes are structured for fun and a challenge—but be certain that the one your child chooses is appropriate for his level of fitness. Before enrollment, be sure the instructor will work with you, will be responsive to your child's unique needs, and will always ensure your child's safety.

# WEEKLY EXERCISE ACTIVITIES

### WEEK 7 AEROBIC ACTIVITY: RECOMMENDED GOALS

Write your goal in the TRIM KIDS AEROBIC ACTIVITY AND FOOD CHECKLIST (page 386). This is the minimum amount of aerobic exercise that you should perform this week. Every day, record what type of physical activity you did and how long you did it. At the end of the week, compare your list with the goals you set at the beginning of the week.

- Red Level: The exercise goal this week is three days per week for thirty to thirty-five minutes each day.
- Yellow Level: The exercise goal this week is four days per week for thirty to forty minutes each day.
- Green Level: The exercise goal this week is five days per week for thirty-five to fifty minutes each day.
- Blue Level: The exercise goal this week is three days per week for thirty to sixty minutes each day.

### AEROBIC ACTIVITY OF WEEK 7: AEROBIC SOCCER

In aerobic soccer, there are no boundaries other than those needed for safety reasons. The ball is always in play. Offensive and defensive players switch places every ten minutes to enable all members to run up and down the field. Only five seconds are allowed to begin play after a goal is made. Special note: Teams are selected as follows—all children line up behind the instructor, coach, or parent who will serve as referee. The referee then alternately assigns the children to one of two colors to designate the different teams (for example, blue and red). This method is efficient and discourages captains and elimination issues such as being picked last for a team.

### WEEK 7 STRENGTH AND FLEX EXERCISES

Read the instructions aloud to your child as he does these exercises, until he no longer needs your assistance.

> ## Recipes for a Stress-Free, Active Lifestyle
>
> - Enroll the entire family in a karate, modified yoga, or tai chi class that meets once a week.
> - At the end of the day, put on some soft, soothing music while preparing a healthy dinner with your child.
> - Go for a long walk with your child.
> - Go outside with your child and work in the garden, pick flowers, or watch birds.
> - Turn on some upbeat music and dance to three songs nonstop with your child.
> - Turn on music videos and try to learn the latest dance moves with your child.

## Strength Exercise 7: Pelvic Tilt

Lie on the floor with your arms at your sides. Bend your knees at a ninety-degree angle to the floor, keeping your feet flat on the floor. That's right. Now press your lower back gently into the floor. Keep your upper body relaxed.

Slowly extend your hips upward, raising them off the floor. Tighten your buttocks and the backs of your thigh muscles (hamstrings) to press your hips upward on the count of four. Your shoulders and feet will balance you as you raise your hips. Keep raising your

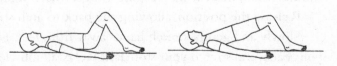

hips until your upper body and thighs align. Hold for one to two seconds. Good job! Slowly return to the starting position to a count of four.

Do eight to twelve repetitions of this move. This exercise works your buttock muscles (gluteus) and your hamstrings.

Common errors your child may make include tensing the upper body.

## Flex Exercise 7: Relax Your Back

Lie on your back. Relax your head and neck. Gently press your lower back into the floor. Slowly bring your knees into your chest, holding the legs behind the knees, and squeeze gently. Keep breathing. Keep your upper body relaxed.

Drop one foot to the floor, keeping your knee bent. Squeeze the other knee gently into the chest.

Slowly pull the knee across your body to stretch the outer hip. Extend the opposite arm, palm down. Turn your head in the opposite direction. Slowly return the knee to the chest. Repeat with the other leg.

Return both knees, and then the rest of your body, to the starting position.

Slowly slide one arm upward along the floor. Stretch your arms in the direction of the head. Repeat with the other arm.

Place arms behind your head and relax your head and shoulders. Tilt your hips upward as you gently press your lower back into the floor. Tighten and hold in lower abdomen.

Keeping the same lower-body position, slowly extend your arms overhead. Do not lift the shoulders, neck, or head. Keep the upper body relaxed. The spine should be completely aligned with the floor, and relaxed.

Continue to hold the stomach tight and press the spine gently into the floor. Begin to "walk" the feet out until the back starts to come up. Tilt the hips again and press the spine into the floor, holding the stomach tight. Over time, your stomach muscles will become stronger, enabling you to achieve and maintain this position. Keep your back flat and spine gently pressed into the floor. Relax your shoulders and head while keeping your stomach tight.

Release the position, allowing the back to arch slowly. Relax your abdomen.

Slowly and gently, stretch hands away from feet. Let your rib cage expand, arch your back, and stretch your stomach. Relax all muscles. Slowly, return the knees to the chest and gently squeeze.

Slowly return to the original stretch position. Drop feet to the floor, keeping knees bent for safety.

Relax all muscles. Slowly return the knees to the chest and gently squeeze. Return to starting position.

Roll onto your stomach. Sit back on your heels while extending arms forward, palms down. Keep your face down, head in line with the back. Gently stretch.

Perform these new Strength and Flex Exercises and the ones you learned previously in weeks 1–7 at least once, but preferably twice this week. Record your progress

| Calcium Content of Common Foods | | |
| --- | --- | --- |
| Yogurt | 1 cup | 400 mg |
| Low-fat or skim milk | 1 cup | 300 mg |
| Calcium-fortified fruit juice | 1 cup | 300 mg |
| Cheese pizza | 1 slice | 200 mg |
| Cheese | 1 ounce | 200 mg |
| Collard greens | ½ cup | 170 mg |
| Soups made with milk | 1 cup | 160 mg |
| Macaroni and cheese | ½ cup | 150 mg |
| Custard | ½ cup | 150 mg |
| Cottage cheese | 1 cup | 145 mg |
| Pudding | ½ cup | 130 mg |
| Ice cream, frozen yogurt | ½ cup | 125 mg |
| Shrimp | 3 ounces | 100 mg |
| Beans | 1 cup | 90 mg |
| Broccoli | ½ cup | 45 mg |

on the TRIM KIDS STRENGTH AND FLEXIBILITY WORKOUT CHART in the appendix ("Forms You'll Need"), on page 388. Every week, you will add another exercise to your program.

Remember to fill out your TRIM KIDS AEROBIC ACTIVITY AND FOOD CHECKLIST on page 386, and try the aerobic activity of the week with the entire family.

## SECTION 3: TIME TO DINE

# NUTRITION NUTSHELL: ABOUT CALCIUM

One of the most important minerals for our bodies—and the one that's most lacking—is calcium. More than half of America's children and adolescents don't consume the calcium they need. Children should consume between 800 and 1,300 milligrams per day; teenagers need 1,500 milligrams per day.

Many foods contain calcium, but dairy products supply the most abundant amounts. Dairy products also provide much-needed vitamin D, which helps the body to absorb calcium. If your child doesn't routinely consume three to four servings of dairy foods daily, chances are good that she isn't meeting her recommended daily allowance. But don't worry—adding calcium doesn't have to mean adding calories or pounds: nonfat, low-fat, and skim versions of dairy products and their higher-fat cousins contain similar amounts of calcium. If your child is lactose intolerant, see your pediatrician.

Conduct a calcium intake check for your child by referring to the list below. If you realize that your child isn't eating enough calcium-rich foods to meet the minimum requirements, consult your doctor about a calcium supplement. Remember, without adequate calcium intake, your child could suffer some serious health consequences later in life. Your child's skeletal framework is forming now. Studies suggest that females especially are at risk of developing osteoporosis and related bone fractures later in life unless they consume enough calcium.

## Week 7 Weekly Menu

*Recipes are given for items in boldface.*

|  | **Breakfast** | **Lunch** | **Dinner** | **Snacks** (1 to 2 choices per day) |
|---|---|---|---|---|
| MONDAY | Fried egg sandwich made with 1 egg fried in nonstick spray and wheat bread (reduced-fat cheese is optional) Salsa (optional) Orange juice—calcium-fortified (½ cup) | Tuna or chicken salad (made with fat-free mayonnaise) in a pita bread pocket with lettuce, tomato, and pickles Fresh fruit in season (1) Milk (½ to 1 cup) | **Easy Black Bean Soup** (1 cup) **Corn Casserole** (½ cup or about a 2-inch square) Tossed salad with 1 teaspoon olive oil or reduced-fat dressing Milk (½ to 1 cup) | Cereal containing fiber (1 cup) and skim or soy milk Cereal-fruit bar (1) Reduced-fat chips (about 15 chips or 1 ounce) with fat-free dip or salsa Wheat crackers (6) with: Reduced-fat cheese (2 slices) |

|  | **Breakfast** | **Lunch** | **Dinner** | **Snacks (1 to 2 choices per day)** |
|---|---|---|---|---|
| TUESDAY | Whole-grain waffle (1) with sliced banana and low-sugar syrup (1 to 2 tablespoons walnuts or pecans optional)<br><br>Scrambled egg substitute (optional)<br><br>Milk (1 cup) | Peanut butter sandwich on whole-wheat bread (1)<br><br>Carrot-raisin salad<br><br>Milk (½ to 1 cup) | **Turkey-Broccoli Divan** (1 to 2 cups)<br><br>Brown rice (0 to ½ cup)<br><br>Fruit cup (½ cup)<br><br>Sliced tomatoes with reduced-fat dressing if desired<br><br>Milk (½ to 1 cup) | Lite cream cheese (2 tablespoons)<br><br>Peanut butter (1 tablespoon)<br><br>Hot cocoa made with skim milk (1 cup)<br><br>English muffin or bagel "pizza": ½ muffin with tomato or pizza sauce and reduced-fat cheese |
| WEDNESDAY | Cottage cheese (½ cup) with canned pineapple chunks (½ cup)<br><br>Cinnamon toast (1 slice)<br><br>Orange juice—calcium-fortified (½ cup) | Leftover **Easy Black Bean Soup** (1 cup)<br><br>Carrot and celery sticks with reduced-fat dip<br><br>Rice cakes—any flavor (8 to 10 small)<br><br>Milk (cup) | Restaurant meal: Grilled or broiled seafood (fish or shellfish) as desired<br><br>Cocktail sauce as desired<br><br>½ cup potato dish<br><br>Vegetables and tossed salad as offered<br><br>Water or calorie-free beverage | Fruit (1 piece fresh, ½ cup canned, or 3 tablespoons dried)<br><br>Frozen fruit bar (1)<br><br>Fruit juice "spritzer": 3 ounces fruit juice mixed with 5 ounces club soda or sparkling water<br><br>Graham crackers (3 squares) |
| THURSDAY | Yogurt shake made with 1 cup yogurt, 1 cup frozen strawberries, banana, and ice (½ cup skim or soy milk for a thinner shake) | Reduced-fat cheese slices with wheat crackers (6 to 12)<br><br>Vegetable soup<br><br>Fresh fruit of choice<br><br>Milk (½ to 1 cup) | **Roasted Pork Tenderloin Cheesy Cauliflower**<br><br>Tossed salad with 1–2 teaspoons olive oil or reduced-fat dressing<br><br>Water or calorie-free beverage | Teddy grahams (½ cup)<br><br>Nuts (3 tablespoons)<br><br>Oatmeal (½ cup)<br><br>Oatmeal cookies (2 small) |

|  | **Breakfast** | **Lunch** | **Dinner** | **Snacks** (1 to 2 choices per day) |
|---|---|---|---|---|
| FRIDAY | Cold cereal containing fiber (1½ cups)<br><br>Banana (1) or berries (1 cup)<br><br>Milk (1 cup) | Fast-food meal:<br>Soft taco (2)<br><br>Tortilla chips (½ cup, or about 15)<br><br>Salsa<br><br>Water or calorie-free beverage | Grilled "veggie" burger (1)<br><br>**Eggplant Sticks**<br><br>Tossed salad as desired<br><br>Fruit cup (½ cup)<br><br>Milk (1 cup) | Air-popped popcorn (5 cups)<br><br>Reduced-fat pudding or ice cream (½ cup)<br><br>Quesadilla (1 tortilla) with melted, reduced-fat cheese, salsa, and fat-free sour cream |
| SATURDAY | Scrambled egg substitute<br><br>Turkey bacon (3) or "veggie" breakfast sausage (2)<br><br>Wheat toast (1 slice)<br><br>Melon (⅓ melon) or berries (1 cup)<br><br>Milk (1 cup) | String cheese, made with part-skim milk, mozzarella cheese (3 to 4 pieces), and dill pickle spears (optional)<br><br>Sliced turkey or ham rolled around the string cheese and pickle spears<br><br>Reduced-fat ranch dressing, as a dip<br><br>Fruit cup (½ cup)<br><br>Water or calorie-free beverage | **Stir-Fry Dinner** (2 to 3 cups) with brown rice (½ cup)<br><br>Reduced-fat pudding or ice cream (½ cup or a small "kiddie-size" scoop)<br><br>Milk (½ to 1 cup) | Rice cakes (10 small or 2 large)<br><br>½ sandwich on whole-wheat bread with turkey, tuna with lite mayo, or reduced-fat cheese<br><br>Soup: vegetable or chicken noodle (2 cups)<br><br>Trail mix (4 tablespoons)<br><br>Yogurt, regular or frozen (4 to 6 ounces) |

| | Breakfast | Lunch | Dinner | Snacks (1 to 2 choices per day) |
|---|---|---|---|---|
| SUNDAY | Cheese toast made with reduced-fat cheese slices (2 pieces)<br>Sliced tomato<br>Orange juice—calcium-fortified (½ cup) | **Chicken Breasts Florentine**<br>Dinner roll or bread (1)<br>Tossed salad as desired<br>Fruit salad made with leftover fruit pieces (1 cup)<br>Milk (½ to 1 cup) | **Leftover Night**<br>Food Units<br>1 to 2 starch-bread<br>Lean or low-fat protein<br>0 to 1 fruit<br>1 milk-dairy<br>1 fat<br>Veggies—unlimited! | |

# Week 7 Recipes

## EASY BLACK BEAN SOUP

Nonfat butter-flavored spray
1 tablespoon olive oil
1 onion, finely chopped
2 garlic cloves, minced
3 to 4 celery stalks, chopped
Two 16-ounce cans black beans, drained
1 cup chicken or other broth, or more for a thinner soup
2 bay leaves
¼ teaspoon hot pepper sauce (optional)
1 cup diced cooked ham or 6 to 8 cooked turkey bacon slices (optional)

Spray the bottom of a large saucepan or Dutch oven, heat the oil, and sauté the onion, garlic, and celery until tender. Add the remaining ingredients and simmer for about 1 hour. Remove the bay leaves and serve.

Makes about 5 cups.

Nutritional Analysis
1 cup: 2 carbohydrate units (180 calories)

## CORN CASSEROLE

Nonfat butter-flavored spray
One 15-ounce can corn
One 15-ounce can creamed corn
8 ounces fat-free sour cream
½ cup nonfat liquid butter substitute
1 egg or ½ cup egg substitute
One 6-ounce package corn bread mix

Preheat the oven to 350°F. Spray the bottom of a casserole. Mix all the ingredients in a bowl and transfer to the casserole. Bake, uncovered, for 50 minutes to 1 hour.

Makes about eight ½-cup squares.

Nutritional Analysis
⅛ recipe: 1 carbohydrate unit, 1 fat unit (125 calories, 6 grams fat)

## TURKEY-BROCCOLI DIVAN

Nonfat butter-flavored spray
1 bunch fresh broccoli, cut in 1-inch pieces, or one 10-ounce package frozen broccoli
4 leftover cooked turkey or chicken breasts, diced
½ cup chicken broth
1 cup skim milk or fat-free half-and-half
2 tablespoons cornstarch
1 cup reduced-fat shredded Cheddar or American cheese
½ teaspoon salt or salt substitute (optional)
½ teaspoon curry powder (optional)
Brown rice for serving (optional)

Preheat the oven to 375°F. Spray the bottom of a baking dish. Microwave or steam the broccoli until tender and transfer to the baking dish. Top with turkey pieces. To make the sauce, whisk the broth, milk, and cornstarch in a saucepan and heat over medium heat, stirring constantly. Bring to a simmer—do not let boil—and stir until the sauce starts to thicken, then add ½ cup of the cheese and the seasonings and heat through. Pour the sauce over the turkey and broccoli and sprinkle with the remaining cheese. Bake, uncovered, for 25 to 35 minutes until heated through. Serve with brown rice if desired.

Makes about four 1½-cup servings.

Nutritional Analysis
1 to 1½ cups (2 to 3 broccoli stalks with turkey slice and sauce): 2 protein units, ½ carbohydrate unit, vegetable group (145 calories, 4 grams fat). The brown rice will add 1 carbohydrate unit for every ½ cup.

## ROASTED PORK TENDERLOIN

*For the marinade*
1 tablespoon Dijon mustard
2 tablespoons dark brown sugar or low-sugar pancake syrup
2 tablespoons water
½ teaspoon garlic powder
¼ teaspoon cayenne pepper (optional)

One 1- to 2-pound pork tenderloin

Mix the marinade ingredients in a bowl. Place the pork tenderloin in a roasting pan and pour the marinade over the top, coating the tenderloin well. Cover and marinate for 10 to 12 hours in the refrigerator. Heat the oven to 400°F and roast the pork in the pan, uncovered, for 20 to 25 minutes on each side, basting several times, until fully cooked.

Makes 6 to 7 three-ounce slices.

Hint: "Pre-marinated" pork tenderloins are sometimes available in the grocery store's meat section for a quick dinner option.

Nutritional Analysis
¾-inch slice (3 ounces): 3 protein units

## CHEESY CAULIFLOWER

Two 10-ounce packages frozen cauliflower, defrosted, or 1 bunch fresh, cut into bite-size pieces
1 can reduced-fat cream of mushroom soup
½ soup can skim milk or chicken broth
6 ounces reduced-fat shredded Cheddar or American cheese (about 1½ cups)
Salt or salt substitute and pepper to taste (optional)
Bread crumbs
Nonfat butter-flavored spray (optional)

Preheat the oven to 375 degrees. Combine all the ingredients and nonfat butter-flavored spray in a baking dish. Top with bread crumbs and spray if desired. Bake, uncovered, for 35 to 40 minutes.

To microwave: Put the cauliflower in the microwave when still frozen and microwave until just tender, 3 to 5 minutes. Add the rest of the ingredients and microwave on medium-high for another 5 minutes.

Makes about 4 cups.

Nutritional Analysis
½ cup: vegetable group (45 calories, 2–3 grams fat), 1 protein

---

## EGGPLANT STICKS

½ teaspoon salt or salt substitute
½ cup water
1 large eggplant, cut into strips and left unpeeled
1 cup fat-free mayonnaise
2 tablespoons skim milk
½ teaspoon garlic powder (optional)
1 cup Italian-style bread crumbs
2 tablespoons grated Parmesan cheese
Nonstick cooking spray
Tomato or spaghetti sauce for serving (optional)

Preheat the oven to 400°F. Fill a zippered bag with the salt and water and add the eggplant. Shake and let sit for about 30 minutes to remove the bitter taste. In a small bowl mix together the mayonnaise, milk, and garlic powder, if using. In another bowl mix bread crumbs and cheese. Rinse, drain, and dry the eggplant. Dip the eggplant in the mayonnaise mixture, then in the bread crumbs. The easiest way to do this is to place the mayonnaise and bread crumb mixtures in separate zippered bags. Spray a baking sheet. Lay the eggplant on the sheet and bake for about 30 minutes, or until tender. Serve with heated tomato or spaghetti sauce if desired.

Variation: This recipe also works well with cauliflower nuggets or zucchini sticks. It is unnecessary to soak the cauliflower or zucchini in salt water.

Makes 24 to 36 sticks (4 to 6 servings).

Nutritional Analysis
Vegetable Group: No limit + ½ carbohydrate unit for every 6 to 8 sticks (50 calories, 1 gram fat)

## STIR-FRY DINNER

1 tablespoon peanut oil
4 cups fresh vegetables such as broccoli, peppers, onions, carrots, and mushrooms, cut into bite-size pieces
One 5-ounce can sliced water chestnuts
3 green onions, white and green parts sliced (optional)
1 tablespoon grated, fresh ginger or ½ teaspoon powdered ginger, or more to taste
4 skinless, boneless chicken breasts, cut into bite-size pieces, or 1 to 2 pounds shrimp, peeled, or 1 to 2 cups chunks of firm tofu
⅓ cup reduced-sodium soy sauce
⅓ cup chicken broth or water
2 teaspoons cornstarch
¼ teaspoon red pepper flakes or more to taste (optional)
Brown rice for serving (optional)

Place a wok or large nonstick frying pan over medium-high heat. Add the oil. When it is hot, stir-fry the vegetables, water chestnuts, green onions, and ginger for about 5 minutes, until crisp-tender. Remove, set aside, and stir-fry the chicken or shrimp until cooked through. Return vegetable mixture to the wok. In a small bowl, mix the soy sauce, water, cornstarch, and red pepper flakes. Pour into the wok and heat briefly until hot and thickened, 2 to 3 minutes. Do not overcook. Serve over brown rice if desired.

Makes about 8 to 10 cups.

Nutritional Analysis
2 to 3 cups: 3 protein units, vegetable group (155 calories, 1–3 grams fat). The brown rice will add 1 carbohydrate unit for every ½ cup.

## CHICKEN BREASTS FLORENTINE

One 10-ounce package defrosted frozen chopped spinach, drained
8 ounces fresh mushrooms, sliced and sautéed in a little olive oil, or one 4-ounce can mushrooms
1 cup cottage cheese
¾ cup Parmesan cheese
½ teaspoon salt or salt substitute (optional)
A few dashes of Tabasco sauce (optional)
4 to 6 skinless, boneless chicken breasts
1 cup egg substitute
1 cup Italian-style bread crumbs

Preheat the oven to 375°F. Combine the spinach, mushrooms, cottage cheese, ½ cup of the Parmesan, and seasonings in a bowl and spread in a baking dish. Dip the chicken breasts in the egg substitute. Mix the bread crumbs with ¼ cup of the Parmesan and roll the chicken in the bread crumb mixture. Lay the chicken on top of the spinach mixture. Bake, uncovered, for 40 to 45 minutes.

Nutritional Analysis
1 breast with the spinach mixture: 4 protein units, ½ carbohydrate unit, vegetable group (185 calories, 6–7 grams fat)

# Week 7 Weekly Shopping List

| Fruits | Vegetables | Meat, Deli | Dried, Canned |
|---|---|---|---|
| Banana | Carrots, celery | Chicken breasts, boneless, skinless (buy a "family pack"— enough for 2 meals) | Breakfast cereal (should contain more than 2–3 grams fiber per serving) |
| Melon in season | Eggplant | | |
| Miscellaneous fruit for snacks | Ginger | | |
| | Green onions | Ham, thick slice (to dice for the Black Bean Soup)— (optional) | Italian-style bread crumbs |
| | Mushrooms, fresh or canned | | Corn bread mix (6-ounce box) |
| | Onion | Turkey cold cuts | Brown rice |
| | Salad greens: | Turkey bacon | Black beans, canned (2–3) |
| |    Lettuce | | Chicken broth or bouillon cubes |
| |    Tomato | | Reduced-fat cream of mushroom soup |
| |    Cucumber, etc. | | Vegetable soup |
| | Vegetables for stir-frying | | Corn, canned |
| | | | Cream corn, canned |
| | | | Water chestnuts, canned |
| | | | Soy sauce, reduced-sodium |
| | | | Tuna or chicken (water-packed) |
| | | | Pineapple chunks |
| | | | Crushed pineapple |
| | | | Fruit cup |
| | | | Raisins |
| | | | Dill pickle spears |
| | | | Ranch seasoning packet |

| Dairy Case | Frozen Food Section | Breads, Miscellaneous |
|---|---|---|
| Milk (skim, 1½%, or soy milk) | Broccoli* (2 boxes) | Whole-wheat bread |
| Egg substitute, eggs | Cauliflower* (2 boxes) | Whole-wheat pita bread |
| Reduced-fat or part-skim cheese slices (less than 5 grams of fat per ounce or slice) | Spinach, chopped | Hamburger buns (for the veggie burgers) |
| | Strawberries | |
| Reduced-fat shredded cheese, Cheddar or American (2 or more packages) | "Veggie" burgers—vegetable-protein hamburger patties | |
| | Waffles | |
| Fruit yogurt | *Substitute fresh if desired. | |
| Orange or fruit juice—calcium-fortified | | |
| Cottage cheese | | |
| Parmesan cheese | | |
| Fat-free sour cream (two 16-ounce containers or more) | | |
| String cheese (made with part-skim milk) | | |

## Staples

Reduced-fat or very low-fat mayonnaise (less than 3 grams fat per serving)

Reduced-fat or very low-fat salad dressings (less than 3–5 grams fat per serving)

Catsup, mustard, pickles, BBQ sauce (regular versions OK)

Low-sugar syrup, low-sugar or all-fruit jelly

Peanut butter (no added hydrogenated or partially hydrogenated vegetable oils)

Nuts

Oil (olive, canola, peanut), nonfat cooking spray, nonfat liquid butter (dairy section)

Lite margarine (first ingredient should be *liquid* vegetable oil—not hydrogenated or partially hydrogenated oil)

# WEEK 7 PORTION CONTROL AND FOOD RECORD PRACTICE

Don't forget to use TRIM KIDS AEROBIC ACTIVITY AND FOOD CHECKLIST to help keep track of your daily intake. Let's practice portion-control checks for one day:

## Thursday:

*Breakfast:*

| | |
|---|---|
| Yogurt shake | |
| Yogurt (1 cup) | 1–2 carbohydrates (1 for plain yogurt or 2 for fruit-flavored yogurt) |
| Frozen strawberries (½–1 cup) | 1 carbohydrate |
| Banana | 1 carbohydrate |
| Milk (½ cup) | ½ carbohydrate |

*Lunch:*

| | |
|---|---|
| Reduced-fat cheese slices | 2–3 proteins, 2 fats |
| Wheat crackers (6–12) | 1–2 carbohydrates |
| Vegetable soup | Vegetables, as desired |
| Fruit of choice | 1 carbohydrate |
| Milk (½–1 cup) | ½ to 1 carbohydrates |

*Dinner:*

| | |
|---|---|
| **Roasted Pork Tenderloin** | 3 proteins |
| **Cheesy Cauliflower** | Vegetables, as desired, 1 protein |
| Salad with 1–2 teaspoons olive oil | Vegetable, as desired; 1–2 fats |
| Sample snacks: | |
| Frozen yogurt (small, 4 ounces) | 1 carbohydrate |
| Raisins (¼ cup) | 1 carbohydrate |
| | |
| Total food units for Thursday: | 9 carbohydrates |
| | 6 proteins |
| | 4 fats |
| | Vegetables |

......................................................
## SECTION 4: TIME TO SUM UP
......................................................

## Trim Kids Weekly Checklist

*Did you remember to:*                     *Yes*      *No*      *Will do it by*

Fill out TRIM KIDS WEEKLY REPORT AND GOAL SHEET?

_____     _____     _____

Fill out TRIM KIDS AEROBIC ACTIVITY AND FOOD CHECKLIST?

_____     _____     _____

Fill out TRIM KIDS STRENGTH AND FLEXIBILITY WORKOUT CHART?

_____     _____     _____

Have your child complete the chart Your Goals?

_____     _____     _____

Practice relaxation exercises with your child for ten to fifteen minutes
at least two times per week?     _____     _____     _____

Practice taking action by helping your child confront stressful
situations and negative thoughts with positive self-talk or the
relaxation response?

_____     _____     _____

Perform the recipes for a stress-free, active lifestyle?

_____     _____     _____

Have your child take the Flex Test?     _____     _____     _____

Review vitamins and minerals, determine your child's calcium intake, and
adjust if necessary?     _____     _____     _____

*Did you remember to:*                    **Yes**        **No**        **Will do it by**

Perform the aerobic activity of the week?

_____    _____    _____

Perform the strength and flex exercises of the week?

_____    _____    _____

By now you know that the Trim Kids Program is a family affair. In week 8, we'll give tips on how to keep all members of the family involved and committed.

# Week 8

# KEEPING IT ALL TOGETHER

## TRIM KIDS ROAD MAP FOR WEEK 8

*This week, after filling out the Trim Kids Forms in the appendix (remember to weigh your child and list your goals for the week), you will practice techniques to help you and your child solve problems and handle pressure from peers, family, and the media. You will read about body types and genetics to help you to tailor the exercise program to your child's individual needs. We'll give you ideas for burning an extra 20 calories twenty times a day; then you and your child will write some ideas of your own. You will learn how to shop for healthy snacks and do a calorie comparison for snack foods. Don't forget to check your child's progress with the Trim Kids Weekly Checklist at the end of the chapter.*

## SECTION 1: TIME TO STOP AND THINK

## STAYING POSITIVE AND SOLVING PROBLEMS

When your family collaborates in the Trim Kids Program, then your efforts are united. To keep the positive momentum going, it's helpful to conduct regular family meetings in which you recognize and reward the supportive behavior of all family members. Avoid reprimanding *any* of your kids for undesirable behavior. Research shows that negative reinforcement will invite all children—not just your overweight child—to act out unpleasantly more often and with more intensity. Research also shows that *a parent's expectations* greatly influence both the child's perception of himself and how he behaves. This suggests that whatever attitude parents maintain will affect how well their children comply with household rules.

Pick a relaxed time to hold the meetings. Evaluate whether you have been giving enough positive attention to the family's healthier eating and increased activity. Then, allow family members to express regret about the things they miss from the old, unhealthy lifestyle. Keep an open mind and discuss issues without judgment.

TRIM KIDS TESTIMONIAL

## A Parent's Perspective

"My wife and I never realized that just by walking a couple of days a week, stretching and flexing with our son, and eating more healthfully, we would see such dramatic effects. We're all happier, healthier, and thinner because of it. Even Sophie, our dog, has started to run in the backyard again!"

Remember that you will have a greater influence over younger family members than over teenagers, who are seeking autonomy. Regardless of age, however, all family members engage more fully in the program when they feel they have a say in the situation.

If the program isn't working as well as it could work, take an honest look at how you're motivating your child and other family members. Do you use guilt or praise? Are you setting a good example? Are you following through with firm household rules? Family meetings are an appropriate time to confront your family and overweight child supportively. Ask for potential solutions, and present some of your own. At this point, you must decide whether you're willing to take control of the situation or allow the family to take a planned vacation from the program. Remember to set a start and stop date if you decide to take a vacation, as it's easy to abandon the family's efforts and never return to the healthier lifestyle you've begun. Conclude by raving about new, healthier family events and eating habits.

Here's a worksheet for parents so you can keep yourself on the right track.

## Positive Parenting, Modeling, and Limits

What are some of the things that you do to set a good example of eating and physical activity for your child?

_____

_____

_____

What is something positive that you can say or do for your child to promote success in the Trim Kids Program?

_____

_____

_____

What are the new house rules you've tried since starting the program?

_____

_____

_____

## Ten Upbeat Tips for Parents

1. Set the example (eat healthfully, become active).
2. Don't coerce or hassle your child.
3. Limit or control high-fat and high-calorie food in the home.

4. Provide positive incentives for your child on a regular basis (lots of praise, and inexpensive rewards such as CDs, tennis shoes, and movie passes).

5. Have plenty of tasty, low-fat, low-calorie foods available.

6. Get the entire family involved in being more active and eating more healthfully.

7. Be prepared for major and minor setbacks—they're inevitable! Discuss problem situations with your child and brainstorm ways to handle them.

8. Initiate activities in the evening and on the weekends by inviting your child to take a walk in the park with you, or take a family bike ride together.

9. Help your child plan an eating strategy for special events such as parties or dances.

10. Assist your child in making healthy choices at restaurants and fast-food spots.

## Pressure in Other Places

With your child, list the *places* where it is easiest to stay on the Trim Kids Program, and why:

_____

_____

_____

_____

List the *occasions and times* when it is easiest to stay on the Trim Kids Program, and why:

_____

_____

_____

_____

List the _places_ where it is hardest for you stay on the Trim Kids Program, and why:

_____

_____

_____

_____

List the _occasions and times_ when it is hardest for you to stay on the Trim Kids Program, and why:

_____

_____

_____

_____

Do you think about these temptations _before_ you are actually tempted?

_____

_____

_____

_____

What can you do to change or avoid these temptations?

_____

_____

_____

_____

# TAILORING EXERCISE ROUTINES TO INDIVIDUAL BODY TYPES

Just as no two snowflakes are alike, so no two human bodies share exactly the same genetic makeup or body proportions. You may have one overweight child among five lean siblings. But the fact that your overweight child may have a genetic predisposition to heaviness doesn't mean she has to live a lifetime of overweight, poor nutrition, poor exercise habits, and medical problems.

Identifying body types can help determine which physical activities are best suited for your child. Remember: no matter what the size or shape of your child, she needs to experience a variety of physical activities in a supportive environment. To begin, figure out which somotype—or genetically determined body type—your child inherited.

- **Mesomorph**: These people have a high muscle-to-fat ratio and tend to have an hourglass-shaped body. The best exercises for mesomorphs include activities that require strength, power, and endurance, such as football, baseball, martial arts, boxing, wrestling, weight lifting, shot put, discus, long jump, ice skating, ice hockey, water polo, sprinting events in track and field, swimming, springboard diving, gymnastics, and tumbling.
- **Endomorph**: This group has a higher fat-to-muscle ratio. Endomorphs tend to be pear-shaped, round, and soft. Endomorphs do well in all types

of middle-distance or moderate-intensity activities, such as swimming, synchronized swimming, dancing, or brisk walking. They are also well suited for the individual sports—martial arts, tennis, archery, bowling, sailing, golf, softball, hiking, snorkeling, scuba diving, water skiing, and middle-distance field events.

- **Ectomorph:** These people are long and rectangular-shaped, typically low in weight and fat. They excel at long-distance events such as field sports, basketball, soccer, football (running back), ice hockey (offense), field hockey, track-and-field long-distance runs, pole vaulting, marathons, triathlons, long-distance swimming, cross-country running, and skiing.

Exercise that's right for your child's age, size, and genetic makeup is determined by many factors. One of these factors is muscle fiber types.

Muscle fibers are generally classified as *slow-twitch* or *fast-twitch*. The percentage we have of each is genetically determined. Those with more slow-twitch muscles are better equipped to partake in moderate- to vigorous-intensity, long-duration exercises such as those defined for ectomorphs (like basketball). Those with more fast-twitch muscles are well suited to high-intensity, short-duration exercises like those suggested for mesomorphs. People with an equal number of slow-twitch and fast-twitch fibers typically excel at middle-distance or moderate-intensity events, although they are typically competent in all types of sports or activities.

After determining your child's body type, notice the activities she gravitates to—those that she likes and is able to master with ease. She will probably independently select activities best suited to her innate abilities, personal preferences, and the positive feedback she receives from coaches, parents, and peers. You may be tempted to limit activities to those she likes most and that are compatible with her body type, but it's important to expose her to many different exercises—all in a nonintimidating, nurturing environment.

Every body type benefits from a variety of exercises, although those benefits may be manifested differently. Genetics determines skin thickness and where fat tissue is stored. So, even if your child's routine has a consistent strength-training component, genetics may prevent her from ever appearing as lean as kids with different genetic profiles, skin, and muscle tissue.

Help your child accept the body she was born with, while encouraging activities of all kinds. Respect your child's own passion for certain activities. Try not to impose your personal preferences. Even short, stocky athletes can excel in basketball if they love the game.

When creating an individual exercise program, remember that:

- Aerobic exercise burns large amounts of fat. The longer you do an aerobic activity, the more your body draws from its fat stores for fuel. It's much better for kids to do an activity *that's easy to sustain for long periods of time* than to do something more intense for short periods. When you maintain an even level of intensity in an activity, you reach what's called *steady state*.
- Steady-state activity is best for older children and adults who want to lose fat, so encourage your older child not to change the intensity of her exercise during a workout. Younger children will naturally start and stop during physical activity, since their body engines are immature and are better suited for intermittent activities. When a young child plays tag (a start-and-stop activity) for a few hours, her total caloric expenditure will be the same as that of an older child performing a steady-state (nonstop) biking session for a slightly shorter or sometimes an equal amount of time.
- It's healthy to accept your body type. Genetics determines not only fat distribution and muscle fiber types but also bone density and heaviness. Some ethnic groups have larger bones and, therefore, carry more weight. Help your child accept the size of her body frame whether it's small, medium, or large.
- Consider the size of her frame when selecting physical activities. For instance, large-framed girls with dense, heavy bones excel in sports requiring strength and endurance such as volleyball, baseball, and basketball. Small-framed boys do well in martial arts, gymnastics, soccer, and sports requiring speed, agility, and strength. Always provide opportunities to try as many different activities as possible, even those that don't appear well-suited to your child's physical makeup.
- Most important, remember that all activity burns calories and improves overall health.

Even though individualizing your child's exercise program according to somotype may be helpful, remember that children gain a sense of mastery when they *succeed* in a behavior. When they feel masterful, they will almost certainly engage in that behavior again.

# WEEKLY EXERCISE ACTIVITIES

### WEEK 8 AEROBIC ACTIVITY: RECOMMENDED GOALS

Write your goal on the TRIM KIDS AEROBIC ACTIVITY AND FOOD CHECKLIST (page 386). This is the minimum amount of aerobic exercise that you should perform this week. Every day, record what type of physical activity you did and how long you did it. At the end of the week, compare your list with the goals you set at the beginning of the week.

- Red Level: The exercise goal this week is three days per week for thirty to thirty-five minutes each day.
- Yellow Level: The exercise goal this week is four days per week for thirty to forty minutes each day.
- Green Level: The exercise goal this week is five days per week for thirty-five to fifty minutes each day.
- Blue Level: The exercise goal this week is three days per week for thirty to sixty minutes each day.

### WEEK 8 AEROBIC ACTIVITY: AEROBIC CIRCUIT

Guide your child through an aerobic station routine. Use a treadmill, a cycle ergometer, a stair climber, a rowing machine, or any of the aerobic activities that we've been working with—side jacks (page 97), heel backs with arms up (page 97), skipping rope, twists, and so forth. Time your child for two-minute intervals at each station followed by thirty seconds to change stations. This could take place in the imagination station with a map describing the different stations. Put on upbeat music and work out together!

### WEEK 8 STRENGTH AND FLEX EXERCISES

Read the instructions aloud to your child as he does these exercises, until he no longer needs your assistance.

### Strength Exercise 8: Dumbbell Press

Lie on the floor with your knees bent and your feet flat on the floor. Hold the weights at chest level with your thumbs in toward the middle of your body and your elbows out and even with your shoulders. Be sure to relax your upper body. Good.

 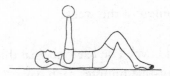

Now gently press your lower back into the floor. To the count of four, slowly extend the weights upward directly above your chest. Turn the weights inward toward your lower body slightly so your arms are fully extended. Good.

Now again to the count of four, slowly return to the beginning position.

Do eight to twelve repetitions of this move. This exercise trains your chest muscles (pectorals).

Common errors your child may make include moving the weights above the face rather than above the chest and arching the back.

### Flex Exercise 8: Modified Butterfly Stretch

Sit on the floor and spread your legs out to each side. Make sure your tummy is tight and your head, neck, and shoulders are relaxed. Slowly bring your feet together and grasp your ankles.

Bend forward as you hold your ankles, bringing your chest and chin down toward the floor. Good stretch! Make sure you look straight ahead and don't roll your back or drop your chin. Hold this stretch for fifteen to thirty seconds.

Return to the sitting position. Repeat this process one more time, holding this position again for fifteen to thirty seconds.

Perform these new strength and flex exercises and also those you learned previously in weeks 1–7 at least once, but preferably twice this week. Record your progress on the TRIM KIDS STRENGTH AND FLEXIBILITY WORKOUT CHART in the appendix ("Forms You'll Need"), on page 388. Every week, you will add another exercise to your program.

Don't forget to fill out your TRIM KIDS AEROBIC ACTIVITY AND FOOD CHECKLIST on page 386, and try the aerobic activity of the week with the entire family.

## EXERCISE ACTIVITY IDEAS

Plan a weekly physical activity routine that uses a variety of sports or exercises. Refer to the cross-training suggestions in week 9 for ideas. This will naturally expose your child to all types of physical activities.

### Twenty Ways to Burn 20 Calories

1. Do twenty abdominal crunches (page 332) slowly (four seconds up, four seconds down) before going to sleep. Follow with gentle stretching.
2. Walk upstairs twice.
3. Do twenty toe raises while standing in line (at the grocery store, for example).
4. Walk briskly to the bus stop and again from the bus to the schoolyard.
5. While standing in front of the television, do forty side jacks (page 97) with large arm movements.
6. Also while standing in front of the TV, do twelve leg squats (page 335) slowly (four seconds down, four seconds up).
7. Walk briskly five times through the school halls.
8. Slowly press your arms above your head fifteen times (four seconds up, four seconds down) while sitting in a chair or in front of the TV.
9. In that same chair, do twelve double leg extensions (page 101) slowly (four seconds up, four seconds down).
10. While watching your favorite television show, do sitting stretches (page 333) for the duration of the show.
11. Walk briskly through the grocery store aisles.

12. March in place for five minutes anywhere!
13. Do fifteen leg curls (page 128) on each leg and follow with gentle stretching each night before bed.
14. Ride your bike to your friend's house.
15. Skip rope for five minutes.
16. Dance to two of your favorite songs without stopping.
17. Help Mom or Dad with the housework for ten minutes.
18. Help Mom or Dad with yard work for ten minutes.
19. Clean out your closet for fifteen minutes.
20. Stand up and do five cheers at your hometown's next football game. The team will probably love you for it!

If you do some of these activities several times a day for a full week, doing a total of twenty-five activities a day, you will burn enough calories to lose one pound (3,500 calories). Choose the activities that are easy for you to do, and do them several times a day to reach your goal of twenty-five per day.

Now list the activities you will do for five to ten minutes that will burn 20 calories.

_____

_____

_____

_____

## SECTION 3: TIME TO DINE

# NUTRITION NUTSHELL: HEALTHY SNACKS AT A GLANCE

Review the following lists with your child so she'll reach for the healthiest snacks available, and don't forget to include those little tidbits on her daily food record.

### *Healthy Snacks*
- Fresh fruit (any kind)
- Unsweetened canned fruit
- Unsweetened dried fruit
- Fresh vegetables with low-fat dip
- Vegetable soup
- Reduced-fat chips (in moderation)
- Pretzels
- Air-popped popcorn
- Whole-wheat crackers (look for crackers that contain 2 or more grams of fiber)
- Rice cakes
- Graham crackers or animal crackers
- Sandwiches (preferably whole wheat) with low-fat toppings or peanut butter
- Bagels (preferably wheat or whole-grain)
- Reduced-fat cheese
- Low-fat yogurt
- Low-fat ice cream or frozen yogurt
- High-fiber breakfast cereals (containing more than 2 to 3 grams of fiber)
- Reduced-fat cream cheese (with bagels or rice cakes)

# Week 8 Weekly Menu

*Recipes are given for items in boldface.*

|  | Breakfast | Lunch | Dinner | Snacks (1 to 2 choices per day) |
|---|---|---|---|---|
| MONDAY | Cold cereal containing fiber (1½ cups)<br><br>Banana (1) or berries (1 cup)<br><br>Milk (1 cup) | Baked beans (½ cup) with reduced-fat hot dogs (2), cut up and mixed with the beans if desired<br><br>Cucumber slices with vinegar, fat-free mayo, or ranch dressing<br><br>Applesauce or canned fruit (½ cup)<br><br>Milk (½ to 1 cup) | Flank steak or turkey breast (marinated in your favorite marinade mix, grilled)<br><br>Cooked corn (½ cup) or corn on the cob (1)<br><br>Vegetables, grilled or steamed as desired<br><br>Tossed salad with 1 teaspoon olive oil or reduced-fat dressing<br><br>Milk (½ to 1 cup) | Cereal with fiber (1 cup) and skim or soy milk<br><br>Cereal-fruit bar (1)<br><br>Reduced-fat chips (about 15 chips or 1 ounce) with fat-free dip or salsa<br><br>Wheat crackers (6) with:<br><br>Reduced-fat cheese (2 slices)<br><br>Lite cream cheese (2 tablespoons)<br><br>Peanut butter (1 tablespoon)<br><br>Hot cocoa made with skim milk (1 cup) |
| TUESDAY | Soft taco made with 1 soft tortilla (heated) filled with scrambled egg substitute, turkey bacon, reduced-fat cheese, and salsa | Peanut butter (1 to 2 tablespoons) and reduced-sugar jelly spread on 4 large rice cakes (or 2 slices wheat bread)<br><br>Fruit yogurt (small, 4 to 6 ounces) | BBQ chicken tenders or drumsticks, skinless (baked with your favorite BBQ sauce) (3 to 4)<br><br>Macaroni and cheese (½ to 1 cup) | English muffin or bagel "pizza": ½ muffin with tomato or pizza sauce and reduced-fat cheese<br><br>Fruit (1 piece fresh, ½ cup canned, or 3 tablespoons dried) |

| | Breakfast | Lunch | Dinner | Snacks (1 to 2 choices per day) |
|---|---|---|---|---|
| TUESDAY *(cont.)* | Orange juice—calcium-fortified (½ cup) | Cucumber slices with reduced-fat dip as desired<br>Milk (½ to 1 cup) | **Candied Carrots**<br>Tossed salad as desired<br>Water or calorie-free beverage | Frozen fruit bar (1)<br>Fruit juice "spritzer": 3 ounces fruit juice mixed with 5 ounces club soda or sparkling water<br>Graham crackers (3 squares)<br>Teddy grahams (½ cup)<br>Nuts (2 tablespoons)<br>Oatmeal (½ cup)<br>Oatmeal cookies (2 small)<br>Air-popped popcorn (3 to 5 cups)<br>Reduced-fat pudding or ice cream (½ cup)<br>Quesadilla (1 tortilla) with melted, reduced-fat cheese, salsa, and fat-free sour cream<br>Rice cakes (10 small or 2 large) |
| WEDNESDAY | Oatmeal (½ cup) with raisins, nuts, and brown sugar (1 teaspoon) or low-sugar syrup if desired<br>Wheat toast, 1 slice<br>Milk (1 cup) | Turkey sandwich in half of a pita bread (add preferred vegetables as desired)<br>Dill pickle spears (optional)<br>Apple (1)<br>Milk (½ to 1 cup) | Leftover steak sandwich made with sautéed sliced beef, peppers, and onions on hoagie roll (1)<br>Sliced or cherry tomatoes with fat-free mayonnaise or dressing<br>Baked chips (15 to 20, small bag)<br>Milk (½ to 1 cup) | |
| THURSDAY | Bagel (½) with peanut butter or reduced-fat cream cheese (1 tablespoon)<br>Berries (1 cup) or melon (⅓ melon)<br>Milk (1 cup) | BBQ chicken tenders (leftover) wrapped in a tortilla (1) with extra BBQ sauce and/or reduced-fat ranch dip<br>Optional: reduced-fat cheese, lettuce, tomato, pickles<br>Fruit cup (½ cup)<br>Milk (½–1 cup) | **Seasoned Lentils** (1 cup)—see week 3 for lentil recipes<br>Carrot-raisin salad<br>Tossed salad as desired with 1–2 teaspoons olive oil or reduced-fat dressing<br>Milk (½–1 cup) | |

| | Breakfast | Lunch | Dinner | Snacks (1 to 2 choices per day) |
|---|---|---|---|---|
| FRIDAY | Cheese toast (1–2 slices) made with reduced-fat cheese<br><br>Turkey bacon (3) or "veggie" sausage links (2), optional<br><br>Sliced tomato<br><br>Orange juice—calcium-fortified (½ cup) | Celery sticks filled with peanut butter, honey, and raisins (optional) mixed with the peanut butter (about 6 sticks)<br><br>Grapes (½ cup)<br><br>Fruit yogurt (small, 4 to 6 ounces)<br><br>Water or calorie-free beverage | **Salmon Cakes** (1 to 2 cakes)<br><br>**Baked Artichoke Hearts** Steamed or cooked vegetables as desired<br><br>Bread or dinner roll, preferably whole wheat (1)<br><br>Milk (1 cup) | Sandwich on whole-wheat bread (½) with turkey, tuna with lite mayo, or reduced-fat cheese<br><br>Soup: vegetable or chicken noodle (2 cups)<br><br>Trail mix (4 tablespoons)<br><br>Yogurt, regular or frozen (4 to 6 ounces) |
| SATURDAY | Pancakes (1–2) with berries (½ cup) and lite whipped topping if desired<br><br>Egg substitute, scrambled (in nonfat, nonstick cooking spray)<br><br>Milk (1 cup) | **Vegetable-Ranch Pasta** (1–2 cups)<br><br>Fresh fruit in season (1)<br><br>Milk (½–1 cup) | Restaurant meal: Pizza (2 slices)<br><br>Bread stick (1, optional)<br><br>Tossed salad as desired with 1–2 teaspoons olive oil or reduced-calorie dressing<br><br>Water or calorie-free beverage | |
| SUNDAY | Omelet made with egg substitute, reduced-fat cheese, and the desired vegetables<br><br>Turkey bacon (3 slices) or "veggie" breakfast sausage (2)<br><br>Wheat toast (1 slice)<br><br>Orange juice—calcium-fortified (½ cup) | Baked ham (1 to 2 slices)<br><br>**Mashed Sweet Potatoes** (½–1 cup)<br><br>Mixed vegetables<br><br>Applesauce (unsweetened) or pineapple (½ cup)<br><br>Milk (1 cup) | **Leftover Night**<br><br>Food Units<br><br>1 to 2 starch-bread<br><br>Lean or low-fat protein<br><br>0 to 1 fruit<br><br>1 milk-dairy<br><br>1 fat<br><br>Veggies—unlimited! | |

# Week 8 Recipes

## CANDIED CARROTS

½ pound carrots, peeled and sliced into rounds, or two 10-ounce packages sliced carrots
¼ cup pineapple, apple, or orange juice or chicken broth
2 tablespoons reduced-fat margarine
2 tablespoons nonfat liquid butter substitute
1 teaspoon cornstarch (optional)
2 tablespoons dark brown sugar or low-sugar pancake syrup
¼ teaspoon salt or salt substitute (optional)

Microwave the carrots with the juice until slightly soft, 2 to 3 minutes on high. In a sauce-pan, melt the margarine and nonfat butter-flavored liquid. Stir in the cornstarch, if using, sugar, and salt or salt substitute and bring to a simmer, stirring constantly. Cook until the mixture thickens and turns golden brown. Add the cooked carrots and juice. Mix well and cook until the carrots are tender.

Makes about 4 cups.

Nutritional Analysis
Vegetable Group: No limit (½ cup = 35 calories, 1 gram fat)

## VEGETABLE-RANCH PASTA

2 packages powdered ranch salad dressing mix
1½ cups fat-free mayonnaise
1 cup skim milk
1 bunch fresh broccoli, cut into bite-size pieces
One ½-pound bag carrots, peeled and sliced
2 red or yellow peppers, diced (optional)
Other favorite raw vegetables (optional)
One 16-ounce bag rotini or spiral (or other) noodles, cooked according
    to package directions

In a large bowl, combine the dressing mix, mayonnaise, and milk. Microwave the broccoli and carrots for about 3 minutes to make a bit tender if desired. Toss the vegetables and noodles with the dressing and chill.

Makes about 10 cups.

Nutritional Analysis
1 cup: 1½ carbohydrate units (140 calories)

--------

## SALMON CAKES

2 six-ounce cans pink salmon, drained
1 tablespoon grated onion or dried onion flakes
½ teaspoon dried dill (optional)
¼ teaspoon salt or salt substitute (optional)
¼ teaspoon black pepper
1 tablespoon Dijon mustard
¼ cup fat-free mayonnaise
1 egg or ¼ cup egg substitute
1 cup cracker or cornflake crumbs or bread crumbs
2 teaspoons olive, peanut, or canola oil
Butter or olive oil–flavored spray

In a bowl, combine all of the ingredients except the oil and spray, reserving ½ cup of the cracker or cornflake crumbs. Form the salmon mixture into about 6 patties and roll them in the reserved cracker or cornflake crumbs. Spray the bottom of a skillet, add the oil, and fry the patties over medium heat until brown on both sides, about 5 minutes total per side. Turn the patties frequently to prevent burning. Spray the patties during cooking as needed. (The patties may be prepared ahead and refrigerated until ready to cook.)

Makes about 4 large cakes.

Nutritional Analysis
1 salmon cake: 3 protein units, ½ carbohydrate unit, 1 fat unit (175 calories, 8–14 grams fat)

## BAKED ARTICHOKE HEARTS

Two 14-ounce cans artichoke hearts, drained
1 tablespoon olive oil
Juice of 2 lemons
2 tablespoons white wine (optional)
2 garlic cloves, minced, or more to taste
¼ teaspoon salt or salt substitute (optional)
Nonfat butter-flavored spray
½ cup Parmesan cheese
¼ cup Italian-style bread crumbs

Preheat the oven to 375°F. Line a shallow baking pan with the artichoke hearts. Mix the olive oil, lemon juice, wine, garlic, and salt in a bowl and pour over the artichoke hearts. Spray liberally. Mix the cheese and bread crumbs together, sprinkle over the artichoke hearts, and spray liberally. Bake for about 25 minutes, until top is browned.

Makes about 3 cups.

Nutritional Analysis
Vegetable Group: No limit (½ cup = 35–40 calories, 2 grams fat)

## MASHED SWEET POTATOES

2 large sweet potatoes, baked and peeled, or one 29-ounce can yams, drained
¼ to ½ cup skim or reduced-fat milk
¼ cup nonfat liquid butter substitute
¼ teaspoon salt or salt substitute (optional)

To microwave: Heat the sweet potatoes in the microwave until hot (they will mash more easily if heated). Mash with a potato masher or ricer until smooth, then add the remaining ingredients. Heat through again if needed prior to serving.

Nutritional Analysis
½ cup: 1 carbohydrate unit (100 calories)

# Week 8 Weekly Shopping List

| Fruits | Vegetables | Meat, Deli | Dried, Canned |
|---|---|---|---|
| Apples | Broccoli | Chicken breasts, boneless (for the chicken tenders) | Bread crumbs |
| Banana | Carrots | | Oatmeal |
| Grapes | Celery | | Lentils (dried) |
| Lemons | Corn on the cob (or frozen) | Flank steak | Noodles—your favorite type (for the Pasta-Ranch Salad) |
| Miscellaneous fruits for snacks | Onion | Ham—thick slice (for baking) | |
| | Peppers (red, yellow) | Reduced-fat (less than 3 grams of fat) hot dogs | Macaroni and cheese mix |
| | Salad greens: | | Baked beans, canned |
| |    Lettuce | Turkey cold cuts | Salsa |
| |    Tomato | Turkey bacon | Meat marinade (your favorite brand for the flank steak) |
| |    Cucumbers, etc. | | |
| | Yams | | Chicken broth or bouillon cubes |
| | Miscellaneous vegetables for snacks | | Artichokes, canned (2) |
| | | | Salmon, flaked, canned (2–3) |
| | | | Applesauce, fruit cup |
| | | | Raisins |
| | | | Crushed pineapple |
| | | | BBQ sauce |
| | | | Teriyaki sauce |
| | | | Ranch seasoning packet (2 or more) |

| Dairy Case | Frozen Food Section | Breads, Miscellaneous |
|---|---|---|
| Milk (skim, 1½%, or soy milk) | Mixed vegetables | Wheat bread |
| Egg substitute, eggs | Pancakes (or buy the mix) | Bagels |
| Reduced-fat or part-skim cheese slices (less than 5 grams of fat per ounce or slice) | | Hoagie rolls |
| | | Whole-wheat pita bread |
| Reduced-fat shredded cheese | | Tortillas |
| Fruit yogurt | | Baked (less than 3 grams of fat) chips |
| Orange or other fruit juice—calcium-fortified | | Rice cakes (any flavor) |
| Fat-free sour cream | | Teddy grahams |
| Parmesan cheese | | |

## Staples

Reduced-fat or very low-fat mayonnaise (less than 3 grams fat per serving)
Reduced-fat or very low-fat salad dressings (less than 3–5 grams fat per serving)
Catsup, mustard, BBQ sauce, pickles (regular versions OK)
Low-sugar syrup, low-sugar or all-fruit jelly
Peanut butter (no added hydrogenated or partially hydrogenated vegetable oils)
Nuts
Oil (olive, canola, peanut), nonfat cooking spray, nonfat liquid butter (dairy section)
Lite margarine (first ingredient should be *liquid* vegetable oil—not hydrogenated or partially hydrogenated oil)

# WEEK 8 PORTION CONTROL AND FOOD RECORD PRACTICE

Don't forget to use TRIM KIDS AEROBIC ACTIVITY AND FOOD CHECKLIST to help keep track of your daily intake. Let's practice portion-control checks for one day:

## Saturday:

*Breakfast:*

| | |
|---|---|
| Pancakes (1–2) | 1 carbohydrate, 2 fats |
| Berries (1 cup) | 1 carbohydrate |
| Scrambled egg substitute | 2 lean proteins |
| Milk (1 cup) | 1 carbohydrate |

*Lunch:*

| | |
|---|---|
| Vegetable-ranch pasta (1–2 cups) | 1½ carbohydrates |
| Fruit of choice | 1 carbohydrate |
| Milk (½–1 cup) | ½–1 carbohydrate |

*Dinner:*

| | |
|---|---|
| Pizza, thin crust (2 slices) | 4 carbohydrates, 4 proteins, 4–6 fats |
| Bread stick (1, optional) | 1 carbohydrate |
| Salad with 1–2 teaspoons olive oil (or reduced-fat dressing) | Vegetable—as desired 1–2 fats |

*Sample snacks:*

| | |
|---|---|
| Baby carrots with fat-free dip | Vegetables—as desired Free |
| Teddy grahams (½ cup) | 1 carbohydrate |

| | |
|---|---|
| Total food units for Saturday: | 11–12 carbohydrates |
| | 6 proteins |
| | 8 fats |
| | Vegetables |

## SECTION 4: TIME TO SUM UP

## Trim Kids Weekly Checklist

*Did you remember to:*          Yes      No      *Will do it by*

Fill out TRIM KIDS WEEKLY REPORT AND GOAL SHEET?

___     ___     _____

Fill out TRIM KIDS AEROBIC ACTIVITY AND FOOD CHECKLIST?

___     ___     _____

Fill out TRIM KIDS STRENGTH AND FLEXIBILITY WORKOUT CHART?

___     ___     _____

Set family meeting times and agree on what will be discussed?

___     ___     _____

Review how to choose alternative behaviors and fill out the form Pressure in Other Places?

___     ___     _____

Determine overweight child's body type, interests, and abilities?

___     ___     _____

Create an individualized exercise routine based on body type?

___     ___     _____

Review Twenty Ways to Burn 20 Calories and make up your own?

___     ___     _____

Review ideas for healthy snacks with your child?

___     ___     _____

*Did you remember to:*                    **Yes      No      Will do it by**

Perform the aerobic activity of the week?

_____   _____   _____

Perform the strength and flex exercises of the week?

_____   _____   _____

Sometimes change is difficult because your child has spent years responding to situations in an unhealthy way. In week 9, we'll show how to overcome typical life-long habits so your child can maximize the benefits of the Trim Kids Program.

# EMOTIONAL PITFALLS

## TRIM KIDS ROAD MAP FOR WEEK 9

*This week, after you've filled out the Trim Kids Forms in the appendix (remember to weigh your child and list your goals for the week), we will discuss the emotional pitfalls of changing behaviors—including social sabotage. You'll find recommendations for cross-training to help prevent exercise burnout. Follow this week's menu plan, try the new recipes and use the weekly shopping list to get what you'll need, and try our delicious snack recipes. Involve your kids in the cooking!*

## SECTION 1: TIME TO STOP AND THINK

## SOCIAL SABOTAGE

Social situations, emotions, and family events are often responsible when our children overeat or remain underactive. These responses have become habitual. This week, you and your child work together to develop healthier solutions so she doesn't overeat and feel bad about herself. For example, one of our patients, Terri, was in the habit of eating a supersize fast-food meal with her soccer team after winning a game. Her equally overweight brother, Jamie, typically indulged in two or three pieces of his grandmother's homemade triple-chocolate cake whenever they visited her. Each child was in the habit of celebrating positive events by eating large quantities of food.

When she followed the Trim Kids Program, however, Terri altered her habits by ordering a kid-size meal—complete with toy—after soccer games. Likewise, Jamie was happy with just one piece of the cake. Their celebration still included food, but less of it.

Austin provides another example of how to alter habitual responses. Austin had always wanted to play football, but because of his weight he was never picked for games at recess, and he lacked the confidence to try out for the playground teams—so he eventually quit trying. After one month on the Trim Kids Program, however, Austin had lost eight pounds and had become more confident about his physical skills. He and his father began passing a football each evening, and the whole family participated in weekend football games. Austin knew his skills were improving, and soon enough, he mustered the confidence to try out for his neighborhood park team. Before long Austin was playing tackle for the playground team and was being chosen regularly for pickup games during recess at school.

Before beginning the Trim Kids Program, your child may have shied away from doing any exercise at all, fearing discrimination from lean peers who could accomplish the same activities with relative ease.

### TRIM KIDS TESTIMONIAL

## A Parent's Perspective

"I just wanted to write in to let you know how Matthew is doing. If you remember, he lost about 60 pounds on the program about four years ago. Well, he's sixteen years old now and he just looks fantastic. His weight fluctuates a little, but he's managed to stay in the same size clothes this whole time. I just wanted to thank you for changing his life."

It's important to find peers that your child feels comfortable with—preferably other active kids who want to stay healthy or maybe lose weight, and who will participate in team sports or other activities at the same pace as your child. Seek out other children in your child's social circles at school, at church, and in

## Keeping Parents Nurtured

To prevent parental burnout, reach out to teachers, coaches, scout leaders, extended family, and friends to form a support network. Try a buddy system in which you team up with a group of other parents of overweight kids to facilitate physical activities, educational sessions, and problem-solving dialogues. Enlist the help of your community—local markets, skating rinks, shopping malls, or restaurants—and check out the programs offered by your county or city recreation department. Almost all are geared toward families, are run by volunteer parents, and are developmentally appropriate for children of different ages. Your local YMCA or religious organization may offer similar opportunities.

We've often wondered if these organizations even know they're helping prevent overweight in children—we thank them, and you as parents should become advocates for these programs. Show your gratitude and support for the healthy opportunities they provide.

If you're one of the unlucky few whose community lacks such facilities and opportunities, consider organizing a parent advocacy group. Rally other parents to encourage schools to improve lunch selections, remove junk-food vending machines, increase physical education time, and, most important, increase recess or free play time.

The key is family and community support—and providing opportunities for fun and fitness for your child.

scouting and other clubs or associations. Arrange regular meetings at a park or in someone's backyard where the kids can play and practice the sports and activities they like.

Younger children are more influenced by parents and family, but older ones seek autonomy and are more apt to listen to friends. Consequently, there may be times when you, as the parent, must intervene to set appropriate limits for your teen and to help him deal with peer pressure to choose unhealthy food. Sometimes, when you become the "heavy," it takes the pressure off the teen. For example, advise your teen to say, "Gee, guys, I'd love to eat some pizza with you, but you know how my mom can be. I think I'll order the salad instead. It will keep her off my back!"

........................................................

## SECTION 2: TIME TO GET ACTIVE

........................................................

# PREVENTING ACTIVITY BURNOUT: CROSS-TRAINING

By now, your child is accustomed to regular activity and exercise. To keep your child interested and to add variety to the routine, this is a good time to introduce cross-training. He'll continue the structured exercise program, but now he'll integrate two or more different types of aerobic and endurance activities into his workout. Cross-training also burns more calories by targeting and using all different muscle groups (including slow- and fast-twitch muscle fibers); this results in an all-over toned appearance (or "buffed," as your kids might call it).

There are four types of cross-training:

1. Continuous cross-training—a regimen without rest, such as jogging, swimming, walking, or cycling. Alternate types of activity by days or by weeks. Maintain intensity consistently throughout the session.
2. Interval cross-training—a workout that draws from a variety of activities interspersed with rest periods, followed by repeating the activities. For example: run very hard for one lap, walk easily for two laps, jog moderately for one lap, run very hard for one lap, and so on. Intensity varies from very high to very low during the workout.
3. Fartlek cross-training—a more casual version of interval training, this free-form training typically occurs outdoors on trails or roads. The cycle of exercise and rest is not predetermined or precisely timed or measured. Instead, it is based on how the individual feels. He could run uphill for ten minutes, walk on a flat area for five minutes, slowly jog downhill and on flat land for fifteen minutes, walk rapidly uphill for twenty minutes, and so on.
4. Circuit cross-training—an approach involving ten to twenty stations of varying calisthenics and weight-lifting exercise, coupled with running or walking.

As your child explores new types of exercises, observe his reactions so that you can monitor the routine: is it right for him, or is it too challenging? Look for the following clues: Is he discouraged or sad? Is he breathing very fast, turning red in the face, and sweating profusely? Is he complaining that his ankles, knees, or other joints hurt? If so, the activity is too challenging. Refine the workout by reducing the time he spends performing the activity as well as the work level, speed, or intensity. Allow him more time to rest, give him extra water, and make sure he's getting enough sleep. To grow properly, children need between nine and eleven hours of sleep per night.

As your child enters this level of the program, negotiate specific rewards for her long-term exercise goals. Find out what she wants—new weights, new clothing for her fit body, a weekend trip to an activity park—in exchange for following her cross-training routine for a specified amount of time. Make the agreement formal by signing a contract that specifies her responsibilities and her reward. Then, see how powerful this incentive can be!

## WEEKLY EXERCISE ACTIVITIES

### WEEK 9 AEROBIC ACTIVITY: RECOMMENDED GOALS

Write your goal in the TRIM KIDS AEROBIC ACTIVITY AND FOOD CHECKLIST (page 386). This is the minimum amount of aerobic exercise that you should perform this week. Every day, record what type of physical activity you did and how long you did it. At the end of the week, compare your list with the goals you set at the beginning of the week.

- Red Level: The exercise goal this week is four days per week for thirty-five to forty minutes each day.
- Yellow Level: The exercise goal this week is four days per week for thirty-five to forty-five minutes each day.
- Green Level: The exercise goal this week is five days per week for thirty-five to fifty-five minutes each day.
- Blue Level: The exercise goal this week is three days per week for thirty to sixty minutes each day.

### WEEK 9 AEROBIC ACTIVITY: CROSS-TRAINING

Plan one week of cross-training or family in-line skating.

WEEK 9 STRENGTH AND FLEX EXERCISES

Read the instructions aloud as your child does these exercises, until your assistance is no longer needed.

## Strength Exercise 9: Lower Back

Lie on the floor on your stomach with your legs extended and your hands alongside your chest, palms down. Bend your elbows and spread your fingers on the floor. Keep your head in line with your body, with face downward.

Using your lower back muscles, slowly and smoothly lift your upper body from the floor as one unit for the count of two. Use your hands for support, but don't push with them. Instead, lift with your back muscles. *Keep your head in line with your back.* Terrific job!

Now, slowly, to the count of two, return to the starting position. Do eight to twelve repetitions of this move. This exercise trains your lower back muscles.

Common errors your child may make include pulling the head back, jerky movements, and pushing with the hands.

## Flex Exercise 9: Butterfly Stretch

Sit on the floor with your legs extended out to each side. Tighten your tummy and keep your head, neck, and shoulders relaxed. Bring your feet together and grasp your ankles. Pull your feet toward your body until you feel a gentle stretch. You're doing great!

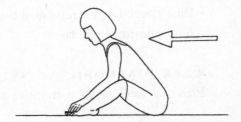

Now place your elbows on your knees as you continue to hold your ankles. Bend forward, looking straight ahead as you bring your chest and chin to the floor.

Press your elbows on your knees as you bend forward. Do not roll your shoulders or drop your head.

Hold this stretch for fifteen to thirty seconds. Slowly return to starting position. Then repeat this process one more time, holding this position again for fifteen to thirty seconds.

Perform these new strength and flex exercises and also those you learned previously in weeks 1–8 at least once, but preferably twice this week. Record your progress on the TRIM KIDS STRENGTH AND FLEXIBILITY WORKOUT CHART in the appendix ("Forms You'll Need"), on page 388. Every week, you will add another exercise to your program.

Don't forget to fill out your TRIM KIDS AEROBIC ACTIVITY AND FOOD CHECKLIST on page 376, and try the aerobic activity of the week with the entire family.

## SECTION 3: TIME TO DINE

# NUTRITION NUTSHELL: FUN IN THE KITCHEN

Involving your child in hands-on cooking activities is a great way to work fun into healthy eating. Food acceptance also tends to improve when the child takes part in selection and preparation. Here are some tips for involving your child in cooking activities:

- Review the recipe and ask the child to help in gathering the ingredients and utensils.
- Begin with simple activities, such as washing fruits and vegetables or separating grapes, and advance according to the child's age and ability.
- Practice measuring ingredients with measuring cups and spoons. This will also help your child become accustomed to various portion sizes.
- Use this time to practice reading food labels—for example, review grams of fat and sugar.
- *Always* have adequate adult supervision, especially when anyone is using sharp knives, a hot oven, burners, or electric appliances. For safety, use table knives whenever possible.

Preparing healthy snacks together is a good place to start involving your child. Here are a few snack recipes to help get you started.

# SUPER-EASY SNACK RECIPES

## YOGURT FRUIT DIP

8 ounces fat-free cream cheese, softened
1 cup vanilla-flavored low-fat yogurt
1 teaspoon vanilla extract
1 teaspoon grated lemon zest or lemon juice
2 tablespoons honey

In a mixing bowl, beat together all the ingredients until smooth. Chill before serving. Serve with your favorite pieces of fruit for dipping.

Makes 2 cups.

Nutritional Analysis
2 Tablespoons: 35 calories, 1 gram fat

## FROZEN GRAPES

Wash fresh grapes well, pick off the stems, place in a freezer bag and freeze for a quick snack.

Nutritional Analysis
½ cup = 80 calories (1 carbohydrate unit)

## FAT-FREE VEGETABLE DIP

One 16-ounce container fat-free sour cream
1 packet powdered ranch salad dressing mix or 1 envelope onion soup mix
Raw fresh vegetables of choice, cut up

Mix the sour cream with the salad dressing. Chill and serve with your favorite vegetables.

Nutritional Analysis
2 Tablespoons = 25 calories, 0 grams fat ("free food")

## QUESADILLAS

Whole-wheat tortillas
Nonfat butter-flavored spray
Reduced-fat shredded cheese
Salsa
Fat-free sour cream
Fillings (optional): chopped tomatoes, jalapeño peppers, sautéed vegetables, and/or grilled chicken pieces

Spray a tortilla and sprinkle with the cheese. Top with another tortilla. Lightly spray the outside of the tortillas. In a nonstick frying pan, grill or pan-fry the tortillas for about 3 minutes on each side, until the cheese is melted. Cut into quarters and serve with salsa and fat-free sour cream.

Nutritional Analysis
1 quesadilla = 200 calories, 2–5 grams fat (2 carbohydrate units, 1 protein unit)

# Week 9 Weekly Menu

*Recipes are given for items in boldface.*

| | Breakfast | Lunch | Dinner | Snacks (1 to 2 choices per day) |
|---|---|---|---|---|
| MONDAY | Cinnamon toast (1–2 slices) with 2 teaspoons lite margarine and a sprinkle of cinnamon sugar<br><br>Fruit yogurt (4 to 6 ounces)<br><br>Orange juice—calcium-fortified (½ cup) | "Chunky tuna cup": solid white tuna (½ cup) mixed with ½ to 1 diced apple, chopped celery (optional), and fat-free mayonnaise (serve with lettuce leaves if desired)<br><br>Wheat crackers (6)<br><br>Grapes (½ cup)<br><br>Milk (1 cup) | Turkey spaghetti made with ground turkey and your favorite spaghetti sauce<br><br>Spaghetti noodles—preferably whole wheat (½ to 1 cup)<br><br>Parmesan cheese<br><br>Fruit cup (½ cup)<br><br>Tossed salad with 1–2 teaspoons olive oil or reduced-fat dressing<br><br>Water or calorie-free beverage | Cereal with fiber (1 cup) and skim or soy milk<br><br>Cereal-fruit bar (1)<br><br>Reduced-fat chips (about 15 chips or 1 ounce) with fat-free dip or salsa<br><br>Wheat crackers (6) with:<br><br>Reduced-fat cheese (2 slices) Lite cream cheese (2 tablespoons) Peanut butter (1 tablespoon)<br><br>Hot cocoa made with skim milk (1 cup)<br><br>English muffin or bagel "pizza": ½ muffin with tomato or pizza sauce and reduced-fat cheese<br><br>Fruit (1 piece fresh, ½ cup canned, or 3 tablespoons dried)<br><br>Frozen fruit bar (1) |
| TUESDAY | Fried egg sandwich (1 egg fried in nonfat butter-flavored spray) with wheat toast and reduced-fat cheese (optional)<br><br>Banana or other fresh fruit (1)<br><br>Milk (1 cup) | Turkey in a pita with tomato, lettuce, cheese (optional), and fat-free mayonnaise<br><br>Baby carrots with fat-free dip<br><br>Raisins (small box)<br><br>Milk (1 cup) | **Ham and Potato Casserole** (1 cup)<br><br>Green beans or your favorite vegetable<br><br>Unsweetened applesauce (½ cup)<br><br>Water or calorie-free beverage | |

| | **Breakfast** | **Lunch** | **Dinner** | **Snacks**<br>**(1 to 2**<br>**choices per day)** |
|---|---|---|---|---|
| WEDNESDAY | ½ bagel with peanut butter or reduced-fat cream cheese (1 tablespoon)<br><br>Melon (⅓ melon) or berries (1 cup)<br><br>Milk (1 cup) | Make-your-own "lunch pizza crackers" with 12 crackers, reduced-fat round pepperoni slices, reduced-fat cheese slices, your favorite tomato sauce (optional)<br><br>Fruit cup or reduced-fat pudding (½ cup)<br><br>Milk (½–1 cup) | Restaurant meal: BBQ chicken (1 breast or leg quarter or 1 to 2 drumsticks) or BBQ sliced beef (2 to 4 slices)<br><br>Baked beans (½ cup)<br><br>Corn on the cob<br><br>Water or calorie-free beverage | Fruit juice "spritzer": 3 ounces fruit juice mixed with 5 ounces club soda or sparkling water<br><br>Graham crackers (3 squares)<br><br>Teddy grahams (½ cup)<br><br>Nuts (2 tablespoons) |
| THURSDAY | Oatmeal (1 cup) with nuts (2 tablespoons), raisins (2 to 3 tablespoons), and brown sugar (1 teaspoon)<br><br>Milk (1 cup) | Grilled reduced-fat cheese sandwich (grilled with nonfat butter-flavored cooking spray)<br><br>Melon cup (1 to 2 cups)<br><br>Milk (½ to 1 cup) | **Chicken and Vegetable Soup** (2 cups or more)<br><br>Wheat crackers (6)<br><br>Tossed salad as desired<br><br>Reduced-fat pudding (½ cup)<br><br>Water or calorie-free beverage | Oatmeal (½ cup)<br><br>Oatmeal cookies (2 small)<br><br>Air-popped popcorn (5 cups)<br><br>Reduced-fat pudding or ice cream (½ cup)<br><br>Quesadilla (1 tortilla) with melted, reduced-fat cheese, salsa, and fat-free sour cream |
| FRIDAY | Scrambled egg substitute<br><br>Grilled ham slice (1) or turkey bacon (2 to 3)<br><br>Bagel (½) or wheat toast (1 slice)<br><br>Sliced tomato<br><br>Orange juice—calcium-fortified ½ cup) | Peanut butter and low-sugar jelly sandwich (1)<br><br>Rice cakes—any flavor (8 to 10 small)<br><br>Grapes (½ cup)<br><br>Milk (½ to 1 cup) | Oven-baked fish or fish sticks (1–2 fillets or 4–6 sticks)<br><br>**Spaghetti Squash**<br><br>Tossed salad as desired with 1–2 teaspoons olive oil or reduced-fat dressing<br><br>Waldorf salad (½ cup)<br><br>Milk (½ to 1 cup) | Rice cakes (10 small or 2 large)<br><br>Sandwich on whole-wheat bread (½) with turkey, tuna with lite mayo, or reduced-fat cheese |

| | Breakfast | Lunch | Dinner | Snacks (1 to 2 choices per day) |
|---|---|---|---|---|
| SATURDAY | French toast (1–2) with low-sugar syrup<br><br>Scrambled egg substitute (optional)<br><br>Banana (1) or berries (1 cup)<br><br>Milk (1 cup) | Leftover **Chicken and Vegetable Soup**<br><br>Wheat crackers (6)<br><br>Fruit cup (½ cup)<br><br>Milk (1 cup) | **Taco Salad**<br><br>Tortilla chips (15 to 20) with salsa<br><br>Water or calorie-free beverage | Soup: vegetable or chicken noodle (2 cups)<br><br>Trail mix (4 tablespoons)<br><br>Yogurt, regular or frozen (4 to 6 ounces) |
| SUNDAY | Cold cereal with fiber (1½ cups)<br><br>Banana (1) or berries (1 cup)<br><br>Milk (1 cup) | Fast-food meal: Kid's meal–size chicken nuggets or tenders (about 4), french fries (kid's meal–size), catsup, and BBQ or sweet-and-sour dipping sauce<br><br>"Kiddie"-size low-fat milk or yogurt shake<br><br>Water or calorie-free beverage if desired | **Leftover Night**<br><br>Food Units<br><br>1 to 2 starch-bread<br><br>Lean or low-fat protein<br><br>0 to 1 fruit<br><br>1 milk-dairy<br><br>1 fat<br><br>Veggies—unlimited! | |

# Week 9 Recipes

## HAM AND POTATO CASSEROLE

Nonfat butter-flavored spray

3 large potatoes, baked and sliced

4 medium carrots, coarsely grated

2 cups cooked ham or reduced-fat or "veggie" sausage, cooked, well drained, and diced

1 can reduced-fat cream of mushroom soup

½ soup can skim milk

1½ cups reduced-fat shredded Cheddar or American cheese

1 tablespoon dried minced onion (optional)

¼ teaspoon pepper (optional)

½ cup bread crumbs

2 tablespoons nonfat liquid butter substitute

Preheat the oven to 350°F. Spray a casserole, then in it layer half of the potatoes and carrots. In a bowl, mix the ham, soup, milk, 1 cup of the cheese, and the seasonings and pour half of the mixture over the potato/carrot mixture. Repeat. Top the casserole with the bread crumbs mixed with the remaining ½ cup cheese and the butter substitute. Bake, uncovered, for 45 to 50 minutes, till heated through and browned.

Makes about 6 cups.

Nutritional Analysis

1 cup: 2 carbohydrate units, 2 protein units, 1 fat unit (270 calories, 8 grams fat)

## CHICKEN AND VEGETABLE SOUP

1 tablespoon olive oil

Nonstick cooking spray

4 skinless, boneless chicken or turkey breasts, cut into bite-size pieces

1 small onion, sliced

4 stalks celery, sliced

4 cups chicken broth

1 cup sliced fresh or frozen carrots

1 cup fresh or frozen green beans

One 8-ounce can diced tomatoes, drained

Any leftover or favorite vegetables

1 bay leaf

¼ teaspoon black pepper (optional)

2 garlic cloves, minced, or more to taste

1 tablespoon cornstarch (optional)

Spray a large saucepan, heat the oil, and sauté the chicken, onions, and celery until the vegetables are just tender. Add the remaining ingredients and simmer for 1 hour (or put in a crock pot and cook for about 6 hours on a low setting). For a thicker soup, mix the cornstarch with 3 to 4 tablespoons water and pour into the soup in the last 20 minutes of cooking. Bring to a simmer, stirring constantly. The soup will thicken as it simmers. The recipe can be doubled or tripled. It freezes well.

Makes about 8 cups.

Nutritional Analysis
2 cups: 2 protein units, vegetable group (100–140 calories, 2–4 grams fat)

·····················································································································································

## SPAGHETTI SQUASH

1 spaghetti squash
½ cup chicken broth
Salt or salt substitute (optional)
Nonfat butter-flavored spray

Preheat the oven to 375°F. To make it easier to slice through the squash's hard outer skin, make a ½-inch slit in the side of the squash and microwave for 5 to 10 minutes before slicing, then put the squash cut side down in a baking dish. Add enough water to cover about one-third of the squash, then cover the dish with aluminum foil. Bake for about 50 minutes, or until the squash is very soft. Discard the seeds and scoop out the inside (the flesh will separate and look like spaghetti as you scoop it out of the skin). Discard the thick outer skin. Add the broth, salt, if using, and butter-flavored spray to the cooked squash and heat through, about 2 minutes.

To microwave: Slice, place cut side down in a dish, add water as directed above, and cover with plastic wrap. Microwave for about 20 minutes, until the squash is very soft.

Patrick's Mom's Spaghetti Squash: Omit the chicken broth and add ¼ teaspoon cinnamon, 2 to 4 tablespoons low-sugar pancake syrup, and 2 tablespoons nonfat liquid butter substitute.

Nutritional Analysis
Vegetable Group: No limit (½ cup = 25–30 calories, 0 grams fat)

## TACO SALAD

1 pound lean ground beef or turkey
1 packet taco seasoning
Lettuce, diced tomato, chopped green onion
1 cup shredded reduced-fat cheese
Fat-free sour cream
Salsa

Prepare the ground meat with the taco seasoning packet according to the package directions. Spoon over the lettuce, tomato, and green onion. Top with the cheese, sour cream, and salsa if desired.

Makes 2 to 2½ cups (4 to 5 servings)

Nutritional Analysis
½ cup taco meat and salad/condiments: 3 protein units, vegetable group (180 calories, 10–15 grams fat)

# Week 9 Weekly Shopping List

| Fruits | Vegetables | Meat, Deli | Dried and Canned |
|--------|------------|------------|------------------|
| Apples | Carrots, celery | Chicken or turkey breasts | Oatmeal |
| Banana | Potatoes | Fish fillets (your favorite kind) | Breakfast cereal (should contain more than 2–3 grams fiber per serving) |
| Grapes | Onion | Reduced-fat pepperoni rounds | Spaghetti |
| Melon in season | Spaghetti squash | Ground turkey (buy a "family pack"—enough for 2 recipes) | Spaghetti sauce (your favorite brand) |
| | Salad greens: | Turkey cold cuts | Pizza sauce (your favorite brand) |
| | Lettuce | | Taco seasoning packet |
| | Tomato | | Diced tomatoes (8-ounce can) |
| | Cucumber, etc. | | Chicken broth or bouillon cubes |
| | | | Vegetable soup |
| | | | Reduced-fat cream of mushroom soup |
| | | | Salsa |
| | | | Tuna (water-packed) |
| | | | Applesauce, fruit cup |
| | | | Raisins |
| | | | Reduced-fat pudding cups |

| Dairy Case | Frozen Food Section | Breads, Miscellaneous |
|---|---|---|
| Milk (skim, 1½%, or soy milk) | Green beans | Whole-wheat bread |
| Egg substitute, eggs | | Bagels |
| Reduced-fat or part-skim cheese slices (less than 5 grams of fat per ounce or slice) | | Whole-wheat pita bread |
| | | Rice cakes (any flavor) |
| | | Tortilla chips—baked |
| Reduced-fat shredded cheese— Cheddar or American (2 or more packages) | | Wheat crackers |
| String cheese made with part-skim mozzarella cheese | | |
| Fruit yogurt | | |
| Orange or other fruit juice— calcium-fortified juice | | |
| Fat-free sour cream | | |
| Parmesan cheese | | |

## Staples

Reduced-fat or very low-fat mayonnaise (less than 3 grams fat per serving)

Reduced-fat or low-fat salad dressings (less than 3–5 grams fat per serving)

Catsup, mustard, BBQ sauce, pickles (regular versions OK)

Low-sugar syrup, low-sugar or all-fruit jelly

Peanut butter (no added hydrogenated or partially hydrogenated vegetable oils)

Nuts

Oil (olive, canola, peanut), nonfat cooking spray, nonfat liquid butter (dairy section)

Lite margarine (first ingredient should be *liquid* vegetable oil—not hydrogenated or partially hydrogenated oil)

# WEEK 9 PORTION CONTROL AND
# FOOD RECORD PRACTICE

Don't forget to use TRIM KIDS AEROBIC ACTIVITY AND FOOD CHECKLIST to help keep track of your daily intake. Let's practice portion control checks for one day:

## Tuesday:

*Breakfast:*

| | |
|---|---|
| Fried egg sandwich | 1 protein, 1 fat (egg) |
| | 2 carbohydrates (2 slices wheat bread) |
| Banana | 1 carbohydrate |
| Milk (1 cup) | 1 carbohydrate |

*Lunch:*

| | |
|---|---|
| Turkey pita | 2 proteins (turkey slices) |
| with vegetables | 1 carbohydrate (pita half) |
| with fat-free mayonnaise | Vegetables—as desired |
| | Free |
| Vegetable soup | Vegetables—as desired |
| Raisins (¼ cup or a small box) | 1 carbohydrate |
| Milk (1 cup) | 1 carbohydrate |

*Dinner:*

| | |
|---|---|
| Ham and potato casserole (1 cup) | 2 proteins, 2 carbohydrates, 1 fat |
| Green beans | Vegetables—as desired |
| Unsweetened applesauce (½ cup) | 1 carbohydrate |

*Sample snacks:*

| | |
|---|---|
| Wheat crackers (6) | 1 carbohydrate |
| with peanut butter (1 tablespoon) | 1 protein, 1 fat |
| with reduced-sugar jelly | Free |
| String cheese, part-skim milk (4 pieces) | 2 proteins, 1–2 fats |

Total food units for Tuesday:       9 carbohydrates
7 proteins
4 fats
Vegetables

## SECTION 4: TIME TO SUM UP

# Trim Kids Weekly Checklist

*Did you remember to:*           *Yes*    *No*    *Will do it by*

Fill out TRIM KIDS WEEKLY REPORT AND GOAL SHEET?

———   ———   ——————

Fill out TRIM KIDS AEROBIC ACTIVITY AND FOOD CHECKLIST?

———   ———   ——————

Fill out TRIM KIDS STRENGTH AND FLEXIBILITY WORKOUT CHART?

———   ———   ——————

Have your child fill out the Twenty-Four Hour Activity Diary?

———   ———   ——————

Review emotional pitfalls and tips to prevent parental burnout?

———   ———   ——————

Create an appropriate cross-training routine?

———   ———   ——————

Involve your child in a hands-on cooking activity?

———   ———   ——————

Perform the aerobic activity of the week?

———   ———   ——————

*Did you remember to:*  ·  ·  ·  ·  **Yes**  ·  ·  **No**  ·  ·  *Will do it by*

Perform the strength and flex exercises of the week?

———  ·  ———  ·  —————————

If you're concerned that you can't take a well-deserved vacation while your child is on the Trim Kids Program, put this book down right now—and go call your travel agent! Life's pleasures don't come to a halt simply because you're living more healthfully. In week 10, we'll show you how easy—and much fun—taking a healthier vacation can be.

# Week 10

**TAKING VACATIONS
AND DINING OUT**

## TRIM KIDS ROAD MAP FOR WEEK 10

*This week we'll be your guide for traveling and vacations while you are on the Trim Kids plan. Try our tips for eating smart on the road and keeping fit on your trip. You'll practice the strength exercises with your child using the resistance band. Use the chart Dining Out at a Glance to choose healthy food on the road. Follow this week's menu plan as much as possible on the road. If you're able to cook while vacationing, try the new recipes and use the weekly shopping list to get what you'll need.*

### SECTION 1: TIME TO STOP AND THINK

## STRENGTH IN NUMBERS: THE POWER OF FAMILY COMMITMENT

By now, you and your family are well into your new lifestyle. The program has proved itself as you watch the weight fall away, and notice that all members of the family are more active, eating more healthfully, and generally feeling good about

## A Child's Perspective

"It was really cool to find out we could go camping and not worry about the program or what we were eating. It's weird, but just knowing that I could have some of my favorite things made it easier to stay on the program. We packed a bunch of healthy snacks and some bats, balls, and scuba equipment. It's the best vacation we've had in a long time."

—Brendan, age ten

themselves. But next week, you're leaving town for the annual family vacation. Does this mean that everything is going to revert to how it was before Trim Kids?

Not at all. It means you can be flexible about the program while still making wise choices. It means you can have a great time on your trip, then get back on the program 100 percent when you return.

You'll need the cooperative efforts of the entire family to make your trip a healthy one. To prepare, discuss food choices and portions. Agree on where you'll eat and when, on the road. If you choose a fast-food place, make sure it has a salad bar and grilled items as alternatives to deep-fried foods. Look over the fast-food list (page 337) for reminders about the healthiest options. Make it clear that even though you're breaking the routine to eat at fast-food restaurants, single portions—rather than double burgers or large orders of fries—are still the rule. Look for fast-food places with play areas, so the kids can also burn some calories.

## EATING SMART ON THE ROAD

Once you reach your destination, stay as true to the nutritional components of the Trim Kids Program as you can. Refer to Dining Out at a Glance (page 338) for tips on healthy choices at restaurants. Review these with your children before leaving so the information is at the forefront of their minds. It's smart to bring along some of your favorite low-calorie foods (fruit, rice cakes, low-fat yogurt, grapes, dried fruit, pretzels) and equipment for activities (Frisbee, ball and bat, soccer ball, in-line skates, football, boom box, and dance music).

When you are staying with relatives, call ahead and let them know the basics of your family's new diet. Ask if they are comfortable cooking within those parameters and how you can help. If they seem reluctant or unable to conform, then simply reiterate to your children that on this trip, they'll have to keep an especially close eye on portions.

If you attend family events—birthday parties, holidays, reunions, anniversaries—that revolve around unhealthy foods, bring your own tasty and healthy dishes. If that's not possible, discuss with your child the temptations she will face. Again, encourage her to limit portions and take responsibility for what she eats. Remind her that one small piece of Grandma's pie is fine, but that's it. Be sure to make positive comments about your child's ability to choose healthy food and to limit portions of high-calorie food. If you see her losing control, take her aside for a firm reminder of her goals and of the success she has shown in meeting them while on the program so far. Suggest alternative foods she can eat. If an occasion is informal, you have the option of leaving if she continues to eat compulsively. Be careful not to embarrass or shame her, either in front of others or after you've gone home. Simply review your goals, remind your child of her successes, and encourage her to adhere to the program.

There will also be times when your child stays with family members without you. Speak with him about the temptations that may arise and how to deal with them. Give your child as much responsibility as he can handle. Meanwhile, talk with relatives about your child's weight loss goals and let them know the new kinds of foods he enjoys. Ask them to avoid all-you-can-eat buffet restaurants. Suggest baking chicken instead of frying. Better yet, provide them with a large jar of dill pickles, a couple of bags of baby carrots, or those fresh peaches your child likes so much. That way, he can always make a healthy choice. It also helps if you send along his Trim Kids food record form so he can keep track of his progress.

When your child returns home, be sure to praise him for choosing healthy food or engaging in activities while away. If you find he's been fed biscuits and gravy, ribs, and unlimited chocolate cake, don't take it out on him. Consider confronting your relatives individually and possibly refuse another visit until they are willing to comply with the program.

Natural consequences will manifest themselves in a positive or negative way. Even while you are traveling, this principle still applies. Remind your child that the natural consequence of overeating is weight gain. Eating healthy foods and reasonable portions of high-calorie foods also reaps natural consequences: he will lose or maintain his weight, feel better about himself, be in control of his habits, and continue to receive compliments from others.

Although you and your family will do your best to stay true to the program, remember that slips are inevitable. The temptations that taunt your child during a well-deserved vacation may be too much to resist. If you think he needs a break, let him have one. Don't lecture him and don't focus on the regression. Rather, make a conscious decision together to take a break, and pick a date to return to the program. A slip doesn't mean going back to the vicious circle of overweight forever. After a child has been allowed some time off, recommitting to the program when he returns home should be easy.

## SECTION 2: TIME TO GET ACTIVE

# KEEPING FIT ON THE TRIP

You may not be able to take your local swimming pool, tennis court, or baseball team with you on your travels, but you can still provide plenty of opportunities for your child to exercise and stay active. In fact, sometimes traveling inspires even more activity, since there are so many new things to do and wonderful sights to see.

If the drive to your destination is lengthy, stop every few hours at town parks, playgrounds, or restaurants with play areas. Allow your children to romp around as long as time permits. Join in and stretch out the kinks. Start a game of tag, bring along a ball and kick it around, or simply lead your family in some healthy stretch and flex exercises. The idea is to keep up the habit of family activity even though you may not be following your typical routine.

Once you arrive at your hotel or another destination, ask if there's a gym on the premises. If so, check the equipment before allowing your child to work out, making certain it's safe and secure. Most kids love the hotel pool, if there is one. Parks and skating rinks are good alternatives to gyms, and most towns offer at least some other forms of child-friendly recreation. If the hotel management has few suggestions and you're stumped, call the local chamber of commerce or visitors' center and ask what's available, where it is, and what it costs.

In summer months when many families travel, it's easy to spend hours strolling through zoos, splashing in pools, and exploring parks. Consider a day trip to the mountains for a long, leisurely hike, some rowing in a fishing boat, climbing trees, or skipping rocks on a lake.

Winter months offer plenty of activities, too. If your family doesn't ski, consider ice skating, snowshoeing, sledding, and even building snowmen. Children's museums provide hours of indoor activities. Or go to the local mall and walk briskly from one end to the other.

Remind your child that natural consequences also come into play if he chooses not to exercise while on vacation. He'll begin to feel sluggish, and it will be harder for him to resume his routine once he's back home. If he remains active by playing or doing his stretches and aerobic workout, he'll have more energy on the trip and will be able to resume his routine at home with ease.

Active families deserve trips that encourage fun and learning. These days, complete vacation packages are available in which kids can learn to sail, ski, swim, hike, play tennis or golf, excavate dinosaur bones—you name it, it's out there! Aside from keeping your kids fit and teaching them new skills, these resorts often include child care for those times when you and your spouse want a little time away. Contact a travel agent to learn more.

## WEEKLY EXERCISE ACTIVITIES

### WEEK 10 AEROBIC ACTIVITY: RECOMMENDED GOALS

Write your goal in the TRIM KIDS AEROBIC ACTIVITY AND FOOD CHECKLIST (page 386). This is the minimum amount of aerobic exercise that you should perform this week. Every day, record what type of physical activity you did and how long you did it. At the end of the week, compare your list with the goals you set at the beginning of the week.

- Red Level: The exercise goal this week is four days per week for thirty-five to forty minutes each day.
- Yellow Level: The exercise goal this week is four days per week for thirty-five to forty-five minutes each day.
- Green Level: The exercise goal this week is five days per week for thirty-five to fifty-five minutes each day.
- Blue Level: The exercise goal this week is three days per week for thirty to sixty minutes each day.

### WEEK 10 AEROBIC ACTIVITY: AEROBIC SOFTBALL

The rules of softball are altered to encourage movement at all times. For example, aerobic softball requires that *all* team members walk or run the bases when a run is scored and perform ten jumping jacks or side jacks (page 97) when the batter gets a strike.

### WEEK 10 STRENGTH AND FLEX EXERCISES

Read the instructions aloud to your child as she does these exercises, until she no longer needs your assistance.

## Strength Exercise 10: Crunches

Lie on the floor with your arms behind your head. Interlock your fingers behind the base of your neck. Bend your knees at a ninety-degree angle, and put your feet flat against a wall. Keep your chin tilted slightly back while relaxing your head in your hands throughout the movement.

Press your lower back gently against the floor. *Hold in your abdomen* while lifting your upper body from the lower trunk on the count of two. *Do not roll your head and shoulders forward.* Look up at the ceiling, keeping your head relaxed in your hands, and hold for one second. Nice. Now, on the count of two, return to the starting position. Keep your elbows pointed outward during the entire exercise.

Do ten to twenty repetitions of this move. This exercise trains your stomach muscles (abdominals).

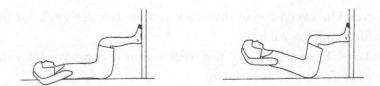

Common errors your child may make include pulling on the neck, dropping the chin, pushing the stomach out, and pushing the elbows forward.

## Flex Exercise 10: Straddle Stretch

Sit upright on the floor with your legs extended forward and your hands alongside your hips. Slowly extend your legs out to the side as far as you comfortably can. Turn your knees and toes up toward the ceiling. Good.

Place your hands behind your hips, keeping your head, shoulders, and trunk in line. Bend from the hips forward until you feel a gentle stretch on your inner thighs. Do not roll your head forward. Do not roll the shoulders forward.

Bring your hands in between your legs and slowly "walk" them forward until you feel a gentle stretch in the inner thigh. Hold this stretch for fifteen to thirty seconds. Release. Now, walk hands over to the left side, reaching for the heel. Hold for fifteen to thirty seconds. Do the same for the right side. Gently release and "walk" hands back to the center and up until you're back in the upright position. Repeat this process one more time, holding each position again for fifteen to thirty seconds.

Perform these new strength and flex exercises and also those you learned previously in weeks 1–9 at least once and preferably twice this week. Record your progress on the TRIM KIDS STRENGTH AND FLEXIBILITY WORKOUT CHART in the appendix ("Forms You'll Need"), on page 388. Every week, you will add another exercise to your program.

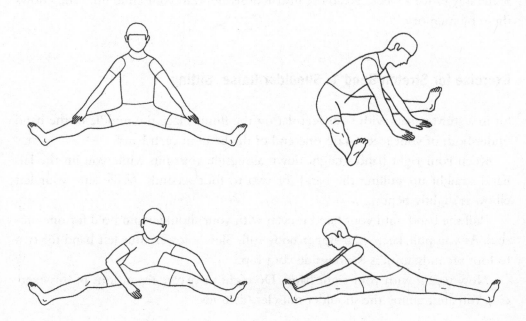

Don't forget to fill out your TRIM KIDS AEROBIC ACTIVITY AND FOOD CHECK-LIST on page 386, and try the aerobic activity of the week with the entire family.

# BAND-AID FOR OUT-OF-SHAPE MUSCLES

Once you're used to the great feeling of toned muscles, it's hard to go back to that loose, flabby feeling. But sometimes it's hard to get to the gym, and you probably don't have the space for big, heavy weights in your room. And what about when you're traveling?

Here are some exercises to do using a stretch band. A stretch band is a large rubber band of sorts. It is usually made of soft latex and is three to four feet long. When you pull on the band, it resists your weight, much as those fancy weight-room machines do. But, unlike weights, this band can be easily stored under your bed, on a shelf, or in your suitcase. See page 234 in "Week 6" for more information on purchasing one.

The exercises below work just like training with weights. Do them exactly as instructed, since the technique is specific and safe. If you do the exercises incorrectly, you may hurt a muscle or joint.

The following exercises should be performed eight to twelve times once and preferably twice a week. Read the instructions aloud to your child until she knows them by memory.

## Exercise for Stretch Band 1: Shoulder Raise, Sitting

Sit in a sturdy chair with your feet flat on the floor. Place the middle of the band under both of your feet. Grasp one end of the band in each hand.

Keep your right hand straight down alongside your hip while you lift the left hand straight up, pulling the band for two to four seconds. Make sure your left elbow is slightly bent.

Pull the band until your hand is even with your shoulder and hold for one second. As you pull, keep your upper body still. Slowly lower your left hand for two to four seconds, until it is alongside your hip.

Now repeat with your right hand. Do eight to twelve repetitions of this exercise. You are training the shoulder muscles (deltoids).

Common errors your child may make include bending the elbows too much or keeping elbows too straight, moving the upper body, or lifting hands too high.

## Exercise for Stretch Band 2: Standing Squat and Pull

Stand with your feet pointing forward, about eighteen inches apart. Place the middle of the band under both of your feet. Grasp one end of the band in each hand while bending your knees, pushing your hips back, and dropping your chest forward. *Your knees should not be in front of your feet.* Keep your head in line with your body and your heels on the floor.

Slowly, over two to four seconds, extend your hips forward and come up to a standing position while pulling the band upward. Keep your elbows straight throughout the entire movement. Great.

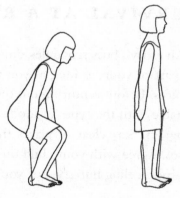

Now slowly lower (two to four seconds), return to the starting position, and do it again.

Do this exercise eight to twelve times. You are training the upper leg muscles (quadriceps) and the buttocks muscles (gluteus).

## Exercise for Stretch Band 3: Reverse Butterfly

Sit in a sturdy chair with your feet flat on the floor. Place the middle of the band under both of your feet. Grasp one end of the band in each hand.

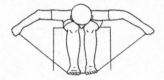

Bend forward until your chest rests on your lap. Keep your head in line with your body and point your face downward. Slowly pull the ends of the band out to the sides and up while keeping your elbows slightly bent. Keep pulling for two to four seconds. Great job!

Now squeeze your shoulder blades together as you stretch the band and feel a slight tension in your upper back and shoulder. Hold for one second. Good.

Now gently and slowly release the band (two to four seconds), returning to the starting position.

Do eight to twelve repetitions of this exercise. You are training the upper back muscles (rhomboids) and the rear shoulder muscles (deltoids).

Common errors your child may make include keeping elbows too bent or too straight, arching the neck, and pulling the band too close to the body.

## SECTION 3: TIME TO DINE

## SURVIVAL AT A RESTAURANT

With today's busy schedules, dining out is part of most people's lives, and it still can be part of yours as long as you and your child plan ahead and make appropriate choices. Before venturing out to a restaurant, wait until you are familiar and comfortable with the types of foods and portions your child can eat in the Trim Kids Program. Stay clear of places that dole out huge portions of primarily high-fat foods. Agree with your child on what to eat before you go out—preferably when he's not feeling hungry—or you may run into a surprise, high-calorie binge!

- Ask how the food is prepared and whether substitutions can be made. Many restaurants offer a vegetable of the day, which can be substituted for extra bread or potatoes.
- Request that sauces and dressings be served on the side. A standard serving (ladleful) of regular salad dressing can contain up to 450 calories and 30 grams of fat!

- Avoid buffet-style restaurants as much as possible!
- If you are hungry, choose a lower-fat appetizer or soup to prevent binge-ing on the bread or on your meal.
- Request that the bread or crackers not be brought to your table until the meal is served.
- Restaurant portions are often very large. To decrease portion size, choose an appetizer as your main meal, or split an entrée with another family member.
- Once you are full, request that the leftover food be removed from the table to prevent ongoing nibbling.

Select items that are:

- Steamed
- Broiled
- Roasted
- Poached
- Grilled
- Cooked in tomato sauce
- Served *au jus*

### Friendly Fast-Food Choices

- Stick to small-size sandwiches and hamburgers. A single hamburger has only about half the calories of a large hamburger and one-third the calories of a super-size burger.
- Hold the mayo. An average sandwich has more than 200 calories (and 20 grams of fat) from just the mayonnaise! Enjoy catsup, mustard, and BBQ sauce instead!
- Skinless chicken, turkey, and ham are the leanest cuts of meat.
- If you are craving french fries, get a "kid's meal" fry (200 calories)—the sandwich is also smaller! A large order of fries contains more than 500 calories, and a super-size order contains more than 700 calories.
- Deep-fat fried chicken or fish can actually have more calories than a greasy hamburger patty!
- A super-size drink contains more than 350 calories and 80 grams of sugar. Get a diet drink, a small juice, or low-fat milk instead.
- Water is free and the best beverage choice!

Avoid items that are cooked in or contain large amounts of:

- Butter or cream sauces
- Gravy
- *Au gratin* or scalloped mixtures
- Cheese sauce
- Fried

## DINING OUT AT A GLANCE

Use the guide below to make healthier choices instead of high-calorie, high-fat restaurant selections. Don't forget to watch portion sizes!

| Healthy Choice | Higher-Fat, Higher-Calorie Choice |
| --- | --- |
| **Appetizers** | |
| Fresh fruit cup | Potato skins, fried cheese |
| Vegetable juice | Fried vegetables |
| Shrimp or crabmeat cocktail | Cream or cheese soups |
| Fresh vegetable relish | |
| Broth or tomato-based soups | |
| **Breads** | |
| Plain or hard rolls | Biscuits |
| French or Italian bread | Garlic or cheese bread |
| Bread sticks, melba toast | Sweet rolls |
| Plain crackers | Corn bread, muffins |

| **Starches** | |
| --- | --- |
| Plain or wild rice | Twice-baked potatoes |
| Baked potato (ask for the toppings on the side) | *Au gratin* potatoes |
| Boiled potatoes or corn | Potato or macaroni salad |
| Beans (red, white, black, kidney) | French fries, hush puppies |
| | Macaroni and cheese |
| **Poultry** | |
| Roast turkey or chicken | Fried chicken |
| Grilled skinless chicken | Chicken cutlets |
| Skinless BBQ chicken | Chicken nuggets or tenders |
| | Chicken-fried steak |
| **Fish and Seafood** | |
| Broiled, grilled, or baked fish | Any fried seafood |
| Boiled crawfish, crabs, shrimp, or lobster | *Au gratin* seafood |
| | Seafood stuffing |
| **Beef and Pork** | |
| Broiled or baked pork chops | Fried pork chops |
| Roasted or sautéed veal | Beef or pork ribs |
| Broiled sirloin steak | Breaded fried veal |
| Baked roast beef (ask for gravy on the side) | Country-fried steak |

| | |
|---|---|
| Baked ham, Canadian bacon | Sausage, hot dogs, bacon |
| | Corned beef |

### Dessert

| | |
|---|---|
| Poached or fresh fruit | All others, including: |
| Angel food cake | Strawberry shortcake |
| Sherbet or sorbet | Ice cream |
| Gelatin | Chocolate pudding |

### Salad Bar

| | |
|---|---|
| Salad greens (lettuce, endive, spinach, etc.). | Regular salad dressings |
| Tomatoes, cucumbers, peppers | Potato salad and macaroni salad |
| Fresh or canned fruit | Croutons |
| Lean turkey, ham | Shredded cheese |
| Low-calorie or fat-free salad dressing | Salami cubes |
| Vinegar | Coconut |

### Chinese

| | |
|---|---|
| Wonton, egg drop, or hot-and-sour soup | Egg rolls, fried wontons |
| Stir-fried dishes with meat, fish, and vegetables (beef and broccoli, moo goo gai pan) | Fried dishes (sweet-and-sour pork, lemon chicken) |
| Hint: request a "dry wok" cooking method to have your dish prepared without oil. | Peking duck |

| | |
|---|---|
| White or brown rice | Fried rice |
| Fortune cookies | Fried bananas |

### Italian

| | |
|---|---|
| Minestrone soup | Buttered garlic bread |
| Pasta with acceptable sauces: marinara, marsala, wine, tomato, onion, garlic, or red clam | Creamy, white, or butter sauce such as Alfredo sauce |
| Chicken cacciatore | Chicken or veal Parmesan |
| Broiled fish or fish in tomato sauce | Italian sausage |
| Italian ice | |

### Mexican

| | |
|---|---|
| Salsa, picante sauce | |
| Soft baked tortillas | Taco chips, fried tortillas |
| Fajitas | Refried beans |
| Chicken or bean enchiladas or burritos (ask for the sour cream and cheese on the side) | Tostados, quesadillas |
| Seviche | Chiles relleños |
| | Mexican fried ice cream |

### Cajun and Creole

| | |
|---|---|
| Okra or chicken gumbo | Fried meat, fish, or poultry |
| "Blackened" fish or chicken | Sausage gumbo |
| Shrimp creole | Shrimp or lobster bisque |

| Boiled crawfish or shrimp | Meunière sauce |
|---|---|
| Chicken or seafood jambalaya | Sausage jambalaya |
| | Étouffée, crawfish, shrimp pies |

# Week 10 Weekly Menu

*Recipes are given for items in boldface.*

| | Breakfast | Lunch | Dinner | Snacks (1 to 2 choices per day) |
|---|---|---|---|---|
| MONDAY | Oatmeal (½ cup) with chopped fruit and nuts (1 tablespoon) if desired<br><br>Whole-wheat toast (1 slice)<br><br>Milk (1 cup) | Tacos (2)<br><br>Lettuce, tomato, salsa<br><br>Fresh fruit in season<br><br>Milk (½ to 1 cup) | Roast chicken (store-bought or home-cooked)<br><br>**Spinach Patties** (2 or more)<br><br>Bread or dinner roll (1)<br><br>Sliced tomatoes with reduced-fat dressing (optional)<br><br>Milk (½ to 1 cup) | Cereal containing fiber (1 cup) and skim or soy milk<br><br>Cereal-fruit bar (1)<br><br>Reduced-fat chips (about 15 chips or 1 ounce) with fat-free dip or salsa<br><br>Wheat crackers (6) with:<br><br>Reduced-fat cheese (2 slices)<br><br>Lite cream cheese (2 tablespoons)<br><br>Peanut butter (1 tablespoon)<br><br>Hot cocoa made with skim milk (1 cup) |

| | Breakfast | Lunch | Dinner | Snacks (1 to 2 choices per day) |
|---|---|---|---|---|
| TUESDAY | English muffin, toasted (½–1) with scrambled egg substitute and reduced-fat cheese<br><br>Fresh fruit in season<br><br>Milk (1 cup) | Chef salad with sliced turkey and ham and reduced-fat cheese (about 2 slices each) with lettuce, tomato, and 2 tablespoons reduced-fat dressing<br><br>Wheat crackers (6)<br><br>Small ("kiddie"-size, 4 ounces) frozen yogurt with fruit topping<br><br>Water or calorie-free beverage | Macaroni and cheese (1 cup) with reduced-fat hot dog (1 to 2)<br><br>Mixed vegetables<br><br>Carrot or celery sticks with fat-free dip<br><br>Fruit cup (½ cup)<br><br>Water or calorie-free beverage | English muffin or bagel "pizza": ½ muffin with tomato or pizza sauce and reduced-fat cheese<br><br>Fruit (1 piece fresh, ½ cup canned, or 4 tablespoons dried)<br><br>Frozen fruit bar (1)<br><br>Fruit juice "spritzer": 3 ounces fruit juice mixed with 5 ounces club soda or sparkling water<br><br>Graham crackers (3 squares) |
| WEDNESDAY | Cinnamon toast (1–2) made with 2 teaspoons lite margarine and a sprinkle of cinnamon sugar<br><br>Fruit yogurt, small (4 to 6 ounces)<br><br>Orange juice—calcium-fortified (½ cup) | Sandwich—preferably whole wheat (½)<br><br>Tomato or vegetable soup<br><br>Air-popped popcorn (3 to 5 cups)<br><br>Milk (1 cup) | Restaurant meal: Spaghetti with tomato sauce (kid's plate if possible—or about 1 cup noodles)<br><br>Meatballs (about 2)<br><br>Parmesan cheese<br><br>Garlic bread (1 slice)<br><br>Tossed salad as desired with 1–2 teaspoons olive oil or reduced-fat dressing<br><br>Italian ice or fruit sherbet (½ cup)<br><br>Water or calorie-free beverage | Teddy grahams (½ cup)<br><br>Nuts (2 tablespoons)<br><br>Oatmeal (½ cup)<br><br>Oatmeal cookies (2 small)<br><br>Air-popped popcorn (3 to 5 cups)<br><br>Reduced-fat pudding or ice cream (½ cup)<br><br>Quesadilla (1 tortilla) with melted reduced-fat cheese, salsa, and fat-free sour cream |

| | Breakfast | Lunch | Dinner | Snacks (1 to 2 choices per day) |
|---|---|---|---|---|
| THURSDAY | Whole-grain waffle (1) with sliced banana or berries<br><br>Egg substitute scrambled in nonfat cooking spray (optional)<br><br>Milk (1 cup) | String cheese made with part-skim milk (about 4 pieces)<br><br>Cottage cheese (½ to 1 cup) with unsweetened applesauce or canned pineapple (½ cup)<br><br>Cucumber slices with reduced-fat dip<br><br>Water or calorie-free beverage | **White Chicken Chili** (1 to 2 cups)<br><br>Tortilla chips (about 15)<br><br>Salsa<br><br>Steamed or cooked vegetables—your favorite or leftover<br><br>Milk (½ to 1 cup) | Rice cakes (10 small or 2 large)<br><br>Sandwich on wheat bread (½) with turkey, tuna with lite mayo, or reduced-fat cheese<br><br>Soup: vegetable or chicken noodle (2 cups)<br><br>Trail mix (4 tablespoons)<br><br>Yogurt, regular or frozen (4 to 6 ounces) |
| FRIDAY | Cold cereal containing fiber (1 to 1½ cups)<br><br>Banana (1) or raisins (add to cereal)<br><br>Milk (1 cup) | Peanut butter (1 to 2 tablespoons) with wheat crackers (12) or rice cakes (4 large) with low-sugar jelly (optional)<br><br>Raisins (small box)<br><br>Baby carrots or carrot sticks with fat-free dip<br><br>Milk (1 cup) | Open-faced sandwich: tuna salad and reduced-fat cheese on half of a toasted English muffin (broiled to melt the cheese)<br><br>Tossed salad with 1–2 teaspoons olive oil or reduced-fat dressing<br><br>Air-popped popcorn (3 to 5 cups)<br><br>Reduced-fat pudding (½ cup)<br><br>Water or calorie-free beverage | |

|  | **Breakfast** | **Lunch** | **Dinner** | **Snacks** (1 to 2 choices per day) |
|---|---|---|---|---|
| SATURDAY | Yogurt shake made with yogurt, frozen strawberries, banana, and ice (skim or soy milk added to make thinner) | Leftover **White Chicken Chili** (1 cup) <br> Grapes (½ cup) or fresh fruit in season <br> Sliced tomato or cherry tomatoes with fat-free mayonnaise or dressing <br> Milk (1 cup) | Grilled steak (filet or sirloin, small) <br> **Baked Sweet Potato Fries** or baked potato (1) <br> Grilled corn on the cob or other favorite vegetables <br> Water or calorie-free beverage | |
| SUNDAY | Pancakes (1–2) with low-sugar syrup and berries if desired <br> Turkey bacon (3) or "veggie" sausage links (2) <br> Milk (1 cup) | **Oriental Chicken with Vegetables** <br> Brown rice (½ cup) <br> Tossed salad as desired with 1–2 teaspoons olive oil or reduced-fat dressing <br> Fruit cup (½ cup) <br> Milk (1 cup) | **Leftover Night** <br> Food Units <br> 1 to 2 starch-bread <br> Lean or low-fat protein <br> 0 to 1 fruit <br> 1 milk-dairy <br> 1 fat <br> Veggies—unlimited! | |

# Week 10 Recipes

## SPINACH PATTIES

One 10-ounce package frozen chopped spinach, thawed and well drained
¾ cup cottage or ½ cup part-skim ricotta cheese
½ cup cornflake crumbs or crushed cornflakes or bread crumbs
½ cup grated Parmesan cheese, plus some for garnish
¼ cup fat-free mayonnaise
2 eggs or ½ cup egg substitute

¼ teaspoon salt or salt substitute (optional)

Dash of pepper

Nonstick butter- or olive oil–flavored cooking spray

2 teaspoons olive oil

In a bowl, combine all of the ingredients except the oil and spray and mix well. Shape into 6 to 8 patties. Spray a skillet, add the oil, and fry the patties over medium heat for about 5 minutes on each side. Sprinkle with additional Parmesan if desired.

Makes 6 to 8 patties.

Nutritional Analysis

Vegetable Group: No limit (1 pattie = 40–50 calories, 1–4 grams fat)

··········································································································································

# WHITE CHICKEN CHILI

Nonstick cooking spray

2 teaspoons olive oil

1 onion, finely chopped

2 to 3 cups leftover cooked chicken pieces, diced (optional)

1 garlic clove, minced

½ teaspoon ground cumin (optional)

One 10-ounce package frozen white corn, thawed, or one 15-ounce can, drained

One 4-ounce can diced green or jalapeño chile peppers

Two 15-ounce cans white northern beans

Reduced-fat shredded cheese, fat-free sour cream, and salsa for serving (optional)

Spray a saucepan, add the oil, and sauté the onions until tender. Add the remaining ingredients and simmer for about 30 minutes. Serve with cheese, sour cream, and salsa, if desired.

Makes 6 cups.

Nutrition Analysis

1 cup: 2 carbohydrate units, 2 protein units (250 calories, 9 grams fat)

## BAKED SWEET POTATO FRENCH FRIES

2 to 3 sweet potatoes
Nonstick cooking spray
¼ cup grated Parmesan cheese
½ teaspoon garlic powder (optional)
¼ teaspoon pepper (optional)

Preheat the oven to 425°F. Cut the potatoes lengthwise into thin wedges (microwave for 1 to 2 minutes to make cutting easier). Spray liberally, place in a zippered plastic bag with the Parmesan and seasonings, and shake. Arrange the potatoes in a single layer on a cookie sheet sprayed with nonstick cooking spray. Bake for about 30 minutes, turning once.

Makes four 2- to 3-cup servings.

Nutritional Analysis
½ cup (about 15 fries): 1 carbohydrate unit (100 calories)

## ORIENTAL CHICKEN WITH VEGETABLES

4 to 6 skinless, boneless chicken breasts
2 zucchini, sliced crosswise
3 to 4 carrots, sliced lengthwise
One 14-ounce can baby corn, drained
2 to 3 green onions, sliced crosswise
⅓ cup low-sodium soy sauce
3 tablespoons hoisin sauce (found in the Oriental foods section of the grocery store) or honey
1 tablespoon fresh ginger, minced, or ½ teaspoon powdered ginger

Preheat the oven to 400°F. Place the chicken breasts and vegetables in a baking dish. In a small bowl, mix the soy sauce, hoisin sauce, and ginger and pour over the chicken and vegetables. Marinate for 30 minutes to 1 hour prior to baking. Bake, uncovered, for about 45 minutes.

Makes 4–6 servings.

Nutritional Analysis
1 breast with vegetables/sauce: 3–4 protein units, ½ carbohydrate unit, vegetable group
(190 calories, 7 grams fat)

# Week 10 Weekly Shopping List

| Fruits | Vegetables | Meat, Deli | Dried, Canned |
|--------|-----------|-----------|---------------|
| Banana | Carrots, celery | Chicken breasts (buy a "family pack"—enough for 2 recipes) | Oatmeal |
| Berries in season | Corn on the cob (or frozen) | | Breakfast cereal (should contain more than 2–3 grams fiber per serving) |
| Grapes | Ginger | Roasting chicken (store-bought or home-prepared) | Cereal-fruit bars |
| | Green onion | | Brown rice |
| | Onions | Reduced-fat (less than 3 grams of fat) hot dogs | Cornflake crumbs (or cornflake cereal to crush) |
| | Sweet potatoes | Steak (sirloin or filet) | Macaroni and cheese mix |
| | Salad greens: | Turkey or ham cold cuts | Oatmeal |
| |    Lettuce | | White northern beans (two 15-ounce cans) |
| |    Tomato | | Diced green chilis or jalapeños (4-ounce can) |
| |    Celery, etc. | | Salsa |
| | | | Dill pickles |
| | | | Baby corn, canned |
| | | | Soy sauce, low-sodium |
| | | | Vegetable soup |
| | | | Tuna (water-packed) |
| | | | Applesauce, fruit cup |
| | | | Hoisin sauce (optional) |
| | | | Reduced-fat pudding cups |

| Dairy Case | Frozen Food Section | Breads, Miscellaneous |
|---|---|---|
| Milk (skim, 1½%, or soy milk) | Waffles, pancakes | Whole-wheat bread |
| Egg substitute, eggs | Mixed vegetables | English muffin |
| Reduced-fat or part-skim cheese slices (less than 5 grams of fat per ounce or slice) | Spinach, chopped | Reduced-fat popcorn |
| | White corn | Tortilla chips—baked |
| | Strawberries | Wheat crackers |
| Fruit yogurt | | |
| Orange or other fruit juice— calcium-fortified | | |
| Cottage cheese | | |
| String cheese (part-skim milk) | | |
| Parmesan cheese | | |

### Staples

Reduced-fat or very low-fat mayonnaise (less than 3 grams fat per serving)
Reduced-fat or very low-fat salad dressings (less than 3–5 grams fat per serving)
Catsup, mustard, BBQ sauce, pickles (regular versions OK)
Low-sugar syrup, low-sugar or all-fruit jelly
Peanut butter (no added hydrogenated or partially hydrogenated vegetable oils)
Nuts
Oil (olive, canola, peanut), nonfat cooking spray, nonfat liquid butter (dairy section)
Lite margarine (first ingredient should be *liquid* vegetable oil—not hydrogenated or partially hydrogenated oil)

# WEEK 10 PORTION CONTROL AND FOOD RECORD PRACTICE

Don't forget to use TRIM KIDS AEROBIC ACTIVITY AND FOOD CHECKLIST to help keep track of your daily intake. Let's practice portion-control checks for one day:

## Tuesday:

*Breakfast:*

| | |
|---|---|
| English muffin (½–1) | 1–2 carbohydrates |
| Scrambled egg substitute | 2–3 very lean proteins |
| Fresh fruit of choice | 1 carbohydrate |
| Milk (1 cup) | 1 carbohydrate |

*Lunch:*

Chef salad:

| | |
|---|---|
| Turkey, ham, reduced-fat cheese | 2–3 proteins, 1–2 fats |
| Salad greens, tomatoes | Vegetables—as desired |
| Reduced-fat dressing (2 tablespoons) | 2 fats (0 fats if fat-free is used) |
| Wheat crackers (6) | 1 carbohydrate |
| Frozen yogurt (small, 4 ounces) | 1 carbohydrate |

*Dinner:*

| | |
|---|---|
| Macaroni and cheese (1 cup) | 2 carbohydrates, 1 protein, 3 fats |
| Reduced-fat hot dogs (2) | 2 proteins |
| Mixed vegetables | Vegetables—as desired |
| Carrot or celery sticks with fat-free dip | Vegetables—as desired / Free |
| Fruit cup (½ cup) | 1 carbohydrate |

*Sample snacks:*

| | |
|---|---|
| Cereal fruit bar | 2 carbohydrates |
| Dill pickle | Free |

| | |
|---|---|
| Total food units for Tuesday: | 10–11 carbohydrates |
| | 7–8 proteins |
| | 6–7 fats |
| | Vegetables |

......................................................
## SECTION 4: TIME TO SUM UP
......................................................

## Trim Kids Weekly Checklist

*Did you remember to:*          *Yes*     *No*     *Will do it by*

Fill out TRIM KIDS WEEKLY REPORT AND GOAL SHEET?

———  ———  —————

Fill out TRIM KIDS AEROBIC ACTIVITY AND FOOD CHECKLIST?

———  ———  —————

Fill out TRIM KIDS STRENGTH AND FLEXIBILITY WORKOUT CHART?

———  ———  —————

Plan your next vacation by contacting a travel agent about activity-related trips? (Once you've decided where to go, mark it on your calendar and get psyched up!)          ———  ———  —————

Review Dining Out at a Glance?          ———  ———  —————

Review Friendly Fast-Food Choices?          ———  ———  —————

Perform the aerobic activity of the week?

———  ———  —————

Perform the strength and flex exercises of the week?

———  ———  —————

Parents: After your child weighs in and fills out the weekly report form, don't forget to review previous goals and set new weekly goals.

# Week 11

# FUN FACTS AND
# RELAPSE PREVENTION

## TRIM KIDS ROAD MAP FOR WEEK 11

*This week, after filling out the Trim Kids forms in the appendix (remember to weigh your child and list your goals for the week), you will read about techniques to prevent a relapse—regaining weight. You will learn about the benefits of individual sports, and how to get the most out of a fitness workout. This week you and your child will use our Trim Kids Menu Plan to create your own one-week menu plan, modify some of your own recipes so that they follow the Trim Kids Nutrition Plan, and make your own weekly shopping list to get what you'll need. Fill out the TRIM KIDS AEROBIC ACTIVITY AND FOOD CHECKLIST. Don't forget to check your child's progress with the Trim Kids Weekly Checklist at the end of the chapter. You've almost finished the twelve-week plan! Make an appointment with your child's pediatrician for next week.*

## SECTION 1: TIME TO STOP AND THINK

# CREATING HEALTHY INDEPENDENCE

There's an old saying: if you give a man a fish, you feed him for a day; but if you teach him how to fish, you feed him for a lifetime. This saying suggests the difference between dependence and independence. Our program advocates fishing lessons from the start.

The more personal responsibility you give your child, the faster she will understand her role in attaining and maintaining her physical well-being. This means letting go enough so she can master the program herself. The sooner she can set and abide by her own limits, the better.

It's important not to take responsibility for your child's actions while she's in the program. You are her coach—not her controller. If she has a bad week, don't blame yourself. Rather, help lead her back on course. In the same vein, when she reaches her goals, don't take credit yourself—give it entirely to her. As is true for any coach, when the team drops the ball, it's not the coach's fault. And when a player scores, it wasn't the coach who threw the winning ball.

One surefire way to break the fishing line between your child and her ability to master this program is to take attention away from her successes. If, for example, you yourself begin losing weight and feeling better as a by-product of this program, be mindful not to steal attention from your child by talking about your success or flaunting your slimmer physique. Redirect the positive attention back to your child by commenting that it is she who inspired you, and the whole family, to become healthier.

Sometimes letting go means allowing your child to make mistakes. This is a tough concept for any parent. But it's essential so that she can understand how the choices she made led to the mistake, take responsibility for where she went wrong, and learn from it. You will sense when your child is ready to make a mistake and take responsibility for it. Try not to intervene. Trust that she'll come out of it in one piece, and of course, be there for her as her coach and loving parent.

Take precautions against unhealthy habits that make children dependent on parents and slow their progress in the program.

*Features of failure:* When your child doesn't reach a goal, it's important to work with her to assess the situation realistically by evaluating her goals. Was a goal too difficult? What was going on in her life that may have made a goal hard to attain? Take a look at the big picture, never refer to her as a failure, and move forward by establishing new, easier goals.

*Parental restrictions:* If things aren't progressing the way you hoped, now's a good time to reflect on the household rules you made and whether or not you enforced them. Restrictions are up to you to initiate, model, and monitor. If your child is straying from the program, it may have more to do with your role as parent and coach than with your child's reluctance to do her part.

*Focusing on negative, unhealthy behaviors:* You already know the rules about positive reinforcement. What was the last positive statement you made to your child? What was the last negative one? How could you have rephrased the negative comment to make it affirming, upbeat, and encouraging?

*Offering no choices:* Is your child better able to take responsibility for herself because she knows that there are always healthy choices available to her? Does she have a list of alternative behaviors visible to her at all times? Do you remind her of these choices? "You can rake the leaves, vacuum the carpet, or spend half an hour riding your bike." Does your child know that she may not be able to have ice cream for dessert, but that there's a delicious array of healthy sweet foods (like strawberries, sugar-free and fat-free yogurt, and watermelon) to choose from? Having choices in every aspect of the program strengthens everyone's commitment and sense of control.

---

### TRIM KIDS TESTIMONIAL

## A Parent's Perspective

"I just don't know what happened. Jimmy did so well on the program last year. I was sure he would stay in the Blue Level and maintain his goal weight. But my dad was hospitalized, and we had to start eating out a lot. Then soccer season ended and softball just didn't seem to be giving Jimmy much of a workout. He started watching a lot more TV. I was so busy at work and with my dad that I guess I just didn't notice those extra 15 pounds until Jimmy was almost back to where he started. We're ready to commit again, and I know we can do it. After all, we did it once before."

# LAPSE, RELAPSE, AND COLLAPSE

Backsliding happens, but to different degrees. Some backsliding is acceptable and easy to manage while some points to danger. Consider the following definitions to determine how to deal with the situation.

- Lapse or slip: Your child engages in an old, unhealthy behavior *once* during a typical week—eating a fast-food meal, for example, or spending an entire day on the couch. Remember: This can be a planned treat.
- Relapse: Your child allows an unhealthy behavior to surface *three times* within a single week.
- Collapse: An unhealthy behavior occurs *every day* of the week. It doesn't have to be the same behavior (such as eating high-fat food), but there is some form of unhealthy behavior every day (eating high-fat food one day, refusing to play outside or do strength exercises the next, etc.).

Clearly, lapses will occur and need to be allowed—even planned. A lapse won't cause weight gain, and as long as you don't punish your child or allow him to criticize himself for the behavior, it will not cause problems. The most important thing is problem solving for future similar situations and either choosing a vacation from the program or recommitting to a healthy lifestyle as soon as possible.

If your child's behavior falls into the category of relapse or collapse, make sure you haven't reintroduced tempting high-fat foods into the house. And take an honest look at how well you've been enforcing the firm rules you've established. If he's not being physically active, why not? Maybe TV and computer games have begun to take precedence over basketball and stretching. It may be time to shore up your energy, call a family meeting, and reassess goals.

One strategy for helping your child stay on track is to reinforce the idea that it's better to get *mad*—and then *glad*. Often, kids fall off the wagon during times of high stress, when others tease them, or when someone calls them fat or lazy. Their typical response is that they get mad first, then feel miserable and turn to food for comfort. They may be thinking, "Bill is right. I can't say no to candy, so I guess I'll go ahead and have another piece."

## It's What You Do All Day That Makes You Overweight!

Overweight People
Do This:

- Skip breakfast.
- Sit at a desk all day.

- Snack on junk food all day.

- Always take the elevator or escalator.
- Walk around with drinks and food.
- Feel physically tired at the end of the day and head for the sofa and TV to relax.

- Eat a large dinner late in the evening.

- Overexert during infrequent exercise sessions.
- Eat midnight snacks.

- Stand impatiently at traffic lights and bus stops.
- Drink soft drinks when thirsty.
- Stand impatiently in store lines.
- *Not* feel hungry until lunchtime.
- Sit in one position for hours.
- Eat fast food three or four times per week.

Normal-Weight People
Do This:

- Eat a healthy breakfast.
- Get up every thirty minutes for two to three minutes of moderate activity.
- Schedule midmornng and midafternoon healthy snacks each day.
- Always take the stairs.
- Eat at the dinner table only.
- Feel mentally tired and go for a walk or ride a bike to reduce stress and unwind.

- Eat a moderate dinner in the evening.

- Exercise moderately most days of the week.
- Sleep soundly because regular exercise reduces stress.
- Shift weight from side to side at traffic lights and bus stops.
- Drink water when thirsty.
- Perform toe raises or shuffles heels forward while waiting in store lines.
- Feel hungry when they wake up.
- Stretch at their desk frequently.
- Eat fast food once every two weeks.

Proving Bill wrong is terrifically more gratifying than giving in to the temptation and proving that he's right. Help your child use his anger to demonstrate that whoever is insulting him is downright wrong; that he *can* resist candy; that he *is* losing weight. Anger can be a productive tool if channeled constructively.

## Avoiding Relapse: Think Ahead!

List below the times, places, or feelings which could cause your family to relapse and keep you from reaching your health and maintenance goals. Examples may include boredom, a sleepover at a friend's house, holidays, or a social event. Discuss ways to avoid these unhealthy temptations.

1. _____

2. _____

3. _____

4. _____

5. _____

Don't let a lapse turn into a relapse—or, worse, a collapse!

## SECTION 2: TIME TO GET ACTIVE

## THE TRIPLE WHAMMY

There are three physiological effects from regular exercise that will help you to maintain your weight loss:

1. Burning calories during exercise.
2. Burning calories after exercise (this is called excess postoxygen consumption, EPOC). You burn calories after exercise because your temperature stays elevated and your body is working to refuel lost oxygen stores.
3. Change in metabolic rate (known as resting energy expenditure, REE) due to change in body composition by increasing the strength, density,

amount, and in some cases overall size of the muscles. Unlike EPOC, which burns calories during the hours after your workout, your resting energy expenditure, REE, is the rate at which you burn calories when you are at rest—no matter how long it's been since you exercised. Remember: muscles burn more calories than fat, so when you work out and develop denser and more trained muscles, you automatically burn more calories!

## THE MPEP ULTIMATE WORKOUT

It's been ten weeks since your child began the Trim Kids Program. If your child has lost at least 15 percent of her starting body weight and is over twelve years of age she can participate in the MPEP Ultimate Workout. First, review the steps below with your child.

1. Warm up—Warm up as usual for three to five minutes. Refer to the MPEP Step (page 146) in "Week 3."
2. Maintain steady state—Regardless of what activity you are doing, bring your speed up to a moderate level and hold it there for forty minutes. If you are walking, keep it at a brisk pace (3 to 4 mph) while swinging your arms. If you are cycling, go for sixty revolutions per minute so that your right foot will push down every second (on a flat road). If you're on a stationary bike, set the pace at level 1, or 25 watts. Swimmers should maintain a slow, easy pace while doing freestyle laps. *Do not speed up or slow down during this period.*
3. Make the MPEP push—After forty minutes at a constant pace, increase your pace as though you were in a race. Continue at this speed until you feel tired, your breathing becomes rapid, or your muscles burn slightly.
4. Cool down—Gradually reduce your speed until you are moving at a slow pace. Continue moving for ten to fifteen minutes, or until your heart rate is normal.

## MPEP Ultimate Workout Time Chart

*Time elapsed (in approximate minutes)*

| 0–5 | 45 | 60 |
|---|---|---|
| **Warm up** | **Steady state—MPEP push** | **Cool down** |

The steady-state phase burns many calories and—especially—fat. While increasing the temperature and metabolism, the MPEP push revs up the body's engine. This can make you feel energized and full of pep. You'll feel this way throughout the cool-down and for hours afterward. You'll also burn calories at a higher rate for several hours after the workout—for as long as twelve hours after the exercise session! The length of this effect is EPOC in action. It depends on both the duration and the intensity of your workout.

Only healthy children who have been engaged in three or more months of exercise conditioning should attempt the MPEP Ultimate Workout.

## EXERCISE ACTIVITY IDEAS: TEAM SPORTS VERSUS SOLO

Research has found that individual goal-based sports may be better for overweight children than competitive team sports, especially during the initial stages of a weight management program. That's because in individual goal-based activities, the child sets a personal goal for himself rather than a goal that depends on competing with another individual or team. For example, swimmers usually aim to exceed their personal best in any given event—to score better than their best score in previous attempts.

Activities that offer children an opportunity to set individual goals include gymnastics, track and field, archery, golf, judo, karate, dance, tai bo, synchronized swimming (solo and duet), springboard diving, and ice skating. Team sports can be beneficial if you select those your child enjoys and to which he is well-suited. Refer to "Week 8" for reminders on which exercises are best for particular body types. As always, make sure the coach and teacher are aware of your child's special needs before signing him up.

Your child also burns calories in doing activities that don't cause him to break into a sweat or become fatigued. Give him the opportunity to participate in less challenging things he can do for hours at a time. Weekends are an especially good time for the entire family to play together. Try golf, badminton, croquet, throwing passes, Frisbee, flying kites, basketball free-throw games (such as H-O-R-S-E), body toning classes, beach volleyball, line-dancing, modified yoga, games in the pool, playing tag, bowling, swinging on the swing set, pulling a wagon full of stuffed animals, gardening, yard work, housework, and more.

## WEEK 11 AEROBIC ACTIVITY: RECOMMENDED GOALS

Write your goal in the TRIM KIDS AEROBIC ACTIVITY AND FOOD CHECKLIST (page 386). This is the minimum amount of aerobic exercise that you should perform this week. Every day, record what type of physical activity you did and how long you did it. At the end of the week, compare your list with the goals you set at the beginning of the week.

- Red Level: The exercise goal this week is five days per week for forty to forty-five minutes each day.
- Yellow Level: The exercise goal this week is five days per week for forty to fifty minutes each day.
- Green Level: The exercise goal this week is six days per week for forty to sixty minutes each day.
- Blue Level: The exercise goal this week is three days per week for thirty to sixty minutes each day.

## WEEK 11 AEROBIC ACTIVITY: FAMILY WATER SPORTS

Choose from water aerobics, water polo, synchronized swimming (water ballet), competitive swimming (races), water skiing, surfing, rafting, snorkeling, scuba, windsurfing, sailing, jet skis.

## WEEK 11 STRENGTH AND FLEX EXERCISES

Read the instructions aloud to your child as she does these exercises, until she no longer needs your assistance.

## Strength Exercise 11: Squat, Standing

Stand tall and erect with your stomach muscles tight. Do not lock your knees. Your hands may be on your hips, or you can use them to hold on to a support. Keep your knees and feet facing forward with about eighteen to twenty inches between your feet.

Slowly, slowly, to the count of four, bend your knees and lean your body slightly forward, bending at the hip while keeping your back straight and your stomach tight. Keep your heels on the ground. Do not allow your knees to extend past your feet. Good job! Again to the count of four, return to the starting position.

Do eight to twelve repetitions of this move. You are training the front thigh muscles (quadriceps), the back thigh muscles (hamstrings), and the buttocks (gluteus).

## Flex Exercise 11: Flex at Your Desk

*If you think you can stretch only at home, think again! Here are some stretches to do at your desk at school. Ask your teacher if the entire class can participate in them. Everyone will feel better for it!*

Turn sideways in your desk or push your chair back. Bend over from the hips and let your chest rest on your thighs. Let your head fall below your knees as your hands fall to the ground. Hold for fifteen to thirty seconds. Inhale as you slowly return to your upright position. Repeat one more time.

Sit with your back straight and flat against the back of the chair. Bring your arms up above your head and interlock your fingers. Keep arms in front of ears. Stretch hands and arms upward toward the ceiling. Hold fifteen to thirty seconds.

Sit with your back straight and flat against the back of the chair. Raise your right arm straight up above your head just to the side of the right ear. Bend your elbow and drop your hand to the back of your neck. Reach up with the other arm and grasp the elbow. Gently pull. Hold fifteen to thirty seconds. Repeat with other arm.

Sit on the edge of your chair. Bring your elbows back and squeeze them together as you lift your chin upward and stretch your chest. Hold fifteen to thirty seconds.

Perform these new strength and flex exercises and also those you learned previously in weeks 1–10 at least once and preferably twice this week. Record your progress on the TRIM KIDS STRENGTH AND FLEXIBILITY WORKOUT CHART in the appendix ("Forms You'll Need"), on page 388. Every week, you will add another exercise to your program.

Don't forget to fill out your TRIM KIDS AEROBIC ACTIVITY AND FOOD CHECK-LIST on page 386, and try the aerobic activity of the week with the entire family.

## TOP TEN TIPS FOR INCREASING PHYSICAL ACTIVITY

1. Encourage your child to move briskly at every opportunity.
2. Enroll your child in structured dance, sport, or movement classes. Make sure the teachers are qualified and discuss your child's condition with the teacher before enrolling.
3. Create an environment for active play both inside and outside the home.
4. Participate in activities the entire family can enjoy together.
5. Expose your overweight child to as many different kinds of activities as possible in a nonintimidating and nurturing environment.
6. Provide opportunities for your normal-weight child to safely climb, run, and jump to help develop muscular strength and bone density.
7. Don't impose adult exercise goals on young children, who have immature metabolic systems.
8. Reserve at least one half day each weekend dedicated to fun family fitness activities.
9. Don't draw attention to sedentary activities with negative comments. Instead, praise your children when they choose active play.
10. Be a good role model. Parents don't have to be thin, but they must set a good example by participating in healthy physical activities.

## SECTION 3: TIME TO DINE

# NUTRITION NUTSHELL: WATER AND WEIGHT LOSS

Water is both essential to your child's health and a wonderful asset to the Trim Kids Program. Water contains no calories, so your child can drink as much of it as he wants. A large glass can stave off hunger and provide much-needed hydration both before and after exercise. Water—which makes up 70 percent of our bodies—is also necessary for processing vitamins and minerals, while keeping stools soft and the urinary tract healthy.

While on the Trim Kids Program, your child should consume between 60 and 86 ounces of fluid each day. Ideally, water should make more than 75 percent of that, while other low-sugar and low-fat drinks can make up the rest.

Be especially mindful of your child's fluid intake during exercise. If he becomes dehydrated, he could experience heat injury and an imbalance in his muscle and blood minerals. Consequently, his endurance will diminish and other problems may occur.

Encourage your child to stay well hydrated by reviewing these tips together.

> ### TRIM KIDS TESTIMONIAL
>
> Do you wonder what happened to Jimmy, whom you met at the beginning of this chapter? Well, we checked Jimmy's height and weight—and his mom was very happy to hear that 5 of those extra 15 pounds were actually due to a one-inch growth spurt. Dr. Kris explained that Jimmy had begun to relapse, but that this had definitely been caught before a big collapse. Jimmy and his mom started coming to our clinic once a month after that. Jimmy kept his food and exercise records faithfully, and after two months he was back on track and had lost most of the weight he regained. Now his mom brings him in to see us about every three months to check his weight and height. His weight is increasing slightly—but so is his height. Now, at fourteen, he's doing great.

- Drink 12 to 16 ounces of fluid before and after exercise to ensure pre- and postexercise hydration.
- Drink an additional 12 to 16 ounces of fluid for every one hour of exercise.

- Water is the best choice for hydration. Sports drinks (with added sugar and minerals) aren't necessary for exercise lasting less than sixty to ninety minutes.
- If you exercise moderately or intensely for more than ninety minutes, you may need a carbohydrate-containing beverage. Dilute a sports drink or fruit juice by adding ½ or ¼ serving of water. We don't recommend high-sugar or full-strength fruit juices, punches, or fruit drinks because they cannot be absorbed as rapidly as water in the bloodstream.
- The longer and more intensely you exercise, the more fluid supplementation you may need.
- Drink cool or cold beverages, since they help decrease body temperature during exercise. They also empty from the stomach faster and are absorbed more quickly, providing rapid hydration.

## CREATING CULINARY DELIGHTS: WRITE YOUR OWN MENU

You've had ten weeks to experience new, tasty, low-calorie foods. Now it's your turn to create menus and write your own recipes!

Feel free to include or adapt the recipes and menu substitutions we've provided. Refer to the healthy cooking suggestions on page 130 in "Week 2." Be daring! The worst that can happen is that your child will give the food an F. That just means he can help figure out the next culinary creation!

Do your best to have your child help you formulate the weekly menu—the more she learns, the better her shopping and cooking skills will be in adulthood.

## SECTION 4: TIME TO SUM UP

## Trim Kids Weekly Checklist

*Did you remember to:*                              *Yes*        *No*        *Will do it by*

Fill out TRIM KIDS WEEKLY REPORT AND GOAL SHEET?

——      ——      —————

Fill out TRIM KIDS AEROBIC ACTIVITY AND FOOD CHECKLIST?

——      ——      —————

Fill out TRIM KIDS STRENGTH AND FLEXIBILITY WORKOUT CHART?

——      ——      —————

Discuss the idea of a planned lapse with your child and move forward with it if necessary?

——      ——      —————

Review the MPEP Ultimate Workout with your older child?

——      ——      —————

Review Top Ten Tips for Increasing Physical Activity with your child?

——      ——      —————

Plan a fun family outing?

——      ——      —————

Write your own menu plan for the week?

——      ——      —————

Record the recipes for your menu plan?

——      ——      —————

Perform the aerobic activity of the week?

——      ——      —————

| *Did you remember to:* | *Yes* | *No* | *Will do it by* |
|---|---|---|---|
| Perform the strength and flex exercises of the week? | ___ | ___ | _____ |

You've got one more week to complete the first session of the Trim Kids Program! Week 12 will help you assess how you've done and where to go from here.

# Week 12

# REASSESSING, RECOMMITTING, AND FORGING THE FUTURE

## TRIM KIDS ROAD MAP FOR WEEK 12

*You'll start this week off—after filling out the appropriate Trim Kids forms, as usual—by bringing your child to the pediatrician's office, where together you will complete the TRIM KIDS QUARTERLY EVALUATION CHART. Compare your child's measures at the beginning of the program with those of today. Compliment and reward your child for any positive changes. This week you will not only review last week's goals and accomplishments but you will also review her twelve-week goals that you wrote in week 1. Reward her for meeting her goals. Discuss any problems or questions with her. You can refer to the TRIM KIDS AEROBIC ACTIVITY AND FOOD CHECKLISTS that you have been filling out each week to praise your child for making healthy selections or to see why she had trouble reaching her goals.*

*This week we give you tips on how to help your child maintain her weight loss. If your child has not yet reached a healthy weight, you will again set a twelve-week goal with the help of your child's pediatrician and the information contained in this week's chapter.*

## SECTION 1: TIME TO STOP AND THINK

Congratulations! You have nearly completed the first twelve weeks of the Trim Kids Program! Chances are good that you've met with many successes, and that your family is healthier and happier.

It's now time to evaluate your child's progress by visiting your pediatrician. The doctor can determine if your child has either lost adequate weight or has grown enough to graduate to the next color-coded level. If she graduates, then reward, reward, reward! Also, set a new three-month goal. Refer to your child's twelve-week goals (page 90). Did she attain some of them? If so, reward her with special (nonfood) gifts such as sports equipment, trips to a water slide, new smaller-size clothing, a camping trip, or some other family adventure. If she is graduating to the next color-coded level of the program, consider printing up a graduation notice or certificate of achievement. These little steps go a long way toward building enthusiasm for the next twelve weeks.

If your child was successful at not gaining weight but needs to remain in the same color-coded level, give as much positive reinforcement as you can. Rave about the efforts she's made and express your faith in her. As you begin a new twelve-week program, brainstorm together an idea for a reward she'll receive upon graduating after this new session.

If you discover, however, that the severity of your child's overweight condition or the percentage of body fat has *increased* since the last visit, then you must recommit to new and more attainable weight-loss goals. Also, try practicing the strategies and behaviors that helped when things went smoothly in the past. You may also want to consider enlisting the help of a professional.

Work with your child so that she doesn't get angry, hopeless, or nervous. Taking a deep breath, reassessing long- and short-term goals, defining rewards, and recommitting to being healthy and happy are all it takes! And remember: everyone who tries to lose weight has setbacks.

Don't be discouraged if you have to revolve through the program several more times before your child meets his goal weight. By now, you have a good handle on the program, know what incentives work for your child, what tempts her to make unhealthy choices, and how to deal with problems. The next three months will most likely be easier than the first three. You are all beginning to master the program. It will simply take as long as it takes, but it's helpful to think in terms of three-month intervals. It's natural that both your overweight child and the family may have a higher commitment to the program at the very beginning than later on. This becomes problematic only if everyone falls back into old eating habits and sedentary behavior. The goal of each session is to integrate lifestyle changes more fully and comfortably so that they become expected and easy.

Each time you begin a new session, practice every component of the program. Establish new goals for each level, for example, because old goals may no longer be relevant. And don't trick yourself into believing that you don't need to make goals, don't need to keep praising your child, or don't need to work at the program fully. It's the *combination* of these elements that makes the program work—not isolated pieces. Eventually, if you continue participating fully, your child will reach his goal weight. Don't forget that she is always growing, that growth is her best friend. For every inch she grows, her goal weight increases by three to five pounds.

Be sure to acknowledge accomplishments of other family members as you end this first session. Take time to celebrate by throwing yourselves a party with your new favorite foods or taking an evening out together.

Before embarking on another session or moving into maintenance, ask yourself these questions:

- As you review the previous twelve weeks, do you feel happy? Confident? Satisfied? Successful?
- Is your child's behavior different? Is she more confident? Are her spirits higher?
- Are you all ready to go for the next twelve weeks?
- Are you committed to helping your child maintain his goal weight?

After visiting your child's doctor, fill out the following form. It will help you gear up for the next twelve-week round!

# Trim Kids Quarterly Evaluation

Name: _____ Age: _____ Today's date: _____

Level: _____

| *3 Months Ago . . .* | *Now . . .* |

Your child's weight was _____ pounds.

Your child's weight is _____ pounds.

Your child lost _____ pounds in the last _____ months!

Your child's height was _____ feet _____ inches.

Your child's height is _____ feet _____ inches.

Your child grew _____ inches in the last _____ months!

Your child's BMI was _____
This value is based on the body mass index charts (pages 21–23).

Your child's BMI is now _____.
This means your child is now in the _____ th percentile for his or her height.

Your child was in level _____, the _____ color.

Your child graduated to level _____, the _____ color.

Based on your child's past height, his or her goal weight was _____ pounds.

Your child's new goal weight is _____ pounds. (Your pediatrician will tell you this.) Bear in mind that your child's goal weight will increase as your child grows.

Your child's percent body fat range was _____ to _____ %.

Your child's range of percent of body fat is _____ to _____ %.

Your child's cholesterol level was \_\_\_\_\_.

Your child's cholesterol level is \_\_\_\_\_. The normal level for children is <170.

Your child's triglyceride level was \_\_\_\_\_.

Your child's triglyceride level is \_\_\_\_\_. The normal range varies by age.

Your child's LDL level was \_\_\_\_\_. This is "bad" cholesterol.

Your child's LDL level is \_\_\_\_\_. The normal range for children is <110.

Your child's HDL level was \_\_\_\_\_. This is "good" cholesterol.

Your child's HDL level is \_\_\_\_\_. The normal range for children is >35.

Your child's waist and hip measurements were \_\_\_\_\_ inches (waist) \_\_\_\_\_ inches (hip)

Your child's waist and hip measurements are \_\_\_\_\_ inches (waist) \_\_\_\_\_ inches (hip)

Your child lost \_\_\_\_\_ inches!

## MAINTAINING GOAL WEIGHT

Although losing weight is your child's first step to a healthier and happier life, keeping it off is the second—and lifelong—objective. Recall that being overweight is a chronic condition, so if your child has reached his goal weight, maintaining it will take diligence both on your part and your child's. Research shows however that support from a health professional during maintenance can help. We also know that children who keep the weight off continue to exercise regularly, use social support, and develop specific problem-solving skills.

There are times when a parent, a child, or both will need help staying true to this new lifestyle. If you sense old habits sneaking back into your child's life (or yours), don't hesitate to get help. There are counselors, exercise coaches, dietitians, friends, family, and support groups—a host of people who will eagerly help you get back and stay on track.

If you are concerned about spending money on professionals, turn to your local bookstore. There are shelves of low-fat, whole-grain cookbooks available from which you can draw years of healthy recipes. Down the aisle, you'll find thousands of helpful books on behavior modification, stress reduction, exercise activities for children, and techniques for overcoming unhealthy habits. Ask your doctor or school professional which ones they think are best. We've listed some resources on our Trim-Kids.com website.

There are other steps you can take as well. If your child is convinced she can eat anything now that her weight is normal, we ask her to take an inventory for one week of calories and fat in meals she eats outside the home, including school lunches. She may be in for a surprise when she realizes that her new, healthy eating habits will ensure a normal weight, but eating regularly at school, fast-food restaurants, and other places she avoided while on the program will sabotage months of hard work and dedication.

You can also enlist the help of the parents of your child's friends. Let them know that she's attained her weight goal and ask them to refrain from offering her high-calorie foods during visits. Most people are more than willing to help a child stay healthy and happy.

Experiencing new things is another way to stay committed to your new life. Have you ever tried Indian food? How about Vietnamese? Has your child been longing to take tennis lessons, but you've refrained for fear of knee injuries? A child who has lost 20 percent of his original weight and has followed the exercise program faithfully should now be able to engage safely in more challenging weight-bearing activities. Refer to "Week 1" for specific exercises suited to different levels of overweight. Keep the program alive by keeping it fun! Branch out and answer those secret longings your child has had to go river rafting, snow skiing, or snorkeling. Or at least start by enrolling the entire family in an introductory skiing lesson!

Review the following with your child to reinforce what has been done and what must continue to be done to stay trim and healthy.


## How to Maintain Your New Weight

By the end of this session of the Trim Kids Program, you will have lost weight by:

- Learning to select healthier food
- Becoming more active and more physically fit
- Changing your eating habits
- Becoming more confident about yourself

Everything you have learned will help you maintain your new weight. Now, answer the following questions with your parents.

## Trim Kids Success Questionaire

1. What changes were necessary for you to lose weight?

   _____

   _____

   _____

2. Which changes were difficult?

   _____

   _____

   _____

3. Which changes were easy?

   _____

   _____

   _____

To maintain your new weight, you must practice the new behaviors or habits that you learned in the Trim Kids Program.

## Rate the Changes

Rate the changes that helped you most.                    Easy          Hard

Recording the foods you ate:                                ❒             ❒

Recording your weight loss:                                    ☐        ☐

Weighing yourself frequently:                                  ☐        ☐

Changing the foods you ate:                                    ☐        ☐

Increasing your daily physical activity:                       ☐        ☐

Becoming involved with sports:                                 ☐        ☐

Going to the playground:                                       ☐        ☐

Doing physical activities with your friends:                   ☐        ☐

---

### SECTION 2: TIME TO GET ACTIVE

## EXERCISE ACTIVITY IDEAS

If left to their own devices, most children would prefer to burn calories outside playing tag, swinging, chasing balls, or throwing themselves into a pile of fallen leaves. Older kids go outside for different reasons: to participate in sports, go for a bike ride, or walk to a mall. Sometimes, however, it's nice to have an option to exercise inside. Exercise machines can provide a good workout while your child watches television or reads. Younger kids aren't as inclined to take such a machine seriously, but it's not out of the question even for them. Roland, a ten-year-old participant in our program, loves the stationary bike. He rides it every day because it's the only time his mother lets him watch television!

### Don't Be Fooled by These Myths about Exercise

Myth: No pain, no gain.

Truth: During exercise, you should feel a gentle burning in your muscles; this indicates fatigue. If you feel pain or discomfort in a bone, joint, or muscle, stop the exercise immediately and consult a doctor.

Myth: "Movie star" exercise equipment and videos are safe and effective.

Truth: These types of items are designed primarily for profit. They have not been researched and could cause severe injury. Stay away from them!

Myth: There are special fat-burning exercises.

Truth: All exercises—except for high-intensity anaerobic activities—burn fat. The longer you exercise, the more fat you'll burn. Fat is lost by creating a caloric deficit; it is not determined by the type of exercise you do.

---

### Rate the Exercise Equipment

You increase the number of calories you burn by using more muscle groups at once. We've rated these exercise machines according to their potential for burning calories.

*****Treadmill, cross-country ski machine, Airdyne® cycle, rowing ergometer

****Stair-climber with handles and support, exercise cycle with handrails

***Outdoor cycle, exercise cycle (incline or upright), stair-climber with support rails

**Arm ergometer

*Stair-climber without support rails

No way! Any gadget (often endorsed by celebrities on TV and in magazines) that promises quick fixes or makes other unrealistic claims.

---

Myth: Spot reducing burns fat in one area.

Truth: There are no exercises that can burn fat in one particular area of the body. You can, however, train a specific muscle or group of muscles for strength and endurance, and this can result in a toned appearance. Being toned is a condition in which muscles remain contracted even when you don't consciously tighten them. So, abdominal crunches (page 332) alone (without other calorie-burning activities or a reduction in how much you eat) won't melt the fat around your waist, although they will help strengthen and firm your abdominal area.

Myth: Strength training makes big muscles.

Truth: Strength training doesn't always result in larger muscles. Rather, genetic makeup, the type of strength training being performed, and the frequency of the training will determine the results. Women especially will probably not develop "big" muscles through strength training. They will create more dense and, therefore, more toned muscles that will make them look leaner and will increase the rate at which they burn calories. Mothers, if you train once or twice per week with your son or daughter, you will be doing yourself and your child a favor.

## SUMMARY

## Recommendations for Preventing Obesity

- Discourage consumption of beverages high in sugar.
- Select healthy fruits and snacks as treats—e.g., grapes and raisins.
- Understand that all food is OK. Some foods are healthy and help children grow tall or big, and some are not. Encourage children to select more of the healthy variety.
- Require that all drinks and foods be consumed only in a designated place—for example, at the kitchen or dining room table.
- Schedule midmorning and midafternoon healthy snacks, and make them attractive.
- Always require children to eat a healthy breakfast.
- Discourage snacking after dinner.
- Create a healthy environment at home: Display and keep within reach nutritious foods naturally low in fat and sugar. Allow infrequent consumption of nonnutritious foods away from home.
- Realize that young children have immature metabolic and musculoskeletal systems. Don't impose adult exercise regimens or goals on children.
- Encourage participation in aerobic activities appropriate for your child's age and size.
- Provide opportunities for young children to safely climb, run, and jump to encourage the development of muscular strength and endurance.
- Families that play together stay healthy together. Reserve at least half a day of each weekend for family physical fitness.

## Recommendations for Treating Obesity

- Obesity is a chronic disease. Treatment should be lifelong. When the treatment is withdrawn, the patient usually regains the weight lost.
- All treatment programs should be closely supervised by a pediatrician or family physician.
- Consult a registered dietitian for specific recommendations about nutrition.
- Praise your child when you observe healthy behaviors.
- When unhealthy behaviors emerge, ignore them, redirect them, or solve the problem.
- Set short-term, achievable goals and reward your child's successes.
- Reevaluate your child's condition every three to six months.
- Replace nonnutritious foods with healthy alternatives.
- Use portion control when healthy eating alone is not enough.
- Replace TV, computer, and video games with indoor and outdoor play.
- Downsize—break large bags of foods into smaller portions.

# WEEKLY EXERCISE ACTIVITIES

### WEEK 12 AEROBIC ACTIVITY: RECOMMENDED GOALS

Write your goal in the TRIM KIDS AEROBIC ACTIVITY AND FOOD CHECKLIST (page 386). This is the minimum amount of aerobic exercise that you should perform this week. Every day, record what type of physical activity you did and how long you did it. At the end of the week, compare your list with the goals you set at the beginning of the week.

- Red Level: The exercise goal this week is five days per week for forty to forty-five minutes each day.
- Yellow Level: The exercise goal this week is five days per week for forty to fifty minutes each day.
- Green Level: The exercise goal this week is six days per week for forty to sixty minutes each day.
- Blue Level: The exercise goal this week is three days per week for thirty to sixty minutes each day.

WEEK 12 AEROBIC ACTIVITY: FAMILY HIKE

If it rains, play laser tag or go roller-skating indoors.

WEEK 12 STRENGTH AND FLEX EXERCISES

Read the instructions aloud to your child as he does these exercises, until he no longer needs your assistance.

## Strength Exercise 12: Standing, Calves

Stand erect with your stomach muscles tight and your hips tilted slightly forward. Hold on to a bar or another stationary object for support.

Slowly, over two counts, rise on the balls of your feet as high as possible. Great!

Now, again over two counts, slowly return to the starting position. Be careful not to lock your knees.

Do eight to twelve repetitions of this move. You are training the calf muscles (gastrocnemius).

Common errors your child may make include failing to rise high enough on the toes and pushing with the hands.

## Flex Exercise 12: Calf Stretch

Stand in front of a wall and place your hands on the wall in line with your chest. Move one leg two to three feet behind the other.

Now bend your front leg and press the heel of the back leg toward the floor until you feel a gentle stretch in the calf muscle. Push on the wall, bringing your head in between your arms, continuing to push the heel backward until you feel a full stretch from your hands down through the heel. Hold this stretch for fifteen to thirty seconds. Looks good. Now, repeat this move with your other leg. Repeat this process for each leg one more time, holding this position again for fifteen to thirty seconds.

Perform these new strength and flex exercises and also those you learned previously in weeks 1–11 at least once and preferably twice this week. Record your progress on the TRIM KIDS STRENGTH AND FLEXIBILITY WORKOUT CHART in the appendix ("Forms You'll Need"), on page 388.

Don't forget to fill out your TRIM KIDS AEROBIC ACTIVITY AND FOOD CHECKLIST on page 386, and try the aerobic activity of the week with the entire family.

## SECTION 3: TIME TO SUM UP

# Trim Kids Weekly Checklist

*Did you remember to:*          Yes          No          *Will do it by*

Fill out TRIM KIDS WEEKLY REPORT AND GOAL SHEET?

_____    _____    _____

Fill out TRIM KIDS AEROBIC ACTIVITY AND FOOD CHECKLIST?

_____    _____    _____

Fill out TRIM KIDS STRENGTH AND FLEXIBILITY WORKOUT CHART?

_____    _____    _____

Visit the pediatrician for a progress check?

_____    _____    _____

| *Did you remember to:* | *Yes* | *No* | *Will do it by* |
|---|---|---|---|

Fill out Rate the Change with your child?

_____ _____ _____

Fill out the Trim Kids Assessment Questionnaire?

_____ _____ _____

Review the myths about exercise with your child?

_____ _____ _____

Perform the aerobic activity of the week?

_____ _____ _____

Perform the strength and flex exercises of the week?

_____ _____ _____

Identify old goals that have become new habits?

_____ _____ _____

What's next? Set new, more challenging goals. Before, you were setting one eating and one activity goal each week. Now that you have graduated to the next level of the program, set a new eating and activity goal every two weeks or monthly. Pretty soon those goals will become lifelong healthy habits.

Parents: After your child weighs in and fills out the weekly report form, you'll need to decide where to go from here. If your child has now achieved a healthy weight, you may only need to set a new eating and activity goal every two weeks—or monthly—depending on your child. If, however, your child's weight still needs some work, it's time to review her previous goals and set new goals for the upcoming week, as she continues with the Trim Kids Program.

# HEALTH FOR A LIFETIME

Rene came to our clinic when she was seven years old, weighing 100 pounds more than what was ideal for her age and height. After losing about 25 pounds, she decided that her problem was no longer severe enough to warrant the rigors of our program, and she decided to drop out.

Ten years later, at age seventeen, she came back—carrying an extra 200 pounds. She has undergone surgery on her legs because of Blount's disease (bowed legs from excess weight) and has been hospitalized for weight-related breathing problems that her doctors considered life-threatening. After becoming involved first in our hospital program and then in our outpatient program, Rene has lost 135 pounds. Both she and her parents see the need for a lifetime commitment to healthy eating and activity. They have agreed to make that commitment.

Settling for temporary accomplishments won't help your child in the long run. Making healthy choices never ends. It is something all of us must do lifelong, whether or not we have a weight problem. It is even more crucial for a child at risk of overweight. When your child reaches his goal weight, celebrate by knowing that he will remain healthy for as long as the family remains committed to the new lifestyle. And celebrate by knowing that your entire family will live a longer, healthier, and happier life together!

**TRIM KIDS TESTIMONIAL**

## A Child's Perspective

"For a long time, I didn't want to admit I was fat. I kept calling myself extra-muscular. I didn't want to go on a diet, and I didn't want to make changes. My parents tried a few things, but they didn't work. Plus, I figured I was OK because I was really active.

"Then one day, I saw myself in a photograph with my friends and I realized that I wasn't just heavyset. I was fat. It upset me, but my mom said it was OK, and that I should start this program.

"I lost weight in the first week. It made me so happy and gave me self-assurance. And I started thinking about the fact that if I stayed heavy, it could affect my health. So I kept with it and now I know I can do just about anything. Before, I didn't think I could, but now I know I can."

—Robin, age fourteen

# Appendix: Forms You'll Need

FORM 1: TRIM KIDS WEEKLY REPORT AND GOAL SHEET, 12 copies. Fill out at the beginning of each week.

FORM 2: TRIM KIDS AEROBIC ACTIVITY AND FOOD CHECKLIST, 12 copies. Fill out throughout the week.

FORM 3: TRIM KIDS STRENGTH AND FLEXIBILITY WORKOUT CHART, 1 copy. Fill out throughout the week.

FORM 4: FORM LETTER—REQUEST TO LIMIT PHYSICAL ACTIVITIES. Use if needed.

# Form 1:
# Trim Kids Weekly Report
# and Goal Sheet

*You'll need to have twelve copies of this form on hand—one for every week. Complete it at the beginning of each week.*

Week number: _____ Date: _____

My weight this week is _____ pounds.

Since last week, I have lost _____ pounds.

Since I began the Trim Kids Program, I have lost _____ all together.★

These are my accomplishments for the past week:★

1. _____

2. _____

These are the goals I achieved in the past week:★

1. _____

2. _____

These are some problems I had this past week:★

1. _____

2. _____

My goals for next week are:

1. Follow the exercise recommendations for my level.

2. Follow the nutrition recommendations for my level.

3. _____

4. _____

Tips for Setting Goals

- Does my goal say exactly what I plan to *do*?
- Do I have control over it?
- Can I tell when I've done it?
- Does it say what I *will* do instead of what I *won't* do?
- Will I be able to reach my goal this week? Can I really do it?

Steps and reminders to help me meet my goals for next week (include who, when, and where):

1. _____

2. _____

My rewards for accomplishing my goals and achieving successes for next week will be:

1. _____

2. _____

3. _____

*In week 1 you will not fill in these blanks.

# Form 2:
# Trim Kids Aerobic Activity
# and Food Checklist

*You'll need to have twelve copies of this form on hand—one for every week. Complete one form during each week, whenever you exercise or whenever you're going to have something to eat.*

Week number: _____  Date: _____

| Day | *My goal this week is to do this many minutes on the following days: | This is the type of physical activity I did each day: | This is how long I did it: | My heart rate was (see "Week 3," page 152): |
|---|---|---|---|---|
| Sun. | | | | |
| Mon. | | | | |
| Tue. | | | | |
| Wed. | | | | |
| Thu. | | | | |
| Fri. | | | | |
| Sat. | | | | |
| *Refer to the recommendations for your child's color level listed in each week. Ask your child to select activities he or she enjoys from the list for the appropriate color level in "Week 1," page 98. | | | | |

1. Fill in your daily portion units.
2. As you consume each unit or portion, place a check mark in the box.
3. Try to stay within your daily allowances.
4. Remember: your calorie level is: _____ (see page 118)

| | I can have _____ carbohydrate units each day.* | I can have _____ meat-protein substitute units each day.* | I can have _____ fat units each day. | I can have unlimited vegetables! |
|---|---|---|---|---|
| Sunday | | | | |
| Monday | | | | |
| Tuesday | | | | |
| Wednesday | | | | |
| Thursday | | | | |
| Friday | | | | |
| Saturday | | | | |

*Refer to the recommendations for your child's color level listed in "Week 2," page 127.

# Form 3:
# Trim Kids Strength and
# Flexibility Workout Chart

*You'll need twelve copies of this form for each of the twelve weeks. Be sure to fill one out each week carefully—and watch your progress! You will being in week 1 by performing one strength and one flex exercise; in week 2, two of each, and so on.*

| Strength Exercise Record | | | Suggested Days: Monday, Wednesday, Friday | | | | | | Rest at least one day between strength workouts. Don't do strength exercises more than three times per week. | | | | | | | |
|---|---|---|---|---|---|---|---|---|---|---|---|---|---|---|---|---|
| Week* | Muscles Working | Pictures of Exercises | Sun. | | Mon. | | Tue. | | Wed. | | Thu. | | Fri. | | Sat. | | |
| Name of Exercise | | | # Reps | Pounds | # Reps | Pounds | # Reps | Pounds | # Reps | Pounds | # Reps | Pounds | # Reps | Pounds | # Reps | Pounds |
| Week 1 — Leg Extension | Quads | | | | | | | | | | | | | | | |
| Week 2 — Leg Curl | Hamstrings | | | | | | | | | | | | | | | |
| Week 3 — Row, Low | Upper Back | | | | | | | | | | | | | | | |
| Week 4 — Overhead Press | Shoulders | | | | | | | | | | | | | | | |
| Week 5 — Bicep Curl | Biceps | | | | | | | | | | | | | | | |

*Listed above each exercise you will find the week number where it is described and illustrated.

| Strength Exercise Record | | | Suggested Days:<br>Monday, Wednesday, Friday | | | | | | Rest at least one day between strength workouts. Don't do strength exercises more than three times per week. | | | | | | | | |
|---|---|---|---|---|---|---|---|---|---|---|---|---|---|---|---|---|---|
| Week | Muscles Working | Pictures of Exercises | Sun. | | Mon. | | Tue. | | Wed. | | Thu. | | Fri. | | Sat. | |
| Name of Exercise | | | # Reps | Pounds | # Reps | Pounds | # Reps | Pounds | # Reps | Pounds | # Reps | Pounds | # Reps | Pounds | # Reps | Pounds |
| Week 6<br><br>Triceps Extension | Triceps | | | | | | | | | | | | | | | |
| Week 7<br><br>Pelvic Tilt | Gluteals/ Hips | | | | | | | | | | | | | | | |
| Week 8<br><br>Dumbbell Press | Chest | | | | | | | | | | | | | | | |
| Week 9<br><br>Low Back Extension | Low Back | | | | | | | | | | | | | | | |
| Week 10<br><br>Crunch | Abdominals | | | | | | | | | | | | | | | |
| Week 11<br><br>Squat | Gluteals/ Quads | | | | | | | | | | | | | | | |
| Week 12<br><br>Standing Calf | Calf | | | | | | | | | | | | | | | |

| Flexibility Workout Chart | | | Suggested Days: You can do flexibility every day. | | | | | | | | | | | | |
|---|---|---|---|---|---|---|---|---|---|---|---|---|---|---|---|
| Week | Muscles Working | Pictures of Exercises | Sun. | | Mon. | | Tue. | | Wed. | | Thu. | | Fri. | | Sat. | |
| Name of Exercise | | | No | Sec | No | Sec | No | Sec | No | Sec | No | Sec | No | Sec | No | Sec |
| Week 1 Shoulder Stretch | Shoulder | | | | | | | | | | | | | | | |
| Week 2 Chest Stretch | Chest | | | | | | | | | | | | | | | |
| Week 3 Upper Back Stretch | Upper Back | | | | | | | | | | | | | | | |
| Week 4 Single Rear Shoulder Stretch | Shoulder | | | | | | | | | | | | | | | |
| Week 5 Lying Quad Stretch | Quad | | | | | | | | | | | | | | | |

| Flexiblity Workout Chart | | | Suggested Days: You can do flexibility every day. | | | | | | | | | | | | | |
|---|---|---|---|---|---|---|---|---|---|---|---|---|---|---|---|---|
| Week | Muscles Working | Pictures of Exercises | Sun. | | Mon. | | Tue. | | Wed. | | Thu. | | Fri. | | Sat. | |
| Name of Exercise | | | No | Sec | No | Sec | No | Sec | No | Sec | No | Sec | No | Sec | No | Sec |
| Week 6 Seated Hamstring Stretch | Hamstrings | | | | | | | | | | | | | | | |
| Week 7 Back | Back | — | — | | | | | | | | | | | | | |
| Week 8 Modified Butterfly Stretch | Hips/ Hamstrings | | | | | | | | | | | | | | | |
| Week 9 Butterfly Stretch | Hips/ Hamstrings | | | | | | | | | | | | | | | |
| Week 10 Straddle Stretch | Hip/Quad | | | | | | | | | | | | | | | |
| Week 11 Flex @ Desk | Back/ Shoulder | — | — | | | | | | | | | | | | | |
| Week 12 Calf Stretch | Calf | | | | | | | | | | | | | | | |

# Form 4:
## Form Letter—Request to Limit Physical Activities

Date _____

Dear _____:

[Name of child]

_____ is currently enrolled in the Trim Kids™ weight-management program. During the first twelve weeks of his/her participation, I am requesting that his/her physical activities be limited to exercise of low to moderate intensity—approximately 55 to 65 percent of maximal heart rate. Please discourage his/her involvement in sprinting and heavy calisthenics. We do encourage exercise of long duration at low to moderate intensity.

This note does not exclude his/her participation in activities appropriate to this recommendation. He/she should be allowed to participate in class with special attention paid to the intensity with which he/she is engaged. Once he/she has achieved a healthy weight condition, he/she can again participate in vigorous activities.

Thank you for your consideration.

Sincerely,


_____
[Physician/health professional]

# Index